OHIO

Its People and Culture

OHIO

Its People and Culture

By
GEORGE C. CROUT
and
W. E. ROSENFELT

Publishers
T. S. DENISON & COMPANY, INC.
Minneapolis

 T. S. DENISON & COMPANY, INC.

Standard Book Number: 513-01570-1
Printed in the United States of America
Copyright © 1977 by T. S. Denison & Co., Inc.
Minneapolis, Minn.

Foreword

Why study the history of Ohio? Within each of us is a quiet wondering and curiosity about those who once shared the same land we now occupy, about those who have known the same cities, the same lakes, streams and woodlands. The answer may be that simple.

The exciting drama of Ohio begins as vast northern glacial ice sheets advance and retreat, depositing soils, moulding hills and valleys, forming our rivers and lakes. The new landscape soon grows deep forests teeming in animal life. Prehistoric peoples come to the land, calling it home and leaving earthen mounds with which to be remembered. Tribes of woodland Indians next know the Ohio country, contributing forever their strange melodic names to the state — Miami, Shawnee, Wyandotte, Delaware, Ottawa, Tuscarora, Seneca.

Frenchmen and Englishmen, adventurers, explorers, soldiers, challenge each other and the Indian chiefs for control of the raw "wilderness empire," but it is for settlers from the thirteen new United States finally to tame the land.

The Ohio of the present seems far removed from its colorful and sometimes chaotic frontier beginnings. Interstate ribbons of concrete crisscross productive farmland connecting busy metropolises. Everywhere growth and vitality in Ohio's industry, agriculture and commerce portray a land of wealth and promise.

The key to Ohio's remarkable progress surely is found in her people, in their labor and creative initiative. Representing diverse nationalities, races and religious creeds, Ohioans early learned peaceably to share their common strength and to build from the riches their state provided. Achievements and sacrifices of past Ohioans, as well as the values they tested, are the proud heritage of present day sons and daughters.

Ohio is our land, a land of excellent schools, great colleges and universities, living churches. Ohio has achieved international recognition for its symphony orchestras, museums, hospitals, and athletic teams. American presidents, astronauts and inventors have called Ohio home. Ohio is rich farmland,

5

green parks, lovely waterways. Its cities are exciting; its villages and towns quietly preserve America's traditions. Beautiful Ohio, our Ohio — yours and mine.

Carl Eugene Bennett, Ph.D.
Executive Director
Middletown Regional Campus
Miami University

Dedication

This book is dedicated to the students in the schools of Ohio today, who will be the leaders of tomorrow. May you find meaning in the study and preservation of your cultural heritage.

The authors

Acknowledgments

Amtrak Intercity Railroad Passenger Service
Delta Queen Steamboat Company
Ford Motor Company, Educational Affairs Dept.
Illinois Historical Society
National Air Museum, Smithsonian Institute
Ohio Dept. of Natural Resources
Ohio Dept. of Economic and Community Development
Ohio Dept. of Transportation
Ohio Historical Society
Ohio Secretary of State
Ohio Bell Telephone
Pioneer Seed Corn Company
Shapiro, Bernstein and Company, Music Publishers

Special Acknowledgment

Special acknowledgment to the late Herbert W. Fall, noted
Ohio artist, for the many historic line drawing illustrations
used throughout the book.

Special Maps and book design by Howard Lindberg

Contents

9

Introduction

A Buckeye is a tree, but in one of the fifty states of the United States it can also refer to a person. The people of Ohio are known as Buckeyes, and Ohio is called the Buckeye state. It is a state whose four seasons present a constantly changing picture of nature in all its beauty, so Ohioans chose as their state song, "Beautiful Ohio."

Long ago Indians lived in Ohio, and it was an Indian tribe, the Shawnees, who first named the Buckeye tree. The word in their language was Hetuck, which means buck's eye, because the Shawnees thought the nut of this tree resembled the eye of a deer. The early pioneers used two simple English words, putting them together to make one word, Buckeye.

When the early pioneers first came to Ohio, they found many Buckeye trees growing along the Ohio River and the rivers which flow into it. This was the first part of Ohio to be settled. The Buckeye tree seemed to grow best on the most fertile soil in the level lands along the rivers. This was one of the first trees to be cut down, and the pioneers found that its wood was very useful. It was a soft wood and easy to cut and carve. They could use the logs to build a cabin as well as to make furniture. Even tableware could be carved from a buckeye block of wood. Bowls, cups and spoons were made from the buckeye wood. Logs could be hollowed out to make troughs to hold maple sap, which the pioneers made into sugar. Ohio babies were rocked in buckeye cradles.

Although the wood was most useful, the nuts could not be used, for they made both people and animals sick. Only the squirrels ate the nuts, for they knew which part was not poisonous. However the people believed the buckeyes would bring good luck so they carried them in their pockets.

When William Henry Harrison, the first Ohioan to become President, was campaigning, some people made fun of him because he was born in a log cabin made of buckeye logs. In the West people were proud of this. They built little buckeye cabins and put them on wagons as part of the campaign. They passed out buckeyes, and girls made necklaces of them. Harrison was elected.

11

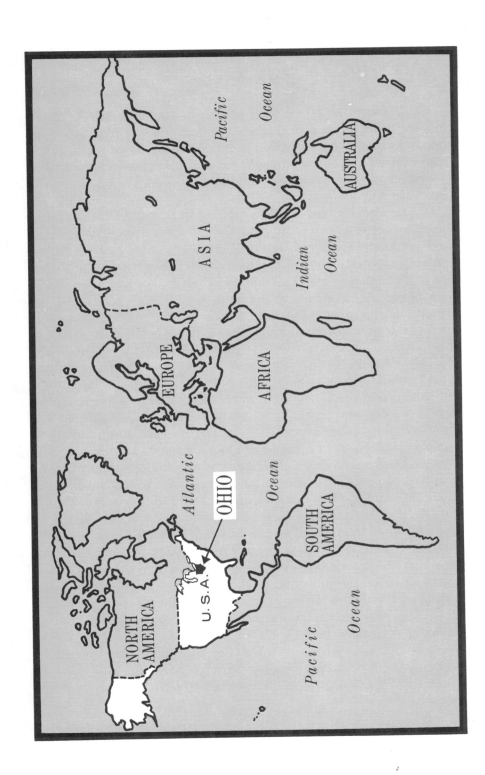

CHAPTER I

The Geography of Ohio

Location

A mountain chain formed a natural barrier between the eastern part of the United States and the great central plain. The Ohio River and its eastern tributaries provided a roadway into this land west of the Appalachian Mountains. Another pathway across New York state led to the eastern shore of Lake Erie. The land called Ohio was between Lake Erie and the Ohio River.

Beginning in the eastern part of the state, descending from the rough highlands to the rolling hills and level plains of central Ohio, the land finally flattens out into a broad, sweeping plain as it reaches the Indiana line.

South of the Ohio River is Kentucky, with its high, rough eastern mountains that cut off good travel routes. The main roads leading to the interior of the continent and finally to the west coast passed through Ohio. Ohio was a funnel for transportation and trade between the east and the west.

More than that, the main routes out of Kentucky ran north and those from the Great Lakes, south to the Ohio River. Ohio, even in the days of the Indians, had become a crossroads. It has been called the "Crossroads" or "Gateway" state, for it is both.

Although Ohio ranks 35th in land area, which means that only 15 states are smaller, it is an important state. In wealth, population, and production it is found among the top six of the 50 states. In Ohio begin the great central plains of the United States. Their fertile lands produce crops that help feed people around the world.

Boundaries

Ohio is easy to find on a map, because its natural boundaries are so clear. Lake Erie is the northern boundary for most of the state. It is one of the five Great Lakes, ranking fourth in size. It

15

is still a large lake, however, being almost 250 miles long, and 30 to 57 miles wide. It covers about 10,000 square miles.

The southern boundary is the Ohio River, which is almost 1,000 miles long, providing a natural boundary for three other states. Such features as lakes and rivers are known as natural boundaries, being made by nature.

The Appalachian Mountains helped make the boundary in eastern Ohio, and so did man. When Ohio became a state Congress decided on the boundaries for Ohio. They used the natural boundaries and man-made boundaries, a result of government surveys. Boundaries are the lines on a map that show the location of a state or any other particular place.

Land Area

To astronauts looking down on our Spaceship Earth, Ohio would be but a dot. To people living in Ohio it seems much larger, for it covers over 41,000 square miles of land, which does not include the land under Lake Erie. Its navigable frontage on the Ohio River and Lake Erie is over 660 miles.

It is not difficult for a geographer to draw a map of Ohio, for it is almost like a square box. But what a big box it would be — 210 miles wide, and 225 miles long.

Terrain

Most of Ohio is a plain covered by deep rich soil, drained by the many rivers of the state, but in some places such as northwestern Ohio, man had to help with the drainage.

While the average elevation or distance above sea level of Ohio is about 770 feet, there is a variety of landscapes. The highest point in the state, Campbell Hill near Bellefontaine, is a limestone ridge rising to 1,500 feet above sea level. Near Cincinnati, in the extreme southwest along the banks of the Ohio River, the land lowers to 440 feet. Ohio has hills, plateaus, and lowlands, all drained by rivers. The differences in elevations are not great when compared to other regions of the nation.

The terrain of Ohio is largely the result of the glaciers which came down from the North and covered almost three-fourths of the land. They ground down great rocks, and the rock particles became rich soil. River valleys, filled with glacial debris became natural filtering plants for water now used in Ohio homes and industries.

While the glaciers did much good by leveling the land, and creating a deep, rich soil in some parts of the state, in other sections it swept away top soil and leaving gravel and rocks.

As the glaciers pushed south, they ran into warmer weather. Since glaciers are great masses of moving ice, the warmer weather and the southern winds slowly melted them. As the edge of a glacier melted, it formed a terminal moraine. A series of hills mark the line made by the moraine, stretching across Ohio from Brown to Columbiana County.

The glaciers changed the beds of old rivers, and created some new ones.

The glaciers even made the watershed across the state. A series of ridges of land was formed, which is called a divide. It is called a divide because if a drop of rain falls on one side of it, the water runs south to one of the rivers emptying into the Ohio River, and from there to the Mississippi and the Gulf of Mexico. If a drop of rain falls to the other side of the divide, it goes by river to Lake Erie. Since the divide does not the separate the state into equal parts, the northern drainage area is much smaller, and the rivers which flow north are shorter.

Landforms

As a result of glaciation, and other physical factors, Ohio can be divided into four physical regions — the Appalachian Plateau; the Central Lowland; the Lake Plains, and the Lexington Plain.

About 45 percent of the area of the state is located on the Appalachian Plateau covering all of eastern and part of Central Ohio. This is an area of rolling lands and hills. In fact, this is often counted as two regions because of the action of the glacier. One section was covered by the glaciers, so it is called the glaciated plateau, and the area not covered by the glacier, is called the unglaciated plateau.

A moraine divides these two areas with an irregular boun-

17

dary line. This hill country of Ohio is beautiful and attracts many tourists. Much of the land is in pasture and provides large graz-

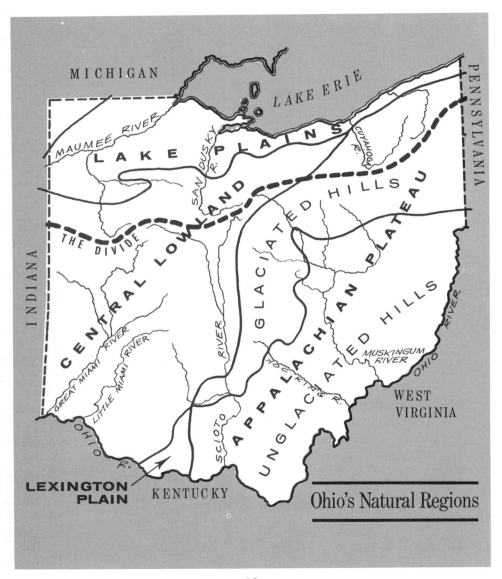

MICHIGAN

LAKE ERIE

PENNSYLVANIA

MAUMEE RIVER

L A K E   P L A I N S

SAN DUSKY R.

CUYAHOGA R.

THE DIVIDE

INDIANA

C E N T R A L   L O W L A N D

GLACIATED HILLS

APPALACHIAN PLATEAU

GREAT MIAMI RIVER

LITTLE MIAMI RIVER

RIVER

UNGLACIATED HILLS

MUSKINGUM RIVER

OHIO RIVER

HOCKING R.

WEST VIRGINIA

SCIOTO

OHIO R.

LEXINGTON PLAIN

KENTUCKY

Ohio's Natural Regions

18

ing areas for livestock. Some of the land is in forests. Since the glacier smoothed off the hills, the unglaciated Appalachian plateau is less rough and easier to travel, as roads are easier to build and maintain.

The central lowland of Ohio is part of a large region which is located in the middle of the continent. In Ohio this region is called the Till plains. These were covered by deposits left by the glaciers, some of the glacial materials being very deep. The glacier not only gave this region good, thick soil, but also left the top of the land smooth, so that it was easy to cultivate even with the crude implements of the pioneers. Level land is also good for building roads and towns.

The southwestern section is known as the Miami Valley, which is one of America's richest farm areas.

In northwest Ohio is a region which narrows to the east, known as the Lake Plains. It is flat and at one time was covered by an ancient lake. Since the land was swampy before being drained, it was known as the Black Swamp region, one of the last to be settled. Now it is heavily settled, and is one of the most productive truck farming areas in the nation.

A region so small that sometimes it isn't listed is the Lexington Plain, or the Blue Grass Region. It extends across the Ohio River from Kentucky covering most of Adams County, and small sections of Highland and Brown Counties. Since it was never covered by the glacier, and rests on limestone rock, its topography is different from other regions.

In some parts of Ohio caves are found. They may be in a sandstone or limestone region. These are formed in an unusual way. When vegetation is in the process of decay, an acid is formed. Rain falls on this material and soaking through, picks up acid. This water then soaks into the cracks in the limestone, and after thousands or millions of years, the cracks become large caves or caverns. Underground streams may form a channel in them before emptying into a river. If water drips down through the roof of a cave, it may leave a deposit called stalactite. If dropping to the bottom of the cave, it may build up a limestone deposit called a stalagmite. In caves these produce a beautiful effect.

19

The land today known as Ohio was here long before man found his way here. Then, how do we know about it? There are people who study the story of the earth through rocks, minerals and other materials. They trace the many changes which have taken place on the earth through millions of years. They study a science called geology, and they are called geologists.

Geologists are important scientists and are still at work, not only studying the secrets of the past as told by reading the stories on rocks, but in discovering new resources. They find where the minerals are hidden. They have found many in Ohio.

The geologists help the geographer by telling him what happened long ago. The geographer is interested in the land as it is used today by animals and man. He studies where man lives and how he makes his living. Since geography is about people, it is one of the social studies. Man is a social being, because he likes to be with other people.

Rivers

To the pioneers coming into Ohio, the rivers were the lifelines of transportation and communication. Since the land was so heavily forested, man had to follow the rivers, and the early settlements were made along the banks of the rivers.

The Ohio River was the most important river flowing into the interior of the midwest. This great river forms a natural southern boundary of Ohio for almost 450 miles. At Pittsburgh, two rivers—the Allegheny and the Monongahela—join to form the mighty Ohio. The Ohio meanders almost 1000 miles before it empties into the Mississippi.

While the Ohio River was the southern boundary of Ohio, it was not one that kept people out, it invited them in. It was an open gateway.

The first settlement in Ohio occurred at Marietta along the banks of the Muskingum. The Muskingum River begins at Coshocton where it emerges from the uniting of the Tuscarawas and Walhonding to be joined later by the Licking River. Although it flows through some hilly country, the bottomlands of the

Hocking River were settled early.

The longest river in Ohio is the Scioto, in the middle of the

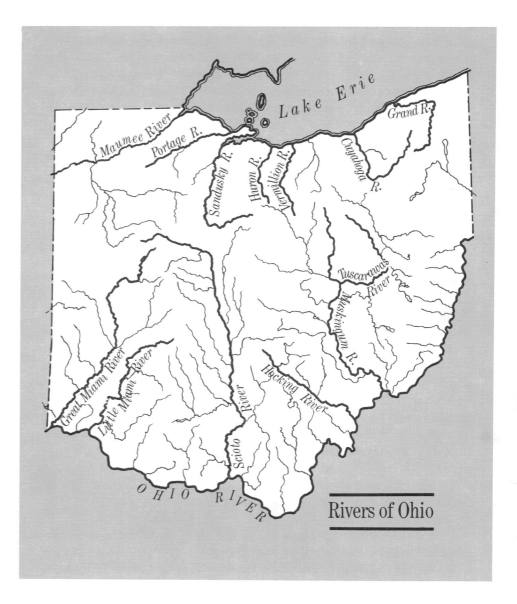

Rivers of Ohio

state, rising in Hardin County. At Columbus it is joined by the Olentangy, and then flows into the Ohio at Portsmouth. The Great Miami River rises also in Hardin County, but flows in a southwesterly direction to join the Ohio near Cincinnati. A sister river, the Little Miami, helps form the Miami Valley. These two rivers never meet, each flowing its separate way to the Ohio. The rivers of northern Ohio are shorter streams which empty into Lake Erie. The most important are the Grand, Chagrin, Cuyahoga, Black, Vermilion, Huron, Sandusky, Portage and Maumee. Another important valley is that of the Mahoning River, while rising in Ohio, flows into Pennsylvania.

Ohio's only important natural lake is Lake Erie, along whose shores have risen many great cities. Ohio's three largest lakes, now used for recreational purposes, were made by man, being constructed to provide water for the abandoned canal system. It is estimated there are about 500 lakes in Ohio, most of them man-made.

Weather and Climate

Ohio lies in the North Temperate Zone. Its climate is classified by people who study weather, meteorologists, as the Humid Continental — Long Summer type.

While the weather is not always pleasant, it is usually moderate, but it can get very hot in summer and very cold in winter. The changes in temperature give Ohioans a vitality which is stimulating. The mean average temperature is around 50 degrees. The growing season which averages 150 to 178 days provides time for the development of most crops. The rainfall which averages between 30 and 40 inches is adequate, and the wettest season is summer when rain is needed for growing crops. A dry autumn gives time for harvest. Winter snows help build up the ground water supply.

Since Ohio is not a large state, the difference in the average annual temperature is only about 5 degrees from south to north. The longest growing season is in the North on the Bass Islands in Lake Erie, then along the Lake Erie shoreline. This might be a

surprise, but due to the moderating effect of Lake Erie's waters
and the direction of the wind, it produces a longer growing sea-

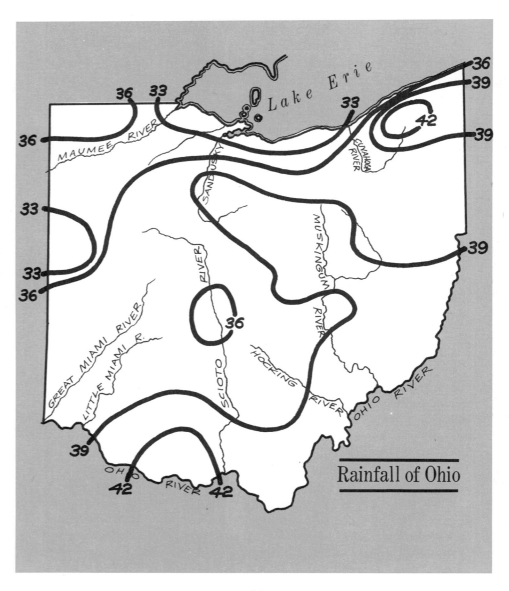

Rainfall of Ohio

son. Due to a lower latitude, the Ohio River country has the next longest growing season.

Being almost half way between the North Pole and the equator, the state has four distinct seasons, with daylight varying during each one. The prevailing winds are from the West, and are known as the Westerlies, but may also come from the northwest or the southwest direction. Occasional tornadoes strike the state, but great destructive ones such as the one that hit Xenia in 1974, fortunately are not common.

Ohio's climate, then, has many characteristics. The temperature changes from season to season, but frequent changes come within a season. In the winter, the cold polar air masses sweep across the state, sometimes bringing below zero temperatures. In the summer, the hot tropical air from the south sweeps in, bringing high temperatures. Buckeyes often experience a range of over 100 degrees during a year.

Clouds are frequent both in the winter and summer, bringing rain or snow and helping moderate temperatures. Since the Ohio climate is so changeable, people watch and listen closely to the weather forecaster. Climate and weather are about the same thing, only weather is for a short time, and climate covers a long period of time.

Natural Vegetation

Long ago most of Ohio was covered by deep, thick forests. It is estimated that about 2500 different kinds of plant life were found in Ohio, including many varieties of trees. Probably 95 percent of the land was wooded.

In general, trees, like the ash and elm, were found in the places with the most moisture, oak trees in the driest spots, and beech forests in areas between.

Swamps, marshes, bogs and prairies were found in the open spaces. Northwestern Ohio had a large Black Swamp, which had to be drained before it could be cleared and settled. Through artificial drainage, many former areas not suitable for cultivation became good farmland.

24

Some of the areas which the pioneer found had been cleared of forests, and were called prairies or meadows. In Ohio there were few such natural grassy places. Most of these were really old Indian fields. When the Indians located their village, they cleared land for gardens and cornfields. When it came time for the village to be moved, the tribe left the cleared land and moved on. The land grew up in tall grasses. The pioneer found these areas and planted them.

Buffalo hunters had wiped out the Ohio herds before 1800.

Since most of Ohio was originally covered with forests, this provided a home for many kinds of wildlife. The black bear, wolves, panthers and wildcats hid in the forest. The deer and wild turkey were plentiful, providing food for the pioneer. Squirrels, rabbits and wild pigeons were ready targets for young boys. Fish swam in the rivers. By the time pioneers reached Ohio, however, most of the beaver had been taken by trappers, and few bison or buffalo were left.

Learning from Maps

Geographers have a way of putting a lot of information in a small space so that certain items will be very easy to find. They make maps. There are many kinds of maps — physical, political, topographic, road and many other kinds. Making maps is so important that there are map makers or cartographers.

Map makers put a great amount of material on a map. Many maps have a scale of miles, which is very simple to use. A piece of string or the edge of a sheet of paper can take the place of a ruler.

On a map there are many different symbols which convey meaning or information. These symbols are usually placed somewhere near the bottom of the map under a heading, known as a legend. By using this legend, the cartographer can communicate with the user. Make a collection of maps, study the legends, and find out what information is being given.

Road maps are most common. By learning to read a road map, a traveller can find his way around Ohio, or the U.S. The State of Ohio publishes an official road map, which should be available to every class. Study its legend. Plan a trip for yourself, for you will need to know how to use a map, when you learn to drive.

LEGEND

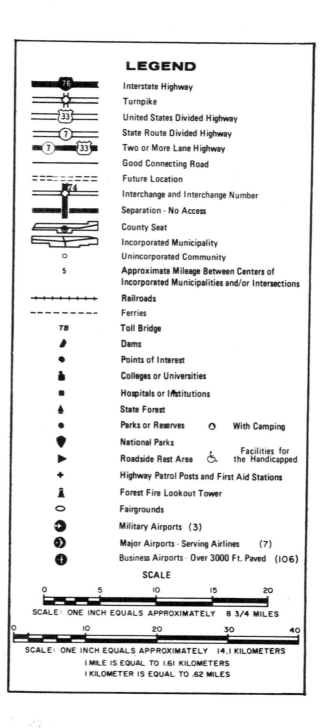

	Interstate Highway
	Turnpike
	United States Divided Highway
	State Route Divided Highway
	Two or More Lane Highway
	Good Connecting Road
	Future Location
	Interchange and Interchange Number
	Separation - No Access
	County Seat
	Incorporated Municipality
	Unincorporated Community
5	Approximate Mileage Between Centers of Incorporated Municipalities and/or Intersections
	Railroads
	Ferries
TB	Toll Bridge
	Dams
	Points of Interest
	Colleges or Universities
	Hospitals or Institutions
	State Forest
	Parks or Reserves With Camping
	National Parks
	Roadside Rest Area Facilities for the Handicapped
	Highway Patrol Posts and First Aid Stations
	Forest Fire Lookout Tower
	Fairgrounds
	Military Airports (3)
	Major Airports - Serving Airlines (7)
	Business Airports - Over 3000 Ft. Paved (106)

SCALE

0   5   10   15   20

SCALE: ONE INCH EQUALS APPROXIMATELY   8 3/4 MILES

0   10   20   30   40

SCALE: ONE INCH EQUALS APPROXIMATELY 14.1 KILOMETERS

1 MILE IS EQUAL TO 1.61 KILOMETERS
1 KILOMETER IS EQUAL TO .62 MILES

CHAPTER II

Ohio's Past

Earliest Hunters

When the early explorers came into Ohio, they found a land of mystery. There were great mounds of earth, some reaching to the sky, and others in unusual forms. In Adams County a mound resembled a great, winding snake, over 1300 feet long. At Miamisburg was a high conical mound, and at Fort Ancient the clear outline of a prehistoric fort. There were hundreds of smaller mounds.

These earthworks were not the work of nature, but had to be made by people. Early scientists mapped and studied these monuments of the past, and later inscriptions were put on markers to describe the earthworks.

When they dug into the mounds, they found other relics or artifacts, such as pottery which were used as dishes, spear and points which were used by the hunters. Knives, scrapers, and even jewelry were found. In burial mounds skeletons of these people of the past were discovered.

Soon special kinds of scientist, called archaeologists, began to study mounds and their contents. An archaeologist can read the past through the artifacts of another culture. He gathers up all the physical items of the past. Then another group of scientists study what was found and the use made of the artifact. People who study such cultures of the past are called anthropologists.

These scientists are still studying and learning new things about the past in Ohio and North America. When the Alaskan pipeline was laid, archaeologists and anthropologists were there to see that nothing important was destroyed. They found out more about how people first came to North America. They now believe that the people who built those mysterious mounds in Ohio came across the Bering Strait, perhaps 50,000 years ago. Then the earth was much colder, more water was locked up in the

Indian Mound
Locations
in Ohio

form of ice, so perhaps there was a land bridge between Asia and North America.

It is believed that the first people to live on earth were on the continents of Africa and Asia, and from there spread out to the other lands. Since early peoples lived by hunting, they had to follow the animals. They wandered from place to place to find food, and were called nomads. Animals became scarce on the plains of Asia, so some of the people followed them as they found their way to the pasture lands of a new continent, North America.

Across the land bridge between the two continents came animals such as the bison, or buffalo, the moose, caribou, bear, musk-ox, and mammoth. There were some places not covered by glaciers. The animals stopped and as the glaciers melted they pushed farther south into the Mississippi and Ohio River Valleys.

This land was a land of promise to early people, for here they could have more food to eat and more skins for clothes, as well as wood to burn to keep them warm, or to provide shelter.

During the thousands of years people lived in Ohio different cultures have developed. The very first people lived by hunting. They led a nomadic life, moving their camping place as seasons changed or as the animals migrated. Since they built no permanent home, they used any type of shelter they could find. Sometimes they found a cave or dug one out of the side of a hill. They were called cave dwellers, and lived in the Stone Age, meaning that the tools they used were made of stone.

Ohio's first people saw the Mammoth from their cave shelter.

Ohio contained one of the most valuable kind of rock found in the whole country. Between Newark and Zanesville is an outcropping of rock known as Flint Ridge. Since flint is hard and brittle, it can be broken into pieces with sharp edges. From it early people could make spearheads, arrowheads, scrapers and knives. These people traveled hundreds of miles to secure pieces of this rock.

The earliest hunters chipped the flint into points, which were put on the end of spears. Hunters used spears to kill the big animals, one of which would provide food for many days for a tribe. Two large animals most hunted were the mastodon and the mammoth, both related to the present-day elephant. They lived along the edges of glaciers. Mammoths were larger than mastodons.

No one knows when or why these giant animals disappeared from Ohio. Perhaps the changing climate affected their foods supply, or the early hunters became such good killers, they destroyed them. It is known that herds of these animals were driven off cliffs and that hunters used fire to force them into lakes, where they could be easily killed. The fact that they lived in Ohio cannot be denied for their bones and skeletons have been found. Through a scientific process called Radiocarbon dating it is possible to determine about how long ago these animals lived.

Archaic People

Just why ancient peoples migrated in large groups from Asia is not known. Near the end of the Ice Age, 10,000 years ago, more people found their way to the Ohio River.

The great, large animals had disappeared, and these people hunted the smaller animals, which took more skill. They invented a new hunting weapon, taking a spear or javelin, thrown by a device called an atlatl. With it they hunted the wild turkey, duck, goose, squirrel, and rabbit. They also liked to fish in the river or gather shellfish. They gathered wild fruits and nuts to add to their diet, but they did no farming.

The Archaic People lived in communities larger than those of the first arrivals. Since they lived more off what the land furnished, they did not move as often. When they did, they made simple boats to travel by river. They often migrated as the seasons changed.

Adena People

Many remains are found of the Adena culture. These people of the woodlands came onto the scene about 800 years before the

Birth of Christ. More is known about them because they were fine pottery makers, as well as makers of tools and jewelry.

An Adena village in Ohio, 1000 B.C.

They received the name, Adena, after the site where archeologists discovered this distinct culture. Adena is near Chillicothe. Since that time, archeologists have found many other places in Ohio where these ancient peoples lived. Even in those times, Ohio was located at the crossroads, and was the home of more Adena people than any other area.

The Adena people liked the rich, alluvial lands along the many rivers of Ohio. Unlike the men and women before them, who depended upon wild animals for their food, the Adena people discovered agriculture. They learned how to take seeds and plant them in gardens, care for them and harvest a crop. They grew beans, squash, pumpkins, and sunflowers. Anthropologists believe that the harvesting and storing of sunflower seed was their most important idea, for they could store it for the winter when other food was scarce. These people were the first farmers in Ohio.

It is not known when people first began to think about religion and life after death, but by the time the Adena people lived

The Ohio Statehouse

State Flag

State Bird (Cardinal)

State Flower (Scarlet Carnation)

State Tree (Buckeye)

Ohio Leads The Way With Modern Highways

Ohio Ports In World Trade

Steel For Industry

Getting Ready For The Ohio State Fair

Ohio Based Research In Communication

Ohio, A Leader In Science and Technology

The Underground Railway, Painting by C. T. Webber Permanent Collection, Cincinnati Art Museum

in Ohio, religious ceremonies were held. They built thousands of mounds, so many in fact, that they became one of the groups of people known as Mound Builders. From the tops of mounds, they observed the countryside. They communicated with other groups by smoke signals. They also used the mounds as places to worship, and burial places.

Hopewell Peoples

Related to the Adena culture, but far more advanced, was the Hopewell civilization. They received their name from a farm owned by Capt. M. C. Hopewell in Ross County on which were found 38 mounds. They were studied carefully by anthropologists.

Fort Ancient on the Little Miami River was one of the sites they developed. It included earth and stone walls, a series of fortifications, places for religious ceremonies, and burial mounds.

The Mound Builder at work.

The Hopewell people lived in communities, which were in contact with each other. They could notify each other of impending danger. They not only hunted and gathered food, they cultivated large areas. In addition to the food plants of the Adena people, they found a new plant—maize, now called corn. It was the best food crop of all. Easily raised and cultivated, it could be stored for winter use in deep food preservation pits which the Hopewell people dug in the earth.

They also discoverd the use of another plant, tobacco. They carved platform pipes from pipestone in the form of animals and birds. They did so well that the carvings can easily be identified today. They used pearl, mica, copper and other materials to make tools and ornaments. They developed pottery-making into an art.

Their religious leaders called shamans conducted services and led dances to commemorate various occasions and events. They built many burial mounds, in which log tombs were made for their leaders.

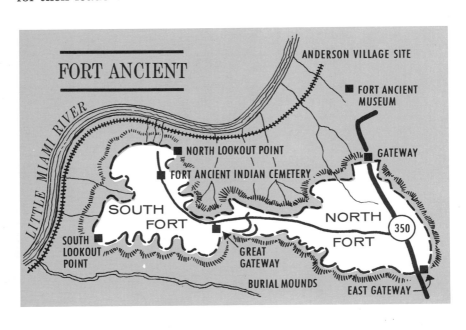

Fort Ancient People

No one knows why this fine culture disintegrated, perhaps some plague swept across the country. Between the close of the Hopewell era and that of the historic Indian period, people continued to live in the area, but in smaller, less organized groups. They lived on some of the same sites as the Hopewell people.

Since they continued to occupy the great Fort Ancient settlement, that name was given to this particular culture. The Fort Ancient people lived in many places, but were most numerous in the valleys of the Miami and the Scioto Rivers.

While they lacked the artistic skills of their ancestors, they did make pottery, ornaments, and pendants. They used bone and stone to make awls, scrapers, fish hooks, and other tools.

Ohio Indians

The story of the ancient peoples who lived in Ohio is pieced together by archeologists and anthropologists. Prehistoric people lived before a written record was made.

When a written record is left, historians, who are writers who study past records and documents, can gather the facts into an historic account. The first such account of people in Ohio was found in a book written by Jesuit missionaries. In 1656 one of them described a tribe of Indians found along the shores of Lake Erie, in fact, the lake was named for this tribe.

During the fifteenth and sixteenth century, Europeans began to explore the new continents in the western hemisphere, North and South America. When the first explorer, Christopher Columbus arrived in 1492, he called the natives Indians. Columbus thought he had arrived among the islands of the East Indies on the other side of the world. Even though he had made a wonderful mistake and discovered a new world, the name, Indians, continued to be used. When explorers finally arrived in Ohio, they used the same name as Columbus did for the natives.

The French first explored the Ohio country. They found the Erie Indians, who were descendants of Iroquois tribes of the East. The Jesuits found them wearing skins taken from the many wild

35

An Indian clan's settlement along an Ohio stream.

cats in the area, so they called them the Cat Nation.

The Eastern Iroquois invaded the land of the Eries, and a fierce battle took place. The Eries had only bows and arrows, but the English traders had sold the Iroquois firearms. Although brave to the end, the Eries could not win against the muskets. The Eries disappeared as a tribe.

For the next fifty years, Ohio became a deserted land, for all were afraid of the mighty Iroquois and their firearms. The Iroquois called it the land drained by the great and beautiful river, in their language, O-he-yo.

As the eighteenth century began, organized Indian tribes moved into Ohio. Despite the fear of the Iroquois, many Indians had to find new homes, for those along the eastern seacoast were being pushed out by European settlers. Ohio was filled with fur-bearing animals, whose skins could be traded for guns, cloth, and trinkets, much desired by the Indians.

One of the most powerful tribes, the Miami Indians, were among the first to move into the Ohio country, due to the encroachment of other tribes on their ancient hunting grounds. They settled in the valley between two rivers, which now bear their name, the Great Miami and the Little Miami Rivers. They also had villages in the valleys of the Maumee and Wabash Rivers. Their first important Ohio village was Pickawillany near the present site of Piqua.

The Miamis were described by the early explorers as kind, and courteous. They cleared large areas for raising corn, their main crop. They were well organized, and such chiefs as Little Turtle were intelligent and good leaders. They were brave warriors in defending what they considered their land. They lived in Ohio for a longer time than any other Indian tribe in historic times. They were finally relocated on a reservation in Indiana, and from there were resettled in Oklahoma.

By 1750 the Indian tribes living in the Ohio country were settled in distinct areas. They belonged to two larger groups called Confederacies. The Miami, Shawnee and Delaware Indians were members of the Algonquin Confederacy, which was friendly to the French. The Iroquois Confederacy, which often sided with the English was composed of the following tribes living in Ohio: the Ottawa, Wyandot, and Mingo, or Seneca.

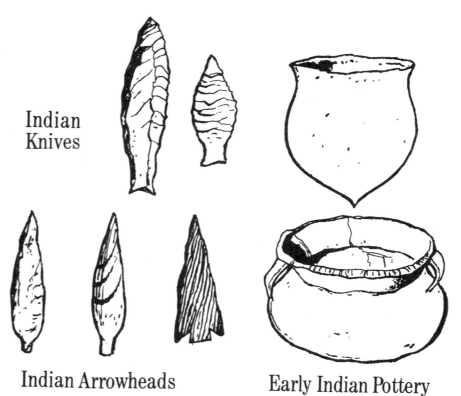

Indian Knives

Indian Arrowheads

Early Indian Pottery

Remnants From Another Culture.

37

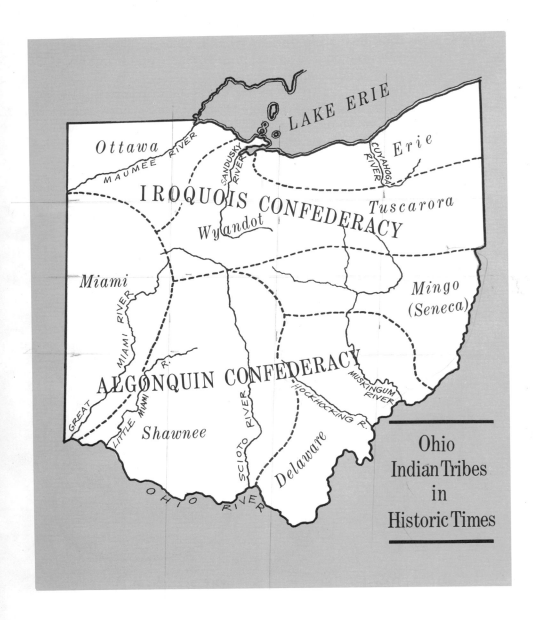

Ottawa

MAUMEE RIVER

LAKE ERIE

SANDUSKY RIVER

CUYAHOGA RIVER

Erie

IROQUOIS CONFEDERACY

Wyandot

Tuscarora

Miami

Mingo
(Seneca)

MIAMI RIVER

ALGONQUIN CONFEDERACY

MUSKINGUM RIVER

GREAT

LITTLE MIAMI R.

Shawnee

SCIOTO RIVER

HOCKHOCKING R.

Delaware

OHIO RIVER

Ohio
Indian Tribes
in
Historic Times

Living also in southern Ohio, east of the Miamis, in the valley of the Scioto River were the Shawnees. They had moved into Ohio from South Carolina and Tennessee. They were the most fearless of the Ohio Indians and put up the fiercest fight against the settlement of the white man.

Shawnee Town at the mouth of the Scioto River, was a major settlement, as was another village called Chillicothe, near the site of the present town. Their chiefs led the battle against the Ohio pioneers. Cornstalk led the Indians at Point Pleasant in 1774; Blue Jacket headed the Indian braves at the Battle of Fallen Timbers; and Tecumseh commanded Indian forces against the Americans in the War of 1812.

The Delaware Indians migrated from their homeland along Delaware Bay, and settled in the Upper Muskingum River Valley. They were a proud people, who gave themselves the name of "Lenape" which in their language meant real brave men. They came to Ohio because the Americans had driven them out of their villages along the Atlantic Coast.

They were the first to be friendly to the white men, perhaps preferring peace to war. They became Christians due to the work of the Moravian missionaries, who set up missions on the Tuscarawas River in the early 1770s. Captain White Eyes was their leader when the missionaries set up their mission church and school.

Across northern Ohio lived those tribes who were members of the Iroquois group. The smallest such tribe in the northwest corner of the state was the Ottawas. They moved down from Canada, and were usually peaceful and friendly.

Pontiac was the most important chief of the Ottawas, being born near what is now Defiance.

The Wyandots, also known as Hurons, moved out of Canada into the valleys of the Maumee and Sandusky Rivers. Their main town was at Upper Sandusky.

While brave fighters, they did not mistreat prisoners. Tarhe, also known as the Crane, was their most famous leader. When the Treaty of Greenville was signed, Tarhe was the chief spokesman for the Indians, and it was he who received the Indian's copy of the treaty.

39

The Shaman or Medicine Man was both doctor and religious leader to the Indians.

While many missionaries taught among the Wyandots, the Methodists gained the most converts and set up a regular mission near Upper Sandusky. John Stewart, an American Black missionary was in charge of the mission.

The Wyandots stayed in Ohio until 1843, being the last tribe to leave the state for a reservation in the West.

The Mingoes, also known as Senecas, settled in the eastern section of Ohio in the area of present-day Steubenville. They later moved westward to the upper Scioto valley.
Chief Logan was the most important chief of the Mingoes.

While these tribes were the most important, there were other smaller ones such as the Tuscaroras Indians, whose name was given to the river along which they lived — the Tuscarawas.

40

Ohio was never thickly settled by the Indians. It is believed that no more than 15,000 Indians ever lived within the boundaries of the state. Modern historians state that the Indians who lived in Ohio in the eighteenth century were not well organized tribes, but more like groups of Indians. They lived in villages and worked together so that they could survive. The explorer, trader, and finally, the pioneer, came into the land. The Indians saw their animals killed, and their hunting ground settled.

The Explorers

"Many, many moons to the south flows a beautiful river," a Seneca Indian Chief had told Rene Robert Cavalier, whose title was Sieur de La Salle. The Chief told La Salle, as he is known, that the river began in their land and flowed to the sea, but the Chief said it took almost a year to make the trip on the long river.

When La Salle heard this he became very excited, for like all explorers, he hoped to be the one to find the Northwest Passage. Columbus had sailed West, thinking that by that route, if the earth were round, he would arrive in the Far East. This was the land of spices, which the Europeans badly needed to help preserve and flavor food in the days before modern refrigeration. Luxuries such as silk and jewels came from this far-away land.

Columbus didn't find the new route to the famed land, for a new continent stood in the way. The explorers following Columbus searched for a passageway across North America, the Northwest Passage. La Salle could not know that such a passage would not be found until 1958, when it was first traveled by an American atomic submarine, the Nautilus, under the ice of the Arctic Ocean.

La Salle thought that the Ohio River might be the passage that explorers were seeking. Little was known of the Ohio country. One French fur trader, Etienne Brule, lived among the Indians in the Great Lakes region. He traveled along the shores of Lake Erie, and is likely the first European to set foot on Ohio soil.

Brule had not gone very far south, and had never seen the Ohio River. La Salle made plans to explore this river. La Salle arrived in Canada from France when he was twenty-two years of age. As he wished to explore Indian country, he learned their language.

La Salle had studied to be a priest and was a member of the Jesuit Order. He wanted Indians to learn about his God, and he also wanted to help his country. He could do both by exploring new lands for France.

When he heard that Father Marquette and Louis Joliet had been successful in exploring land along the Illinois River, he asked the Governor of New France for permission to explore lands farther east.

The Governor gave La Salle permission, if he agreed to pay all his own expenses, which meant that he had to sell about everything he owned. With this money, he bought supplies, and hired seventy men to go with him. It was a summer day when La-Salle finally started on his trip south to find the Ohio River.

At times boats and supplies had to be carried, most usually they used the waterways. They saw trails and rivers never before

Sieur de La Salle

42

traveled by Europeans. While they had brought some food with them, most of the time they lived off the land, killing wild game and eating wild nuts and berries. Since the diary kept by La Salle of this expedition was lost, no one knows his exact route.

The warm summer days turned to the cool ones of autumn, and then snow began to fall. One day his canoe came around a big bend of the river on which they were traveling. La Salle looked ahead, and saw a great river into which this one flowed. He shouted for his men to hurry. He had found it — the Ohio River which the Indians had told him about, and it was larger and more beautiful than he had hoped. The year was 1669.

When the expedition reached the falls of the Ohio at what is now Louisville, the men were tired and wanted to return home. Without La Salle's permission, they slipped away during the night, leaving him alone in the wilderness. La Salle found his way back to Montreal alone.

La Salle made other journeys through the new land of the West. On later expeditions he was accompanied by another explorer, Henri de Tonty, whom the Indians called Iron Hand, because he had lost a hand in battle and used an iron hook in its place. The two men were a good combination.

Ten years after discovering the Ohio River, La Salle and Tonty followed Lake Ontario to the Niagara River, where they erected a warehouse to store furs. They built a ship called the "Griffin" which was to sail on the Great Lakes to gather the furs collected by the French traders from the Indians. The "Griffin" was the first European vessel to ever sail on Lake Erie. After being loaded with furs from a trip around the lakes, a storm arose, and the "Griffin," disappeared forever.

La Salle was not on the ship, and while he regretted the loss, he continued to make explorations in the name of the King of France. His last expedition took him down the Mississippi River. He claimed that all the land drained by the Ohio and Mississippi belonged to France. Since the king of France at that time was named Louis, La Salle called the land Louisiana.

When he returned to France he told the king of the new land, and was given permission to make a settlement at the mouth of

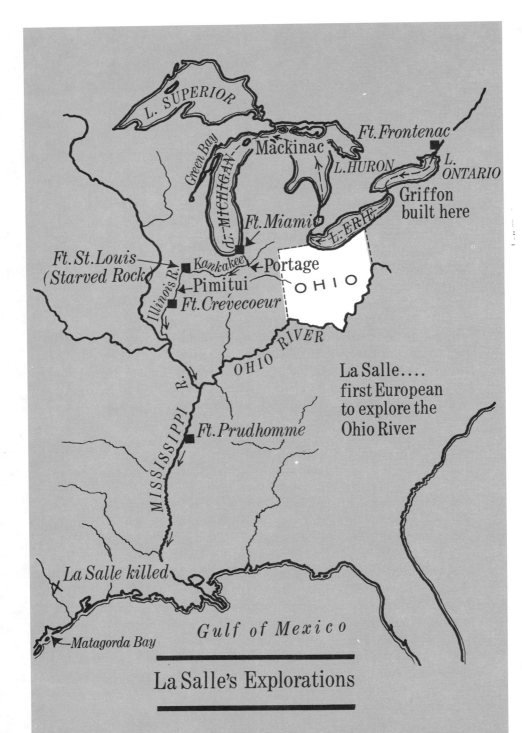

La Salle's Explorations

the Mississippi. He made a mistake and landed in 1687 at Matagorda Bay in Texas. The men with him became so angry at his mistake, that they murdered him.

The English were interested in the Ohio country, so they would not accept the claims of La Salle and the French that it belonged to them.

French trading posts could be found on the major rivers of the Ohio country. Their flag flew over many Indian villages. The French had developed a large fur trade with the Indians, for there was a good market in Europe for furs, as the winters were cold.

French trappers and fur traders in the Ohio country.

Fur Trader and his pack train in the Ohio wilderness, 1750.

45

The English were also good fur traders. The Indians liked to trade with the English, for they gave them more goods for their furs. They liked the shiny beads and the brighter colored cloth, as well as the guns and liquor they could obtain from the English. The French were angry. They said that the English had no right to come on their land to trade with the Indians. They reminded the English that La Salle had discovered and explored the Ohio valley.

The French soon realized that they would have to make their claims to the Ohio country clearer to both the English and the Indians. In June, 1749, they sent out an expedition from Montreal headed by Captain Bienville de Celoron, a French army officer. The expedition was a large one of over 200 men made up of priests, soldiers, and friendly Indians.

They traveled in large birch bark canoes, and stopped at the mouth of each important tributary flowing into the mighty Ohio river. At each, Celoron and his men would go ashore. They put on a show for the Indians watching, wishing to impress with their

French expedition under Celoron on Ohio River, 1749.

46

power. Celoron appeared in a fine lace coat, trimmed in gold that shone in the sunlight. His men marched out, and Celoron proclaimed in a loud voice: "The King of France owns all the land drained by the Ohio."

After that Celoron nailed a piece of tin to a big tree, proclaiming this French land. The final part of the display was planting a lead plate a foot long and half as wide. The plate stated that the land belonged to France. After the plate was buried at the mouth of the river, the priest said a prayer. Muskets were fired. A clerk carefully wrote down what was said.

While the Indians enjoyed the show, they did not know what it meant. The English watched knowing what it meant, but not planning to accept the French claim. Celoron was surprised to find so many English in the Ohio country.

Finally Celoron and his men had gone as far down the Ohio as the mouth of the Great Miami River. Here they stopped and buried the last of the six leaden plates. They went up the Miami to Pickawillany, the main village of the Miami Indians, who were friendly with the English. Celoron tried to persuade the Miamis to join with the French, but they refused.

When Celoron returned to Canada, he had bad news for the Governor. Both the Indians and the English had refused his order to leave Ohio lands. Now the Governor was worried.

The English believed that a land should belong to the ones who settled it. There were very few Frenchmen in Ohio, and they traveled about trading for furs. France was a larger country than England, and a better farming land, so its people were less likely to migrate to the New World. The English, however, were looking for fertile land to farm.

The English saw the rich farm lands along the rivers of the Ohio Country. As early as 1748 the Virginians founded the Ohio Land Company, and planned to send 100 families to the Ohio region.

The Ohio Company looked for a man to explore the great river valley, who could make his way through the great forests and survey parts of the best land. They wanted a man who could record what he saw, and who could deal with the Indians. They found such a man in Christopher Gist.

Christopher Gist party in the Ohio wilderness, 1751.

Gist had spent his boyhood on the Yadkin River in North Carolina. He had lived on the frontier and he knew the ways of the forest. He started out with compass and pen. Traveling with him was a good friend, a Black scout. One day they heard a shot, and were surprised to find another old friend, a trader, who decided to go with them. The three men arrived at a village at the forks of the Muskingum, the present location of Coshocton. From the roof of one of the building flew an English flag.

In this village lived over one hundred families. Many English traders made it their home base. Gist also found another trader friend here, George Croghan, from Pennsylvania, which like Virginia, claimed part of the Ohio country.

Gist then made his way to Pickawillany, where he found the Indians friendly to the English. Here in 1750 Gist conducted a Christmas service for the fur traders and the Indians, the first such service held in Ohio. They made their way back passing through an Indian Village, Hockhocking, now the site of Lancaster. On their way to this village they passed along the Great Buffalo Swamp, now Buckeye Lake. Other stops were made in the Circleville and Portsmouth areas as they are known today.

Christopher Gist kept a careful account of all he saw and heard in a diary. Under the date of January 15, 1751 Gist wrote: "We left Muskingum and went five miles to the White Woman's Creek, on which is a small town, this white woman was taken away from New England, when she was not above 10 years old, and has an Indian husband and several children. Her name is Mary Harris . . ."

Mary Harris was the first white woman to live in Ohio, being one of the prisoners carried off on a savage Indian attack on Deerfield, Massachusetts. She was adopted by the Indians, and taken West with them. She grew up as an Indian maiden, and learned to love her new land. She married Chief Eagle Feather.

Mary Harris was well liked by the Indians, and the place where her group lived was known as White Woman's Town, at the point the Walhonding and the Tuscarawas form the Muskingum River. It is now called Coshocton.

One day Chief Eagle Feather went to war, and when he came home he brought with him a young, new wife as was often the custom among the Indians. Eagle Feather called his new wife, "Glowing Star" but Mary named her, the Newcomer. The two women did not get along well, and the Newcomer asked Mary to leave, but Chief Eagle Feather did not want her to do so.

One night Glowing Star decided to kill Eagle Feather. After the murder, she was tracked down by Eagle Feather's braves. The spot where she was captured and killed is now called Newcomerstown.

Mary Harris lived on for many years, and is buried in the Ohio country which she loved.

A few years after Gist returned to Virginia, in 1754, war broke out between the English and the French. Both sides claimed not only the Ohio country, but all the lands drained by the Ohio and Mississippi Rivers.

While the Indians disliked both the English and the French, and wished that they both would leave, most of them remained loyal to the French. The French seemed to offer less danger to their way of life. The French were satisfied to trade with them, but the English wanted to settle and farm their hunting grounds. Many of the Indians who had been driven out of their lands in the East knew what English settlement meant.

The Governor of Virginia asked George Washington, who had surveyed land in the Ohio country, to go back to Ohio to warn the French that they were on Virginia land. Christopher

Gist was asked to accompany him. They found the French and delivered the message, but the French refused to leave.

Washington and Gist returned to Virginia. The next year the Virginians decided to build a fort where the Allegheny and the Monongahela come together to make the Ohio River. Today this is the location of Pittsburgh. Before the English could finish the fort, the French took it over and called it Fort Duquesne, in honor of the governor of New France. Washington tried to retake the fort, but was defeated. This was the first battle of the French and Indian War.

It was a long war, finally Fort Duquesne was retaken by the English, and renamed Fort Pitt, in honor of a British leader. After a great battle between the French and English at Quebec in Canada, the English won the war. It ended in 1763 with the English the rulers of Canada as well as the land claimed by the French in the Ohio Valley.

The English and the settlers were very happy about the treaty of peace, but the Indians were not. They felt that both the French and English were wrong, for neither owned the Ohio country. The Indians believed they owned the land, and they wanted all white men to leave Ohio.

One of the tribes of Indians living in Ohio was that of the Ottawas, who had a strong chief and a clever leader, brave, wise, and cruel.

He had a plan to drive the white men out of the Ohio country. His grand plan was to get all the Indian tribes together, and each group would attack a special fort or settlement and wipe it out. At a given signal all would attack at once and since the white man would be outnumbered, Chief Pontiac thought his plan would succeed.

Pontiac gave the signal and the war began. Fort Sandusky was the first fort to fall, and soon eight others were taken. White men were killed and women and children taken prisoners. It was the worst attack the English had ever seen. Soon only three English forts remained: Fort Detroit, Fort Pitt and Fort Niagara.

Pontiac decided to take Fort Detroit himself. Pretending to be on a friendly mission, he and his braves entered the fort with guns hidden under their blankets. When Pontiac came in, he noted the English were fully armed, so he knew he could not attack inside the fort. He did not know how the English knew, but an Indian maiden had forewarned the English of Pontiac's plans.

Pontiac had lost, and escaped to the Illinois country, where he made another unsuccessful attempt to defeat the white man. A few years later he was murdered by an Indian enemy.

The English sent a large army into the Ohio country under the command of Henry Bouquet. Seeing so many soldiers, the Indians knew they were lost. They asked for a peace meeting. Almost fifty chiefs came to a place near Coshocton, and pleaded with Bouquet not to go any further.

Colonel Bouquet told the Indians they could have peace under one condition. They must return all white prisoners of war taken during the French and Indian War and by Pontiac. The Indians agreed, and sent out messengers telling all tribes to bring their prisoners to the meeting place on the Muskingum. When the prisoners came it was one of the saddest scenes in history. Many had been held for many years and did not recognize their own parents. Some had married Indian husbands. Some had been treated well by their Indian foster parents and loved them. After the meeting Col. Bouquet told the Indians to go home and live in peace.

The English who lived in America began to call themselves Americans. The young people in the colonies had never seen England. Although they still spoke English and kept many English ways, they were a new people— they were Americans.

As time went on they wanted more and more freedom. Since they lived so far from England, they wanted to make their own laws and levy their own taxes. Great Britain and its King thought the people in America should pay more taxes, for the English had spent a large amount of money to provide troops and supplies in fighting the French and Indian Wars.

The people in the 13 colonies finally decided to fight for their independence from England. The long war was called the American Revolution.

Before the American Revolution began, Virginia and Pennsylvania both laid claims to the Ohio lands. To press Virginia's claim as well as to stop the Indian attacks on white settlers, Lord Dunmore, Governor of Virginia decided to send out an expedition. The Indians were defeated at Point Pleasant, and agreed to peace terms. One Indian, Chief Logan, refused to agree to the terms. When they marched against his village and killed his people, he answered with an eloquent speech considered one of the finest ever made by an Indian.

Lord Dunmore's War made Virginia's claims stronger, and brought a few years of peace to the frontier. As the soldiers were on their way back to Virginia, they stopped at Fort Gower on Nov. 5, 1774. Here they heard of the trouble between the Americans and British in the East. The men agreed upon the Fort Gower Resolves in which they took a stand for liberty and American rights.

Some historians believe that Point Pleasant marked the beginning of the American Revolution and that the Resolves furnished ideas for the Declaration of Independence.

During the Battle at Point Pleasant, one of the men killed was Richard Trotter, who had married Ann Bailey. Ann was born in Liverpool, England, emigrated to America, and then came west. Upon the death of her husband, she vowed that she would devote her life to driving the Indians from Ohio.

Ann Bailey was Ohio's first woman frontier scout and soldier. The Indians called her the Great White Squaw, and believed she was protected by the Great Spirit. Others felt she was so peculiar and filled with hate, that they called her, Mad Ann Bailey.

When a frontier fort ran out of ammunition, she traveled over 100 miles through Indian country to another fort to get the needed gunpowder. Through her effort the fort was saved.

One of the men who had fought in Lord Dunmore's War was a native Virginian, George Rogers Clark, born just two miles from Jefferson's home. Trained in surveying, he knew the land in the Ohio River Valley. He was a friend of Daniel Boone, who taught him the ways of the Indians.

When the American Revolution broke out, George Rogers Clark realized the importance of keeping the western lands under

American control. Even if the Americans won in the East, England could claim the land west of the mountains as part of Canada.

The important forts were at Detroit on the Detroit River; Vincennes on the Wabash River; and Kaskaskia on the Illinois River. Clark knew that no American settlement would be safe with these in English control.

With the encouragement of Patrick Henry, Governor of Virginia, Clark with 175 soldiers set out for Kaskaskia, which he took without firing a shot. Then Clark went up the river to Cahokia, and it, too, fell. His next move was against Vincennes. In one of the Revolution's most daring campaigns, Clark and his men marched through cold, and flooded lands to surprise the defenders. The women of the village, hoping for an American victory made 20 American flags. Clark and his "Long Knives" the name given the soldiers by the Indians, due to the sharp long knives they carried, made the force appear much larger, and captured the British force.

George Rogers Clark

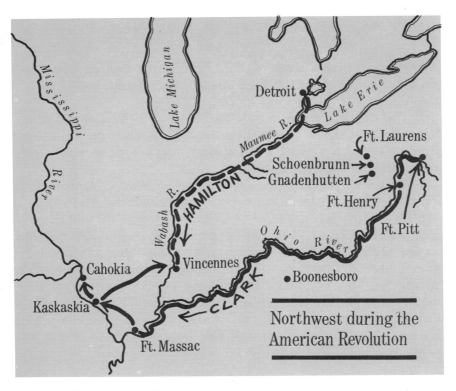

Northwest during the American Revolution

At Vincennes, Clark found his most important prisoner, General Henry Hamilton, the English commander. He was nick-named, the "Hairbuyer" because he bought white scalps from the Indians.

Clark's campaign against the English in the west ended in a most important victory. Without this military action, the Ohio lands would have remained part of British Canada. When the final peace treaty was made, the Americans claimed the land of Ohio was part of the U.S.

Helping Clark in his campaigns was a famous Indian scout of the Ohio country. Simon Kenton, born in Virginia, spent his life on the frontier. During the French and Indian War he served as a scout for the English. He helped Daniel Boone build the fort at Boonesborough. He later served as scout for St. Clair and Anthony Wayne. In tribute to his contributions on the Ohio frontier, the town of Kenton in Hardin County bears his name.

Other military actions took place in Ohio during the American Revolution. In 1778 the Americans built a fort, the only one in Ohio during the Revolution. Fort Laurens, on the Tuscarawas River, was abandoned after fierce Indian and English attacks.

In 1779 the Americans carried out a successful attack against the Shawnees on the Little Miami River. They were gathering there for an invasion of Kentucky, and the defeat changed their plans. The following year, George Roger Clark again fought the Indians and the British at the Battle of Piqua, gaining another victory.

All white men and Indians did not hate and distrust each other. A few white men respected the rights of the Indians, and believed that both could live together in peace in the Ohio lands. One of these men was a Christian missionary, David Zeisberger, the leader of the Moravian Brethren.

Chief White Eyes of the Delaware tribe welcomed Rev. Zeisberger to their land in Eastern Ohio, where the missionaries began to build a village. Since it was near a spring, the town was given a German name, Schoenbrunn, which meant Beautiful Spring. This was the first English settlement in the Ohio country. The large church built of logs held 500 people and its bell was the first one in Ohio.

A school was built, so the Indians could learn how to read and write. The missionaries wrote a spelling book in the Delaware language.

The beautiful Tuscarawas Valley where the villages were located was a dangerous location. It was halfway between the white American settlements along the Ohio River, and the strong Indians tribes in northern Ohio. True to the new Christian teachings, the Delaware Indians tried to remain on friendly terms with the English, the Americans, and all the other Indian tribes.

One of the main villages was called Gnadenhutten. In 1781 the English assisted by some friendly Wyandot warriors arrived in the village, and forced the Christian Delawares to leave their village. They were taken to a place near Sandusky, but were without enough food to last them through the winter of 1782.

Late in February some of the Delawares were permitted to go back to harvest their corn which was left unpicked. While there, a force of soldiers from Pennsylvania, thinking the Christian Indians had raided their settlements in the western part of that state, attacked them. They locked the Indians in two big buildings. A vote was taken, and the soldiers decided to kill every Indian in Gnadenhutten.

Ninety Christian Indians were killed the next day. Only two small boys managed to escape to tell the terrible story of the Gnadenhutten massacre.

Even the tribes who had been friendly with the Americans were angry. They took revenge in raiding the white men's settlements. Colonel William Crawford organized a militia force to fight the Indians. The Indians with help from the British forced Crawford to retreat. During the retreat, Crawford and some of his men were taken prisoners. Crawford was cruelly tortured and finally burned at the stake. The Indians had their revenge but they did not stop, now they were more determined than ever to drive the white man from Ohio.

Even though the American Revolution had ended in the East with the surrender of Cornwallis at Yorktown in 1781, the English continued their attacks in the West. It was September, 1782, when they fought their last battle in the land where the Ohio flows.

Captain Andrew Bradt led about 300 Indians and a number of English soldiers in the battle for Fort Henry.

Fort Henry was defended by only 18 men with some women and children. Among the defenders of the Fort was a young girl, who had just finished school in Philadelphia and had come west to visit her brother, Colonel Ebenezer Zane, who was in command of Fort Henry on the Ohio River. It was an important outpost, being at a site where Indian trails crossed. Many times settlers in the area rushed to the fort for safety.

When the last attack came, the settlers were in the fort. Among those helping the English and Indians were the most hated men in the West, the Girty Brothers. They were considered to be Americans, yet they were traitors to their fellowmen.

The battle raged between those attacking the fort and the ones within the stockade. The guns were kept hot, while the courageous women helped load them.

On the second night under siege, the Americans found their powder running low. There was some gunpowder stored in Col. Zane's house outside the fort. Without this added supply, Fort Henry would have to surrender.

Between the needed powder and the fort was an open space about 180 feet wide. Colonel Zane asked for a volunteer among the men. The mission was dangerous, for if hit by a bullet the powder would explode and blow up the person carrying it.

When she heard the call for a volunteer, Elizabeth Zane spoke up. The men protested that it was not a girl's job, but Elizabeth reasoned that not a single gun or man could be spared. The Colonel agreed, and Elizabeth Zane changed her clothes to light ones, so she could run faster. As the gate was thrown open, she bounded out across the open yard. The Indians were surprised to see "a squaw" running for the house, and did not shoot at her, not knowing her mission.

She reached the house, took a tablecloth and fastened it around her waist. Into it she emptied a keg of powder. Holding the cloth up she rushed out the door.

Now the Indians knew what she was doing, so they showered her with bullets. Some went through her clothing, but none hit the powder or the brave girl. The gate opened, and the men pulled her inside to safety. Now there was enough powder to continue the battle.

After three days, the Indians and their English allies left, Fort Henry was saved by brave Elizabeth Zane. She lived for many years after this heroic deed. At Martins Ferry the school children collected money and built a monument in her honor.

In 1783 a peace treaty was signed with Great Britain, ending the long, bitter war. The land west of the mountains, Ohio, was a part of the new nation, and was known as the Territory of the Northwest. The American flag flew over the land.

Before settlers could move into the Ohio lands, the U.S. government had to set up certain rules. These rules or laws were in a legal document called Ordinances. These Ordinances provided for the survey and sale of the land to citizens of the new country. They also provided for the dividing of the large ter-

The Northwest Territory
Showing the year each state was admitted

ritory, the Northwest, into five states, Ohio, Indiana, Illinois, Wisconsin and Michigan.

Thomas Jefferson and his committee wrote the Ordinance of 1784, which provided a plan for a temporary government until states were formed. The Land Ordinance of 1785 set up the regulations for surveying and selling the land. The Northwest Ordinance of 1787 set up the plan for government.

The Northwest Territory was ready for permanent settlements.

CHAPTER III

Ohio's People

Before the United States government was ready to open the Ohio country for settlement there were already thousands of frontiersmen in the West. They were called squatters and some had found the best land, but they had no legal claim to it. Congress sent General Josiah Harmar out to Ohio to order them to leave.

Some of the frontiersmen went far inland, looking for furs and hides, which they usually bought from the Indians. Most of them were hunters themselves, roaming the forests, killing and skinning the wild animals. They lived out of a pack, carried by one horse, while other horses carried the furs collected. These men learned to live off the land, wild game furnished them food, along with the nuts and berries of the forest.

These hunters and fur traders wandered from place to place, learning the ways of the forest and the paths that led through it. They were of great help to the pioneers moving westward. Their frontier was farthest from civilization.

The wood rancher came next but he remained closer to the eastern boundary of the Ohio country. He was often a man with a wife and children, and likely to be descended from people who came to America from Scotland or Ireland. If he could find an abandoned Indian field, or an area already cleared, he marked off a farm by cutting marks in trees at the four corners of the land with a tomahawk.

The wood rancher cut logs for a cabin, and barns or shed that he needed. With tree branches, rails and posts he built pens to keep in his animals, usually cows, sheep, and horses. In daytime the cattle would be let out to graze on the forest floors, which grew some grass. On the cleared land, the pioneer grew corn for his family and cattle, as well as vegetables for table use.

The wood ranchers drove their cattle to market, the cattle or hogs living off the land as they traveled. Some drove them over Appalachian Mountains, and others down to New Orleans, or to a Fort where there was a ready market.

Since he had not purchased the land, he claimed the land by what was called "squatters' rights." Before the English lost legal control of the land at the end of the American Revolution, the white man was not permitted to settle in the Ohio country. Even the law and treaties with the Indians could not keep the squatter out.

How many there were is not known. One officer sent to order settlers off the land, estimated that there were 600 families living in rude cabins along the Muskingum and Hocking Rivers. He also noted that perhaps 1500 people were along the banks of the Miami and Scioto. These frontiersmen were the first Ohioans.

When driven from their land, some were able to buy the land back from the land company or the government, and continue to develop it. Others moved on farther West into unknown and unmapped country. They hoped that the new family with legal title to the land would pay them something for the improvements they made.

The family with legal ownership of the land wanted to farm it and grow crops. Large trees in the forest were girdled, let to die, then chopped down and burned, so that more land would be available for farming.

The farmer on the frontier grew just about everything he needed. His flock of sheep clothed his family, as the wife made the wool into clothing, as she did the fibers of the flax plant. Logs were cut into lumber. Wheat and corn were ground into meal and flour. Most of the family's food and clothing were home grown or homemade.

Salt, gunpowder and tools were purchased from the money obtained from selling some surplus crops, hogs or cattle. Since a family could produce about all its needs, this was called the subsistence farm.

At first the United States government did not find many buyers for the land in the West. Since money was needed to get the new government started, Congress decided to sell some of the land to land companies. They could resell the land and organize groups of people willing to venture West. Families would be more willing to travel as part of a larger group, as there would be more protection for them. The Indians had not yet given up their dream of driving out the intruding white settler.

In March of 1788, the Continental Congress charted the Ohio Company to help develop the Northwest Territory. The company purchased over 1,000,000 acres of land located on the north side of the Ohio River, which they planned to resell to settlers.

Two men stand out among the directors of the Ohio Company. Manasseh Cutler was the minister of a church at Ipswich, Massachusetts, from which one of the first groups left for the Ohio Country. Dr. Cutler insisted that provision be made for the support of education in the new western lands, and that in Ohio slavery should be "forever prohibited." Although he never lived in Ohio, he visited it often.

The other man led the actual settlers to Ohio. General Rufus Putnam, an old soldier of the Revolutionary War, organized the first party to make a permanent settlement in the new land. Leaving Massachusetts in December 1787, his party traveled to Pittsburgh where they built boats to go down the Ohio.

The largest boat built was called the "Mayflower," after a famous ship in American history. It was much smaller, only 50 feet long and 12 feet wide, carrying 50 tons. Its sides were thick so that Indian rifle balls could not sink it. On April 1, they started down the Ohio, and six days later arrived at the mouth of the Muskingum River, where Fort Harmar stood. The party landed, and after a night's rest began building a village in the wilderness.

At first they thought they would call the town Muskingum after the river, but the people thought the name of Marietta would be better. It was named to honor Queen Marie Antoinette of France, the country which had helped the Colonies win their independence.

The settlement at Marietta grew very rapidly, and before 1788 had ended, there were 132 people living there, and the new year brought 152 more. By 1790 Marietta had over 80 log houses.

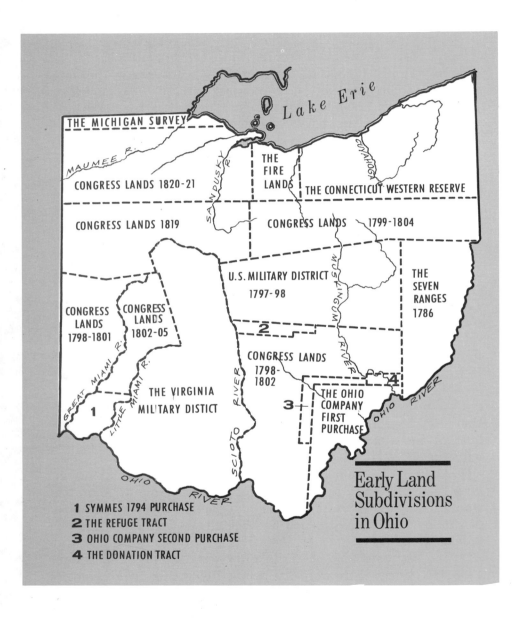

THE MICHIGAN SURVEY

Lake Erie

MAUMEE R.

CONGRESS LANDS 1820-21

THE FIRE LANDS

CUYAHOGA

THE CONNECTICUT WESTERN RESERVE

SANDUSKY R.

CONGRESS LANDS 1819

CONGRESS LANDS 1799-1804

U.S. MILITARY DISTRICT 1797-98

MUSKINGUM RIVER

THE SEVEN RANGES 1786

CONGRESS LANDS 1798-1801

CONGRESS LANDS 1802-05

2

GREAT MIAMI R.

LITTLE MIAMI R.

THE VIRGINIA MILITARY DISTICT

1

CONGRESS LANDS 1798-1802

SCIOTO RIVER

3

THE OHIO COMPANY FIRST PURCHASE

4

OHIO RIVER

OHIO RIVER

RIVER

1 SYMMES 1794 PURCHASE
2 THE REFUGE TRACT
3 OHIO COMPANY SECOND PURCHASE
4 THE DONATION TRACT

Early Land
Subdivisions
in Ohio

General Rufus Putnam acted as Governor of the new colony. From a big tent which he had taken from General Burgoyne during the American Revolution, he conducted the affairs of the colony, and saw that the rules were carried out. He was a wise and good leader. Later President Washington appointed him Surveyor-General of the U.S., and he directed the survey of the Northwest Territory. He completed the first map of Ohio in 1804. He did so many things to help Ohio grow into a great state that he is called the "Father of Ohio."

It wasn't long until new villages were being planned in the Ohio wilderness. About 12 miles down the river from Marietta a town called Belpre was cut out of the forest. Up the Muskingum at Waterford and Wolf Creek communities began.

The first western land rush was soon on. In the first two years, 1788-1790, over 10,000 settlers came into Ohio. Some stopped at Marietta and the Muskingum villages, and others floated on past to a second group of settlements in the Miami Country, drained by the two Miami Rivers.

Judge John Cleves Symmes, an American Revolutionary war leader and then a member of Congress, purchased a large tract of land between the Big and Little Miami Rivers in western Ohio. He chose Benjamin Stites to lead the first party into the Miami lands. He arrived in Nov. 1788, followed by the Symmes party in early 1789. Columbia and Losantiville, now Cincinnati, and North Bend were founded. Due to the danger of Indians, Fort Washington was erected at Cincinnati to protect the frontier.

The Scioto Company obtained a large grant of land along the river of that name. In order to sell off the land, the company sent an agent to France. Due to the French Revolution some Frenchmen thought it would be wise to leave the country. They purchased land, and in 1790 about 500 left France for their new land.

The Scioto Land Company platted a town with 80 cabins, calling it Gallipolis, or city of the French. Unfortunately, Gallipolis was on land owned by the Ohio Land Company. Not wishing to move to the Scioto lands, the Frenchmen paid again for their land. Congress tried to right the mistake by establishing the French Grant.

The state of Virginia had reserved a large tract in Ohio for their military men, who had been paid during the Revolution with promises of land in the Ohio country. These soldiers and their families moved into Ohio.

In the period of 1790 to 1800 many settlements were made in the Ohio country. As early as 1789 an officer at Fort Harmar noted that in a 20 day period that not less than 100 people a day were emigrating to Ohio. By 1800 Ohio had almost 50,000 people.

During this decade, 1790-1800, many settlements were made in the Ohio country. In 1791 Manchester on the Ohio River was settled, taking the name of an important city in England. In 1796 a pioneer village started at Chillicothe in the Scioto River valley. In 1797 Franklinton, named after Benjamin Franklin, was settled at the junction of two rivers in central Ohio. In 1795 Dayton was surveyed, and soon the Miami Valley was dotted with small villages.

During this same decade, the most important settlement in the northern part of Ohio was made by the Connecticut Land Company. When Connecticut turned over its claims to Ohio, it reserved about 3,000,000 acres for sale to its own people. A section of the Western Reserve, was called the "Firelands." Located at the western end, land in this tract was to go to residents of Connecticut who lost their homes or businesses due to the action of English soldiers during the American Revolution.

The pioneer family arrives in Ohio, 1796.

The Connecticut Land Company was formed, and sent out an exploration party headed by General Moses Cleaveland. Cleaveland, was born in Connecticut and studied law at Yale. Led by a black hunter and trapper, Joe Hodge, the Cleaveland party located a good place for a town site where the Cuyahoga River flowed into Lake Erie.

After planning the town, Moses Cleaveland went back to his home state. Cleaveland was founded in 1796. The first winter after Cleaveland and his party left, only two men remained in the settlement, living in one log cabin. The next year three families arrived, and by 1800 Cleaveland had started to grow. A newspaper dropped a letter out of the town's name and it became Cleveland.

In 1798 John Young started a settlement which became Youngstown, and in 1799 Warren and Ravenna appeared on the map. However, in the early history of Ohio, most of the people who came West stayed close to the Ohio River, which was the great highway into the area. Northern Ohio developed more slowly, but once it got started, Cleveland became the state's largest city.

As the Indians watched the Ohio River, each day they saw more and more white settlers coming down its waters. They became worried as they saw their hunting grounds being turned into farms. To stop this emigration, the Indians refused to honor the treaties they had made. They went on the warpath.

The Miami Indians were among the most powerful of the tribes, and had the best warriors. They lived in western Ohio and decided to fight for their homeland, and drive out the intruders.

The settlers feared the attacks of the Indians, and built blockhouses to which they could go when the Indians appeared.

Since there were less than 600 regular troops to protect the pioneers, Congress gave President Washington power to call out the militia of Kentucky, Pennsylvania and Virginia. They were to report to Fort Washington at Cincinnati, under the command of General Josiah Harmar, a Revolutionary War veteran.   About 1500 soldiers reported and were trained at Fort Washington. The soldiers then went up the Miami Valley, burning the Indians' crops and destroying their villages. They marched up through the

Maumee Valley, in what is now northwestern Ohio, into the big Miami villages. They were defeated by the Indians under the command of the great Indian Chief, Little Turtle. The defeated Americans returned to Fort Washington.

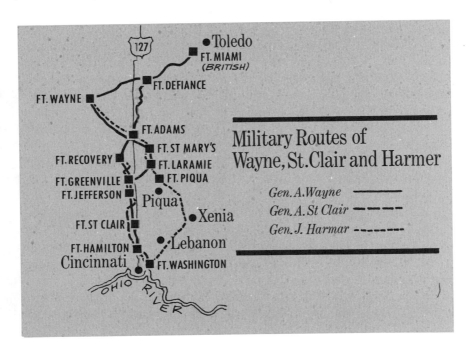

Military Routes of
Wayne, St. Clair and Harmer

Gen. A. Wayne ————
Gen. A. St Clair ————
Gen. J. Harmar ————

This encouraged the Indians, who became more daring and made more frequent attacks. No white settlement in western Ohio was safe. President Washington ordered the territorial governor, Arthur St. Clair, an officer who had served under Washington during the Revolution, to lead the attack against the Indians himself.

General St. Clair trained an army of about 3,000 men. He was given better equipment and guns for the new campaign, which he began in 1791. He moved up the Miami Valley with care, but Little Turtle had scouts watching every move. By the time they made contact with the Indians some of St. Clair's army had become ill, and gone home and others had just deserted.

66

In a surprise attack, St. Clair, himself ill, was caught off guard. After four hours of fighting his army was defeated, with 600 Americans killed, and about 300 wounded. It was the worst defeat ever met at the hands of the Indians by an American commander. The Girty Brothers, as well as some Frenchmen from Canada had helped the Indians. The second great battle of the Indian Wars was over, and the Indians were again the victors.

President Washington was so angry he relieved St. Clair of his command. The Ohio country was in more danger than ever, no cabin was safe.

Washington ordered General Mad Anthony Wayne, so called because he was quick to anger, to the West. He was one of the best generals in the Revolution, and could think fast under fire.

General Wayne got his men together and trained them carefully. He said that no rule should be broken, and that men could not desert without facing the death penalty. He drilled his 2500 men at Pittsburgh, then brought them down the river to Fort Washington. They marched north and built Fort Greenville. At the site of St. Clair's defeat Wayne ordered Fort Recovery built. Wayne continued to march northward, and deep in Indian country built Fort Defiance.

Little Turtle told the Indians, that General Wayne could not be defeated, and he refused to lead the Indians against him. Blue Jacket, a Shawnee Chief, commanded the 2,000 Indian warriors.

The great battle took place at a spot near the Maumee Rapids, not far from present-day Toledo. A bad storm had struck the area a few years before, uprooting many trees. The Indians thought the place they called Fallen Timbers, would be a good one for battle. The fallen trees would give them many places to hide, and horses could not be used among the logs on the ground. Wayne moved his 3,000 men up. They were not afraid, and came forward with gun fire, wave after wave. The Indians could not stop them, and did not even have time to reload their guns. The battle fought on Aug. 20, 1794 was over in less than one hour, and went down in history as the greatest victory ever won over the Indians.

General Wayne then asked that the Indian leaders meet with him at Fort Greenville the next year. Some 1100 Indians came to the peace conference, and after two months a treaty was made. One great chief, Tecumseh, was not there. All the tribes agreed to the Treaty of Greenville.

The Treaty of Greenville established a line across the northern part of the state, starting at the Cuyahoga and Tuscarawas Rivers. Lands north and west of the treaty line belonged to the Indians. Many Indians lived here, and at times would make raids into the Ohio villages, usually to obtain supplies or horses. The Indians slowly disappeared from Ohio, but in 1825 there were still 1500 here.

At last the Indian danger appeared over, and thousands of people swarmed into the Ohio country, so many, that in 1803 Ohio was admitted as the nation's 17th state.

This marked the beginning of a new generation in the Ohio country. The frontier generation which had come into a wilderness far from civilization had opened the land. The new pioneer generation would settle and cultivate the land. During this new generation the population of Ohio would increase from about 50,000 to over half a million.

Some young frontiersmen had explored the Ohio country seeking out the best lands for future settlement when the Indian danger was over. One such man was Daniel Doty, who had arrived in Columbia in 1789, taking part in the Indian wars in western Ohio. While scouting for wild game, he came upon an open land, which had been cleared by the Indians along the Miami River. He built a lean-to on the spot, and decided when the land was safe, he would return there with his family.

After the signing of the Treaty of Greenville, Daniel Doty returned to the land called the Great Prairie, north of Fort Hamilton. He purchased the land upon which he had built his lean-to, and in 1796 completed a log cabin. At that time his family consisted of only two boys, but later it was to grow to twelve children. Daniel Doty's children were all pioneers.

The Dotys built their own log cabin. The work started with the cutting of large trees. When the logs were trimmed and

Daniel Doty and his boys return from the hunt.

smoothed they were ready to use in the cabin. One day some men came from several miles away to help Doty put up or "raise" his cabin. With the logs in place, Doty could finish it himself. With thick clapboards, he made a stout door, which he hung on wooden hinges and fastened with wooden pegs. There was a wooden latch with the leather string hanging through it.

The furniture for the cabin was homemade. Large wooden slabs, split from a tree, supported by four round legs made from hickory saplings set in auger holes were used to make a table. Three-legged stools, made in the same way, served as chairs. Three legs were better than four on a rough, uneven wooden floor. The bed was built with rough logs, with the bottom made from clapboards, and covered with bear skins.

The fireplace was the center feature of the cabin. It furnished both light and heat for the cabin. It was also the cooking stove, and pots were hung on hooks over the blazing fire. Every day a bubbling pot of mush was made. Clapboards, supported by wooden pegs stuck in the logs of the cabin near the fireplace were used as shelves for the pewter dishes, spoons and wooden bowls. The pioneer's gun was always ready above the mantle. The gun provided wild game for food, as well as protection against Indians.

Although there was plenty of good food for the pioneer family, it was not as great a variety as people enjoy today. Daniel Doty killed bear, deer, turkey, geese, ducks, quail, squirrel, rabbit and pheasant. Deer and bear provided both fresh meat and pelts or skins. Deerskin was used by Betsy Doty to make clothing and moccasins for the family

Pioneer men hunted deer in the forests for meat.

The hominy block was a useful item. It was a short log hollowed out to look like a bowl. Shelled corn was put into it and cracked into small pieces with a wooden hammer. After the corn was reduced to a meal, it was made into Johnny cake and mush.

As the Doty's expanded their farm they had to clear the forest. First the underbrush, and then the small saplings were cut and burned. The large trees were girdled by cutting a wide strip of bark off all around the tree. This killed the tree, for when it was dead it was easier to cut down and burn. Two or three men could burn off more logs in a day than they could chop in a month. The fire would burn day and night, and at night it could be seen for miles.

By 1800 sheep and hogs were brought to Ohio. The hogs ate up the surplus corn. Their meat could be smoked and cured for winter use, or it could be sold. Wool from the sheep found a market in the woolen mills.

At first the Doty family used oxen, for they were cheaper than horses and could work harder and pull heavier loads. When injured in work, they could be shot and used for beef. The hide was tanned for leather.

The pioneer family had to cooperate or work together. Daniel Doty planted crops, cut timber, cleared land, and hunted. Betsy, his wife, kept house, spun wool, wove cloth, cured meat, made soap and candles. The children divided up the chores, the older one taking care of younger brothers and sisters.

There were thousands of pioneer families in the Ohio country who lived like the Dotys. The pioneer generation faced many problems in the new land. While there were a few old lands, cleared by the Indians, and some natural open spaces, almost 95 percent of the land was covered with forests. Felling the trees, and getting land into cultivation was a very difficult job. Building homes, and barns with the few tools available was hard work. Women and men worked from sun up to sun down. It took physical stamina on the frontier.

Inside view of a pioneer's cabin.

Life in the Ohio country was at first very lonely, for the families often lived many miles apart. Most pioneers missed the social life which they had enjoyed back home.

As a result of this need, there developed a new kind of community life. The pioneers were very hard-working and busy people; it seemed there was always some work that needed to be done. They learned to develop a social life that combined the need to be with other people, and at the same time do valuable work. They combined work and pleasure.

Typical Ohio home on the Frontier.

One of the first such activities was the log rolling. The man cut down the trees, and then neighbors came to help roll them into one great pile to burn. At night as the fire lighted up the land for miles around, dancing and games would take place, after a big meal prepared by the women.

The house raising for a new family was another frequent reason for getting together. The new settler got his logs together for a cabin, and the neighbors came to help raise it into a cabin. This was something that one man could not do himself. Usually after the cabin was up, there would be a big dinner, and the chance for the young men to see the girls home.

Weddings were a major social event on the frontier, and people gathered for miles around. Sometimes a wedding lasted for three days, with all kinds of activities such as a bear hunt, shooting, and racing, along with feasting. The bride and groom could expect to have many tricks played on them, and a serenade before the families headed for home.

Making of maple sugar was another time neighbors might get together to share the work and the fun at the sugar camp.

The making of apple butter provided another social event for the women in particular, as did the quilting bees. Spinning bees were sometimes held.

Much social life centered on the school. Students from one school often competed against those of another in a spelling bee, or a ciphering match. Singing schools were conducted at night by the teacher or a singing master, providing an opportunity for young men and women to meet, with the ride home in a horse and buggy or a sleigh.

The pioneer provided most of the things needed for himself and his family from his land. There was wild game in the forest. Corn and wheat were milled into meal and flour, made into bread.

Beginning of Ohio industry, the Grist Mill.

The log house replaced the log cabin as a home as the land was cleared and the family prospered.

The garden furnished vegetables, and trees were planted to provide fruit. Flax was grown, and its fiber used to make a linen thread. The wool from the sheep provided yarn to weave into cloth. From the forest came lumber for building, and wood for burning. This was called subsistence farming.

As the pioneers cleared more land, soon a surplus of grain developed. A market for the crops was available in other parts of the U.S. and the world, but most farmers had no way to get their surplus yield to market. A transportation system was needed. If the pioneers could sell the surplus they could use the money to buy things that they needed. This would raise their standard of living, and add to the pleasure of life.

Just as the frontier generation fought the Indians and the English, the pioneer generation faced the same problem. Although defeated, the Indians were still determined to drive the white settlers out of the Northwest Territory. The English still held hopes of building an empire in the western lands and holding it as part of Canada.

One very important Indian Chief had refused to sign the Treaty of Greenville. He was of the Shawnee tribe and in the Indian tongue his name, Tecumseh, meant "shooting star." He was born at the site now known as Xenia. His father, also a Shawnee Chief, fought under Pontiac. Both his father and older brother had been killed in war, and his tribe were driven from their homes by the soldiers of George Rogers Clark. Tecumseh had a brother, called the Prophet, for the Indians thought he had the gift to foretell the future.

Tecumseh had no reason to like the white man, who was driving the Indians from their hunting grounds. Hunting was the only way they knew to make a living. Tecumseh noted the great emigration of the pioneers to the Ohio country, and believed that the only hope of the Indians was to unite against the invasion.

Tecumseh and his brother went from tribe to tribe asking the Indians to unite, and drive out the invaders. Their first attack was on the boats carrying new settlers coming down the Ohio River. In less than 20 years, they had seen the boats on their river which brought about 250,000 new settlers to the Ohio country.

After Ohio became a state, General William Henry Harrison became Governor of the rest of the Northwest Territory, responsible for its safety. He talked often with Tecumseh, but was unable to persuade him to live in peace. Tecumseh said that the Indians could not live up to the treaties they had made, and that no Indian could give away the land of their fathers.

General Harrison knew that this would lead to war. Tecumseh was a wise leader, and a clever and strong fighter. He was also a good speaker. He respected the white man and asked his warriors not be be cruel to prisoners. He just wanted them to leave the land.

Tecumseh and the Prophet decided to move farther west, and settled along the Tippecanoe River, where it flows into the Wabash, near what is now Lafayette, Indiana. Even here the Indians were not let alone, for the white man began to move in. Tecumseh then went South to ask for Indian help in stopping the white man's advance westward.

Hoping to strike the Indians before they could organize, in November 1811, General Harrison and his men decided to attack.

Since Tecumseh was away, the Prophet had to lead the warriors. The Indians were defeated, and knew that they could not make the settlers leave their country. General William Henry Harrison became the great hero of the Battle of Tippecanoe, and was known as ' "Old Tippecanoe."

This battle marked the beginning of another war with England. Many pioneers felt that the English were stirring up the Indians against the Ohio settlers, and that they were helping Tecumseh. The pioneers felt that England had no right to keep forts in the Northwest Territory, for by treaty the land was part of the U.S. Ohioans thought that by driving out the English, they would also end the Indian menace.

A group of men in Congress, called the "War Hawks" agreed with the Ohio pioneers and demanded that England leave the Northwest. Great Britain had not lived up to other parts of the treaty which ended the American Revolution, so there was more than one reason for going to war.

In 1812 President James Madison declared war, known in history as the War of 1812, although it lasted until 1814. Much of that war was fought in the Northwest and Ohio.

General William Hull, governor of the Michigan territory, was appointed to invade Canada, for many Americans believed that the U.S, could take it away from Great Britain. Ohio Governor Meigs sent about 2,000 men to join Hull at Dayton. From here they marched to Detroit, but when the British attacked, General Hull surrendered the fort.

General Hull was in disgrace, and the Americans turned to General William Henry Harrison, whom the President appointed commander-in-chief. Harrison began to build up the army, and strengthen the frontier posts. Harrison moved to Fort Meigs on the Maumee River. The English under General Proctor attempted to take the fort, but were repulsed.

The English then decided to attack the smaller Fort Stephenson, located near the present site of Fremont. It had only a few blockhouses in a stockade, surrounded by a ditch. Fewer than 200 men under Major George Croghan, then only 22 years old, were stationed there. Harrison had told Major Croghan that if he saw the British approaching to destroy the supplies, burn the fort, and retreat.

General Proctor arrived with 1200 soldiers and Indians, with ample gunpowder and supplies. He demanded surrender, but Major Croghan, would not desert the fort or surrender. The English began the attack with five cannon.

Inside the fort was only one cannon called "Old Betsy," which was moved from place to place to make the enemy believe that there were several. Thinking the British would attack the fort at its weakest spot, Major Croghan placed "Old Betsy" there. The attack came just where planned, and "old Betsy" filled with shot and pieces of spikes and iron showered the invaders, who ran for their life, as the Indians sped for the forest.

One of the reasons for the successful defense of the Fort was information that Major Croghan had of the plans for the attack. Nancy Whittaker, born of pioneer Ohio parents who had built the first American home near what is now Fremont, married a British soldier.

Nancy told her mother of the British plans, and Elizabeth Whittaker relayed them to the commander of Fort Stephenson. "Old Betsy" today stands guard at the Birchard Public Library at Fremont, on Croghan Street.

General Harrison welcomed the victory, and hoping for a rapid end to the war, took his army across Lake Erie to Malden, Ontario. Seeing the Americans coming, General Proctor destroyed the fort and took up defenses at a little river called the Thames. Here the Americans and English, with their Indian allies, met. General Harrison again met Tecumseh, leading the Indians. Tecumseh gave the order to attack, and above the fighting his voice could be heard. When it was silenced, the Indians knew it was all over. Their leader was dead, and the Indian power gone forever in the Northwest and Ohio.

The news of the death of the great warrior, Tecumseh, may have brought a moment of regret to Rebecca Galloway of Old Town, near the present city of Xenia, Ohio. The young lady in 1807 decided to hold English classes for the Shawnees at her home, hoping this would help bring about peace between the Indians and pioneers.

77

One of the most regular of Rebecca's students was Chief Tecumseh, who was interested both in English and Rebecca. He proposed marriage, but she was much younger than he, and had another man in mind. Not wanting to hurt the Chief's feelings or endanger the peace, she tactfully replied she would marry him, if he would give up his way of life and adopt the white man's dress and ways.

Duty would not permit him to do this. Tecumseh smoked his peace pipe and rode away, never to see Rebecca again.

The other important campaign of the War of 1812 was on Lake Erie. The English had six armed ships on Lake Erie, and the Americans wanted to see these ships gone. Commodore Oliver Hazard Perry was given the assignment of driving the English from Lake Erie. Perry had gone to sea when he was 13, and by the time he was seventeen, he was an officer. In 1813 Perry with 50 sailors started on his plan to drive out the English. Perry directed the building of the ships to be used in the battle. A large number of the men with Perry on this expedition were black seamen.

By September, 1813, Perry was at Put-in-Bay harbor with his fleet of nine ships. Both sides had about the same fire power and the same number of men. Commodore Perry took a blue flag from his sea chest, on which were the words, "Don't Give Up the Ship." These words had been spoken by Captain Lawrence, after whom Perry had named his flagship.

The two fleets met. When Perry's flagship was wrecked, he moved over to another, the Niagara, and continued the battle until the English hoisted the white flag of surrender. Perry then wrote a famous note to General Harrison: "We have met the enemy and they are ours."

Although the American victories resulted in the English leaving the Northwest, the Americans were not strong enough to march into Canada. At the end of the War, the U.S.-Canadian border remained as it had been before the conflict. The Indians now knew they could never regain their lands.

Finally the tribes who had lived in Ohio were moved west of the Mississippi River. In 1843 the Wyandots were the last Ohio Indians to leave for reservations in the West.

The pioneer generation had disposed of two major problems in the Ohio country—the English and the Indians. The action of their leaders had also disposed of another problem facing the new United States.

As the lands were settled in the rest of the continent to the west and southwest, the question arose as to whom they should belong. One man, Aaron Burr, a former senator and vice-president of the United States, was accused of planning an independent nation in the southwest through seizing Spanish territory. However, this was never proven to be his real intent, and Ohio's first Governor, Edward Tiffin, felt Burr's plans might be treason. Burr was not a well-liked man because he had killed Alexander Hamilton in a duel over political differences.

Ohio became involved in this plan because Aaron Burr on a trip down the Ohio and Mississippi Rivers, stopped at the home of Harman Blennerhassett. Blennerhassett, who had a beautiful estate on what today is known as Blennerhassett's Island, listened with interest to Burr's plans and promised to help him.

Blennerhassett was to provide boats, food, guns, and ammunition for a proposed expedition of about 500 men. When he began to order so many supplies to be shipped to his island home, Ohio authorities became suspicious.

The Ohio legislature gave Governor Tiffin the right to seize the supplies at the island, and called out militia units. Burr and Blennerhassett escaped, but their beautiful island home was burned to the ground. The men were later captured and a trial was held. The government of the U.S. was not able to prove the men guilty, but their lives were ruined.

The real plans of Burr will never be known, but all citizens of the nation now accepted the idea that any new territories settled by Americans would eventually become new states in the Union.

By 1830 Ohio had almost 1,000,000 people living in the state, with most of them living on farms. There was one large city in the state, Cincinnati, with almost 25,000 people. At that time Cleveland had 1,076 people. Ranking below Cincinnati, were four other towns with about 3,000 people— Zanesville, Steubenville, Dayton and Chillicothe.

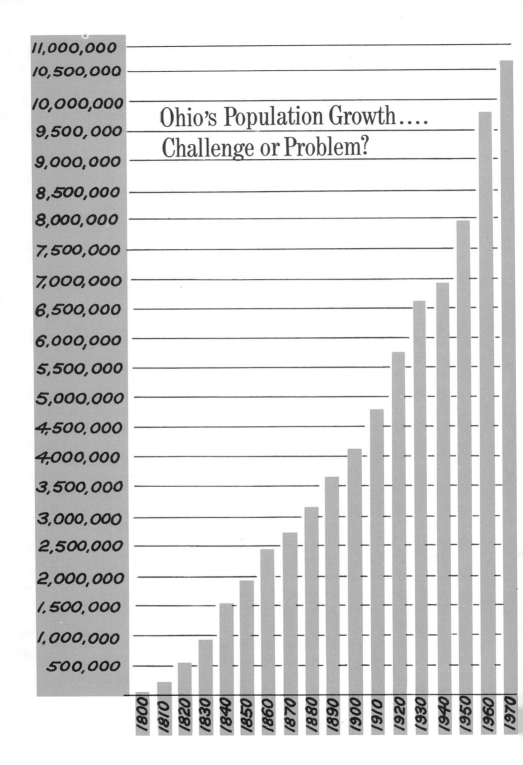

Urban and Rural Population Percentages, 1800-1960

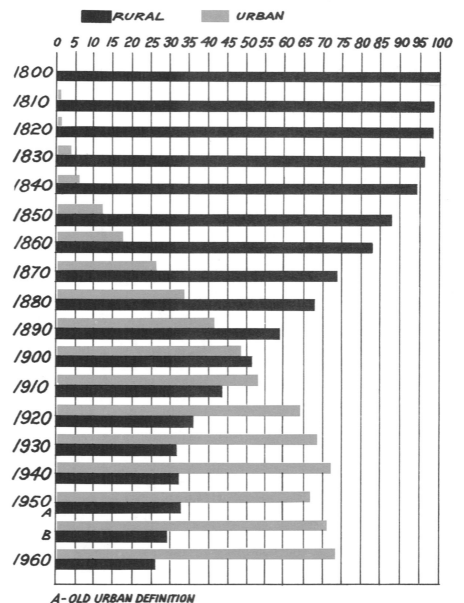

A - OLD URBAN DEFINITION
B - NEW URBAN DEFINITION

While many children had been born in Ohio, most of the adults at the time of the 1830 Census were from other states. They came to Ohio to find a better way of life, which meant making a better living for their family. They began to think of themselves as Ohioans because as a group of people in the new western state they shared common interests and goals.

The first immigrants came from other states, often coming in groups and settling in the same area. This way they would be among their old friends and neighbors. Since New Jersey was a small state, many came from there. Massachusetts, an old state, complained about so many of its citizens going West that they had the "Ohio fever." The soil was better in Ohio and attracted many of the Bay State's farmers. Connecticut with its reserved land in the West sent many of its residents into new Connecticut where they built towns and churches like those at home.

New York and Pennsylvania were listed as the birthplace of many early Ohioans. The Virginia Military tract of reserved land for that state's people, attracted many. Virginians who had emigrated to Kentucky, later moved on up into Ohio where the land was more fertile and level, making it easier and more profitable to farm. This was one of the largest groups in early Ohio.

Pennsylvania Germans and Scotch-Irish born in the U.S. were among the first Ohioans, but after 1830 more and more Irish and Germans came directly from Europe, referred to by them as the "old country."

The Irish first found work in helping to build the canal systems of Ohio, and being poor, they lived along the canal in temporary housing called "shanty towns." After completing the canal many went to work on the waterway, some rising to be captains of boats. Other Irish continued in construction trades, and helped build the railroads of Ohio and the nation. So many came, that sometimes they met with prejudice. Stores and newspaper advertisements at times listed at the end of a notice of need for help: NINA. This meant "No Irish Need Apply." Most of the Irish who came were Roman Catholics, and some Ohioans objected to their religious preference.

During the last century so many Germans came to Ohio that they became the largest group of immigrants in Ohio. They were good farmers and knew how to locate the best farming land. The names of some of their towns show their origin—New Bremen, New Bavaria, Minster (named for Munster) and Germantown. Germans were also tradesmen and lived in cities, usually in a German section. The "Over the Rhine" section of Cincinnati was one of these as well as the German Village section of Columbus and Hamilton.

The French were among the earliest settlers of Ohio. French Canadians also came south to Ohio to work in the lumber industry. For a short time a religious group, the Mormons, settled at Kirkland, Ohio. Welsh and Scotch also settled in the Ohio country.

While people with English ancestors were among the first to settle in Ohio, soon they were a minority, being joined by people whose ancestors had come to America from many countries.

While most of the foreign immigrants came from Great Britain and countries of northern Europe before the Civil War, after that war immigrants began to pour in from southern and eastern Europe. People came from Italy, Austria, Hungary, Russia, Poland and Greece. By this time northern Ohio was growing rapidly, as the industries there needed workers. Most of the immigrants settled in the northern part of the state, especially in the Cleveland area.

By 1910, a third of the people of Cleveland had been born in Europe. By 1920 the Polish immigrants represented the largest group. They were hard workers and found jobs in industry, particularly the steel mills.

New workers migrated to southern Ohio also. Most of them came from Appalachia. As mining became mechanized, fewer workers were needed. These people found jobs in Ohio. They did not have to travel very far coming from Kentucky, Tennessee, and West Virginia.

The people now called Ohioans came from everywhere. By the first decade of the twentieth century, Ohio had become the home of about 30 different nationalities. Each nationality made up what is called an ethnic group. A study of your family history will probably reveal that you have ancestors from different lands.

NATIVITY OF POPULATION OF OHIO—U. S.
CENSUS 1850,

England	25,660
Ireland	51,662
Scotland	5,232
Wales	5,849
Germany	111,257
France	7,375
Spain	28
Portugal	7
Belgium	103
Holland	348
Turkey	1
Italy	174
Austria	29
Switzerland	3,291
Russia	84
Norway	18
Denmark	53
Sweden	55
Prussia	765
Sardinia	15
Greece	0
China	3
Asia	6
Africa	7
British America	5,880
Mexico	26
Central America	12
South America	41
West Indies	86
Sandwich Islands	1
Other Countries	544
TOTAL FOREIGN	218,512
Unknown	4,359
Aggregate	1,980,427

At first ethnic groups tried to forget their special customs and celebrations and become Americans. The U.S. was thought of as a "melting pot" that would make all people alike. Then these ethnic groups came to realize that a person could be a good citizen and still enjoy the rich culture of their own people. America was a land where people could be different, but respected.

The different ethnic groups are now proud of their own culture, which is made up of the customs and traditions passed on from one generation to the next through hundreds of years. Among the items which help make up a particular culture are clothing, food, religious beliefs, games, recreation, festivals, dances, and language.

When all these different groups settled in Ohio, they kept some of the most important parts of their culture, and other Buckeyes began to enjoy them also. In this way the culture of Ohio was made more interesting and varied, and life was more fun for everyone. So that all could communicate, one language was used and taught in the schools. English is a rich language and widely used throughout the world, so all Ohioans thought it a good idea to continue to use that language.

At first the new immigrants had a difficult time to adjust to their new life. Some of the older groups made fun of the new ones because of their different culture and even called them unkind names. As years went by, no one knew or cared from which country they had emigrated.

One group of people, however, who came to Ohio had a more difficult time in gaining acceptance for the color of their skin was different. While all groups had met prejudice, black people faced it more than other Ohioans. Black people had lived in America longer than most Ohioans, as their ancestors began to migrate to the new world in 1619. Some of their forefathers had fought in the American Revolution. Crispus Attucks, a Black man, was the first to be killed in the Revolution. These people, called Negroes, instead of migrating from Europe, had come from Africa.

The Black man had been part of Ohio's history from its beginning. One had accompanied Christopher Gist into the Ohio country in 1750. Black soldiers had joined Anthony Wayne's army as it marched up the Miami Valley in 1794. In 1817 John Stewart, a Black Christian, began his work among the Wyandot Indians.

Before the Civil War, most Black people lived in the Southern part of the U.S., working on farms and plantations. They were held as slaves and were not free to move. Some, however, were freed by understanding owners, and others escaped.

The founders of Ohio were opposed to slavery. The Northwest Ordinance of 1787 prohibited slavery. The first Constitution of Ohio stated that the Constitution could never be changed so as to introduce slavery. A Cincinnati newspaper editor expressed the feelings of early Ohioans when he stated that slavery was "an evil in and a disgrace to our country."

In early Ohio there were few Negroes. One of them was Richard Stanhope, George Washington's servant and valet. In his will, Washington gave Stanhope his freedom and claim to a piece of land Washington owned in the Ohio country.

After the Northwest Ordinance opened the way, free Afro-Americans came into Ohio. They settled in about twenty-five different communities. The first of these was New Guinea, settled in 1810, which later became part of Alliance. This settlement was made up of about two hundred people, most who belonged to a religious group, Christ's Disciples. The Quakers set up a school and one of them acted as teacher for the Black children.

The Census Report of 1820 reported that 5,000 Negroes lived in the new state. By 1850 the Negro population had grown to 25,000 which represented less than two percent of the population. Some Negroes had farms, but most of them worked in cities. Many worked on the wharves or on the steamboats at Cincinnati.

By 1870 there were 60,000 Negroes in Ohio. Many lived in northern Ohio, which had few Black people in the early years. As Cleveland and other Lake Erie ports grew, Black men found jobs at the docks as well as other places. Oberlin College had opened its doors to Negroes early in its history.

As more and more mechanization came to the fields of the South, less labor was needed. Black families continued to move northward to find employment. Problems developed when more

Black people moved North than there were available jobs. Then they had to live in low rent parts of the cities, where housing had deteriorated. These sections were known as slums, or ghettoes. Ohio is still trying to find jobs for all its citizens by attracting new industries. It is building new homes and apartments to replace the old buildings, but it will take many years.

Black people have become the largest minority in Ohio. In the largest city, Cleveland, they represent a third of the population. They take great interest in Cleveland's city government and hold almost one-third of the seats on City Council. Black people now hold many important positions in Ohio.

It was a long struggle in Ohio, and the rest of the U.S., for all people to enjoy the same rights and opportunities. There are still more changes needed, but much has been accomplished.

The first two generations of Ohioans, were busy building the farms and towns. By 1825 the pioneer's children were growing up and beginning to build their own homes. This new generation saw a very rapid growth in Ohio, and during this period Ohio became the third state in population in all the U.S.

This new generation had to plan for the growth of business and industry to provide jobs for those coming to the state. They had to set up a transportation system, resulting in the canal system, and railroad lines, as well as improved roads.

This pre-Civil War generation also wanted to improve the quality of life. They started a free, public school system, libraries, and colleges. The biggest problem of this generation was to be that of slavery.

Across the Ohio River, both Kentucky and Virginia, (West Virginia was not yet a state), permitted slavery. The Ohio River was the river of freedom for many Black people for once across the river, they were free. There were people in Ohio such as John Rankin, whose house was located on a hill at Ripley in Brown County, who would help them.

As early as 1815 the first anti-slavery society was formed in Ohio. A religious group, the Quakers, joined by other churches, believed that slavery was morally wrong. Ohio had an anti-slavery newspaper.

Most Ohioans believed that slavery was wrong, but they did not know how to abolish it in the South. The U.S. Constitution protected slavery as it existed there. In 1817 the American Colonization Society was formed. It planned to resettle the freed slaves in Africa. Several branches of it were formed in Ohio, and it gained wide support.

The people who thought that slavery should be abolished at any cost, were called Abolitionists. Again the Quakers had an important part in this movement. Theodore D. Weld married Angelina Grimke, who along with a sister, Sarah, were leaders of the Abolitionists. Weld, a minister, came to Cincinnati and gained the support of the students of Lane Theological Seminary for the American Anti-Slavery Society. The students went out into the city to help the 2500 Negroes living in Cincinnati by setting up schools. When the trustees of the college objected, most of the students withdrew.

Some of these students transferred to Oberlin, which had agreed to permit the Anti-Slavery organization at its college, and also promised to admit Negroes to its classes. This was the first college in the U.S. to take this action.

On the North side of the Ohio River, there were many people who would help the Black people escape. They helped runaway slaves to reach Canada, away from the danger of being caught and taken back to slavery. Although it was against the law, many Ohioans felt so strongly against slavery that they would take the chance. The method used to help the slaves to escape was called the Underground Railroad.

The Underground Railroad received its name from an unhappy slave owner, who had one of his Black men escape by swimming across the Ohio River. The owner followed the man in a boat, but when the slave reached the Ohio bank, he just disappeared. The owner couldn't understand where the slave had gone, and remarked that the slave must have been carried off on an "Underground Railroad."

The Underground Railroad was not underground and it wasn't even a railroad. It was a group of Ohioans working together to help Black people escape from slavery.

The stations on the Underground Railroad were houses and barns where a slave could be hidden. Houses had hidden closets and secret rooms in basements; there were sliding door panels. Sometimes there were secret tunnels from one house to another, perhaps even under a road.

Rankin House on Liberty Hill, overlooking Ohio River. Major station on the Underground Railroad.

A farmer hides a family of runaway slaves in his barn, a station on the Underground Railroad.

Regular trails crossed through the state. Stations on the north shore of the Ohio River welcomed the Black refugees. The Rankin house stood as a beacon with a light in the window. Levi Coffin, who ran a store in Cincinnati, is said to have helped over 3,000 slaves escape. There was about 25 stations along the southern shore of Lake Erie. Some free Ohio Negroes helped people of their own race escape. Alfred Greenbrier owned a large farm near Cleveland. His farmhouse contained secret hiding places for Black people, and although he was under suspicion, he was too clever to get caught with runaway slaves. John Malvin owned a boat, which was most useful in getting slaves safely across the lake. He was an important person on the Underground Railroad.

In the ten years before the Civil War, more trouble developed between the North and the South. A Republican Party formed in 1854 which was against slavery. A Fugitive Slave Act, passed by Congress, forced Ohioans, by law, to return runaway slaves. This most Ohioans refused to do.

One Black woman, Margaret Garner, showed how determined she was that she and her children not live under slavery. When the Ohio River was frozen in January 1856, so that it could be crossed on foot, she, her husband and four children crossed to Cincinnati.

After finding a hiding place in the home of a Black man, slave hunters and officers surrounded the house. She killed one child before being caught. She was given to her owners under the Fugitive Slave Law. On return, she jumped into the river and tried to drown herself and her youngest child, a mere baby. She did not succeed in drowning herself, but her child was lost. Margaret Garner said she would rather her children and herself be dead than be slaves.

In 1859, when John Price, a fugitive slave, was caught at Oberlin it caused another incident which showed how Ohioans felt about slavery. Price was taken from Oberlin to Wellington. When the news of Price's capture was known, over 500 Ohioans gathered at Wellington to save him. They captured him from the officials, and after hiding him in the home of Oberlin's President, finally saw that he reached Canada and freedom.

A few of the citizens who took part in the rescue were identified and arrested. The Judge ruled that the Fugitive Slave Law was the law of the land and must be obeyed. He said it was wrong to disobey the law. Many people in Ohio disagreed for they believed the law was wrong. The Judge was not renominated for his job.

The person who best described life under slavery and helped the anti-slavery cause was Harriet Beecher Stowe. While living in Cincinnati she met and worked with people on the Undergound Railroad. She listened as the slaves told their stories. One of the slaves, Eliza Harris, is a character in the book, "Uncle Tom's Cabin".

"Uncle Tom's Cabin" was the most influential book ever written on slavery. It told of the hardships of the slaves and how they suffered. The book was made into a play which was the most popular one of the nineteenth century. After reading the book, most Ohioans agreed that slavery should be ended in all the U.S.

Another Ohioan, John Brown, who lived at Akron, decided he would do something more than talk or write about slavery. He planned to free the slaves. In order to get guns and ammunition, he and a group of followers, attacked the army depot at Harper's Ferry.

John Brown gained entrance to the place, and took some guns. The United States troops soon caught him, and John Brown and some of his helpers were hanged. He became a hero to those who did not believe in slavery, and they began to sing the song, "John Brown's Body," an anti-slavery song.

While a student at Otterbein College in 1856, Benjamin Hanby, wrote the most popular song of the Abolitionist's, "Darling Nellie Gray."

On a bright, cool crisp day in September, 1859, a visitor came to Ohio. He made several speeches in major cities giving his views on the most important problem facing the nation at that time — slavery. The new Republican Party was looking for a candidate, and they found him in the person of Abraham Lincoln. The next time he came through Ohio he was on his way to Washington as the new President. Over 50,000 people greeted him in Cincinnati, and at Columbus he spoke to the General Assembly.

Lincoln's last trip across Ohio was a sad one. It was when President Lincoln's funeral train made its way slowly to his Springfield, Illinois home.

Although not a native Ohioan, Lincoln was a man of the Old Northwest. He was born in Kentucky, crossed southern Ohio on his way to his childhood home in Indiana, and as a young man moved to Illinois. With the election of Lincoln, the issue of slavery in the U.S. had reached the point that only war could solve the problem. The Civil War began in April 1861. The southern states decided they would secede from the Union and set up their own country, which they called the Confederacy.

Ohio played a most important part in the Civil War. Before it was over, three out of every five Ohio men between the ages of 18 and 45 as well as thousands of others, older and younger than those ages had served. Almost 320,000 Ohioans were Union soldiers.

Many young boys signed up as Drummer Boys, often becoming fighting soldiers. Each Company was permitted two field musicians. This made room for drummer boys such as Johnnie Clem, who was the youngest and most famous of these drummer boys.

Johnnie Clem was a nine-year old boy at Newark, when the Civil War broke. Although he was only 30 inches tall, he was determined to join the army. At first he was turned down by the recruiting officer. This did not stop him. He ran away from home, and finally found a regiment that would accept him. He waited for sometime before he officially signed up, afraid he would be sent home. The men of his regiment outfitted him, bought him a gun and a drum.

He saw his first big action at the Battle of Shiloh when his drum was hit by a shell. Then Johnnie grabbed his gun and began firing into enemy lines. His bravery inspired others, and his story was told from campfire to campfire. He became known as the "Drummer Boy of Shiloh."

Finally he was captured and taken prisoner of war, but managed to escape. He then returned to his regiment, and was promoted to Sergeant.

After the War, through his friendship with General U.S. Grant, he was admitted to West Point despite the fact he was too short to meet their standards. He became a General in the U.S.

Army and served in many places. Finally he retired as the last Civil War soldier to leave army service. He died in 1937 and rests at Arlington.

Ohio women also played a part in the Civil War. Born on a farm in Knox County between Frederickstown and Mount Vernon in 1817 was a girl named Mary Ann Ball. In 1849 she changed her name by marrying Robert Bickerdyke of Cincinnati. She studied nursing at Oberlin College, first showing her nursing skill in caring for the ill in the cholera epidemic which swept Ohio.

She had two strong beliefs. She felt that women should be able to do any work that they were qualified to do, and that the Negro should be free and have an equal chance in life.

While living in Cincinnati, she helped in the Underground Railroad. When the Civil War broke out, she heard that the soldiers were being poorly fed and that there was no one to care for the sick. She went to a Camp commanded by General W.T. Sherman of Ohio, and began her work. She stayed with Sherman throughout the years of the Civil War. She saw that the men were supplied with good food and with needed medical supplies.

After a battle, she would be on the battlefield looking for the wounded. Black and white soldiers received the same professional care. She worked hard to make the field hospitals more sanitary. Her devotion to the common soldier earned her the name of "Mother Bickerdyke" for that is what she was to thousands of Civil War soldiers.

When the war finally ended she rode her faithful horse, "Old Whitey" in the victory parade in Washington, and none of the great generals received more cheers than Mother Bickerdyke.

Since the Civil War was being fought to end slavery, the Negroes of Ohio wanted to help. One regiment, the 127th Ohio Voluntary Infantry was made up of over 5,000 free, Black soldiers. With the Black population of Ohio about 37,000, including women and children, this was a high percentage of volunteers.

Some Ohio Negroes also served in other regiments. At first Congress did not pay Black and White soldiers the same pay, but within a year they corrected this inequality.

The Ohio Negro regiment took part in many battles, including those of Yorktown, Richmond and Petersburg. They were praised for being brave fighters. Some of the black soldiers rose in the ranks to become officers. Four Ohio Negro soldiers were awarded the Congressional Medal of Honor. They were Milton M. Holland of Athens, Robert Pinn of Massillon, and James J. Brownson and Powhatan Beaty of Delaware.

Since Ohio was providing so many soldiers, as well as supplies for the War, the South planned to invade the state. Led by General Kirby Smith, 12,000 Confederate soldiers came up through Kentucky, finally reaching the Ohio River. General John H. Morgan was on his way North to join his forces with those of General Smith.

Ohioans were afraid that invasion might come at any time, for only the river stood between them and the Confederate forces. Cincinnati, "Queen City of the West," was the prize they were after. The city called for help. President Lincoln sent General Lew Wallace, who was not only a fine soldier, but a writer. The minute he arrived in Cincinnati, it was placed under military law. All citizens were called to the defense of the city. Men and boys from all of southwestern Ohio, grabbed their guns and rushed to Cincinnati. Since they brought any gun available many of which were used in hunting, the defenders took on the name of "Squirrel Hunters."

Ohio men marched across a pontoon bridge over the Ohio and fortified the hills of northern Kentucky. When General Smith saw the preparations which had been made to defend the city, he thought it wise not to make the attack.

The following year, General John Morgan, leader of what became known as the Morgan Raiders, did cross the Ohio River. With 2500 men he brought the war to Ohio. He crossed the Ohio River in Indiana and made his way around the City of Cincinnati, wishing to avoid the strong defenses of General Ambrose Burnside.

Across southern Ohio, Morgan's Raiders rushed, taking food and horses as they went. Soon 100,000 Ohio men were chasing Morgan's men. Morgan rushed to reach the Ohio River, but about half of his raiders were captured. For a short time Morgan and the remainder of his men continued the raid, but they, too, were caught, and sent to the Ohio Penitentiary. General Morgan even managed to escape from the prison, but once back across the Ohio River, he never returned.

While most Ohioans supported Lincoln and the Union, there were a few who wanted the South to win. One of these, Lottie Moon, of Oxford, acted throughout the war as a clever spy for the Confederacy. Her story is one of daring and excitment.

From Ohio came the leaders who would win the war. President Lincoln had tried several generals during the Civil War, but none of them could produce the victory he wanted. Finally he turned to General Ulysses S. Grant, who had graduated from West Point, and had seen service in the Mexican War. It was not until he commanded the western compaign that Grant showed what he could do. Lincoln felt that he was the Union's best General, so he was given command of all forces.

A Civil War Cann n. A war that divided a nation.

Finally Grant brought an end to the Civil War. When General Robert E. Lee surrendered. Grant was kind to him and his soldiers. When the war was over Grant was still a young man. Although he wished to return home, the people asked him to become President. They elected him twice to that position.

Another great leader from Ohio was General William Tecumseh Sherman, also a graduate of West Point and veteran of

95

the Mexican War. Sherman shortened the war by his plan to march through Georgia and cut the South in two. He destroyed railroads and anything which would help the South continue the war. Soon the Confederate army found it impossible to continue to fight.

General Philip H. Sheridan, from Somerset, had his boyhood dream realized when he was given an appointment to West Point. Sheridan played an important part in winning the war.

Other Ohioans helped President Lincoln win the war. Edwin M. Stanton from Steubenville served as Secretary of War. Salmon P. Chase, a former Ohio Governor, became Secretary of the Treasury. Ohio Senators John Sherman and Benjamin Wade supported Lincoln in Congress.

Historic Marblehead Lighthouse

Winning Football, A Tradition In Ohio

Football Hall Of Fame, Canton

Ohio, A Center For Outdoor Sporting Events

Pastoral Scene In Rural Ohio

Enjoying Outdoor Ohio

Ohio Water Is For All To Enjoy

Enjoying One Of Ohio's Natural Beautie

CHAPTER IV

Transportation and Communication

Transportation

When Ohio's first people, the Mound Builders, came into the region they followed the natural highways. These were the rivers and streams which drained the valley or the Great Lakes.

These early people learned to build canoes using the bark of the birch trees over a frame of tree branches. A more sturdy canoe was made with a large log, gouging out the inside and then burning out more of the wood. These dugout canoes could carry heavy loads. A birch bark canoe was so light that one man could carry it over his head, as he walked from one stream to another over a piece of land called a portage.

Ohio had many places of portage, for there is a watershed across the state. Opposite the major rivers flowing south to the Ohio, there were others flowing north to Lake Erie. Over 30 well-defined trails followed these waterways.

In addition to these natural routes, the first Ohioans found other trailways. At one time large buffalo herds roamed Ohio. These heavy animals going from place to place looking for food, fresh water, and salt licks, made primitive trails with their hoofs. They found the easiest routes from place to place avoiding the thick forests.

A path or road which was made by animals beating it out and packing the earth, is called a trace. The Indians followed these traces, knowing they would lead to food and water. Then the pioneers followed the Indian trails, and the traces became wagon trails. Some of these traces and trails are now used as roads, and account for the winding highways in some parts of Ohio.

Both Mound Builder and Indian made frequent use of the water and land trailways through Ohio. By following the Ohio River to the Mississippi, they were able to trade with the people of the Gulf of Mexico, and some shells used in their craft work came from there. They obtained copper from the Great Lakes region, and various other materials from widely scattered places. Indians visited Ohio to obtain the best flint.

Arriving in Ohio, the pioneers found a primitive transportation network to serve as the beginning of a new and better one.

The early pioneers followed three roads to the Ohio country. There was the northern route from New England, beginning in the Boston area. It followed the Mohawk Valley from Albany to Lake Erie or veered south to the headwaters of the Allegheny River and then to the Upper Ohio. The Middle Route passed through southern Pennsylvania to the Ohio River at Pittsburgh, and then down the Ohio. The Southern Route led from Richmond, Virginia to Kentucky through the Cumberland Gap. With the opening of the National Road, people from Maryland and Virginia followed it. Those coming from Western Pennsylvania or Kentucky came into Ohio at the most convenient point.

The freight wagon was used by early Ohioans to get their produce to market.

Ohio Indians watch flatboats going downstream around 1800.

Most of the pioneers came by the northern or middle route. The average migrant bought or built a wagon. The Conestoga wagon was used most, for it carried a heavy load. With a canvas top and sturdy bed, it could be caulked so as not to leak when streams were forded. It received its name from Conestoga, Pennsylvania where the first ones were built.

Horses or oxen were used to pull the wagons. Often a cow or two was tied on the back. Roads were narrow, often with stumps left in them. Log bridges were built over some streams, and in later years ferries came into operation.

After arriving at Pittsburgh, the pioneer sold his wagon and bought lumber to build a flatboat. While building the boat, the family lived in a tent, or some kept their wagon for a time living in it and under it.

Flatboats came in all shapes and sizes, being nothing but a large log raft with sides. Most had two sheds on them, one for the family at one end, and one for the livestock at the other. A large sweep, or oar, served as a rudder. The boat drifted with the current downstream.

The flatboat had a long history on the Ohio River. The first one appeared on the river around 1780 and the last one disappeared around 1850. They came in all sizes, some being 20 feet long and others, 100 feet, and they varied in width from 12 to 20 feet. The average boat carried about 500 barrels of produce, such as flour or pork.

If the flatboat were headed all the way to New Orleans it would likely be a larger, better built boat, and covered. If the boat were headed only for Kentucky, it was usually smaller and covered only about one-third of its length, as well as being made of less sturdy timber. Such a boat was called a Kaintuck boat or an ark, while the larger ones were called Orleans boats.

Since the flatboat could not make the return trip up the river, it was sold at its destination. Wood from flatboats was used to build Fort Washington at Cincinnati, and many houses at New Orleans were made from the sturdy timbers of the flatboats, as well as were some of the sidewalks. Flatboats in the later years for the Orleans destination were built at Gallipolis, Marietta, and Cincinnati.

One of the disadvantages of the flatboat was that it would only go down river. Soon another boat was on the Ohio River, it was the keelboat, which could go both downstream and upstream.

The keelboats were smaller than the flatboats, usually 40 to 80 feet long and 7 to 10 feet wide. It was built on a keel, or a long thick plank. Ribs crossed the keel and wood covered it. Long and narrow they moved fast. They had a cabin and cargo box, and often partly covered.

Poling a Keelboat upstream.

Going downstream was easy in a keelboat, but it was much harder going upstream. It was done in several ways. If the water was not too deep, the men put poles down to the bottom and pushed the boat along. If they could get the boat near shore, they towed the boat from the shoreline. If the wind was right, the keelboatmen even used sails. The keelboatmen were professional river men, for it took great strength to work on them. They learned the best routes to take down the river, avoiding many of the tree trunks and snags in the river, which caused almost a fourth of the flatboats to sink before reaching their destination.

These men were the toughest men in the Ohio country. They were feared by the early settlers, paying little attention to the law. They fought for fun. Known as the King of the Keelboatmen was Mike Fink.

He was always seen with a red feather stuck in the band of his old hat. His face was tanned from the sun, and his arms were strong and his chest wide. One could hear him yell from his boat, "Look out for Mike Fink, I'm half wild horse, and half alligator!"

Mike was the best known of all the river keelboatmen. Born in Pittsburgh, he roamed the forests around Fort Pitt, living with his family in one of the huts around the fort. By the time he was 12 years old he could shoot well, and when the fort was under attack, Mike helped defend it. He became such a crack shot that he won most of the prizes at the shooting contests.

Mike liked to watch the boats go up and down the river. One day some men from a keelboat provoked a fight with Mike, and before it was over, Mike Fink whipped the whole crew. The Captain gave him a job, and from then on Mike was a keelboatman, and finally became Captain of his own boat. When a gang of pirates attacked his boat, Mike and his men not only defeated them, but burned down their hideaway.

One day there came chugging down the river a new kind of boat. It was run by steam. Mike yelled at the boat, and then he tried to race it, but it just went on past Mike's keelboat. Mike Fink knew that a new day had come to the Ohio River. He did not like these new steamboats, and he thought too many people were coming into the Ohio country. Like Daniel Boone, Mike Fink, too, headed toward the new West.

Robert Fulton built a steamboat, the "Clermont" which made its first trip on the Hudson River in New York in 1807. He proved that boats could be propelled by steam. Soon after that the Ohio Steamboat Navigation Company was organized to build and operate steamboats on the Ohio and Mississippi Rivers. The first steamboat on the Ohio was called the "New Orleans."

The "New Orleans" left Pittsburgh on Oct. 11, 1811, and two

days later was at Cincinnati. After many delays, it finally arrived in New Orleans.

While the "New Orleans" could get down the Ohio River, its engines were not powerful enough to push it upstream any distance, so it remained in service in the calm, lower waters of the Mississippi. Henry Shreve was the first steamboat builder to install a new type of engine in a steamboat, giving it enough power to push its way back up the river against the current. His steamboat, called the "Washington" was the first of thousands that would use the Ohio-Mississippi waterway. The age of the steamboat had begun. In 1818 the "Walk-in-the-Water" went into service on Lake Erie.

The Ohio River became a very important transportation route as the Midwest grew and the nation expanded to the Pacific Ocean.

One of the people who watched the steamboats go by at Cincinnati was Stephen Collins Foster. His brother was a steamboat Captain, operating a steamboat agency, which made arrangements for transporting cargo as well as passengers. Stephen was hired as a clerk, and from the windows of his small office he could look down on the wharves— at a time when over 500 steamboats were on the Ohio River.

Stephen Collins Foster was more interested in writing songs than in bookkeeping, and while at Cincinnati he began to compose some that became popular. His songs often reflect the years he spent in Cincinnati. After leaving Cincinnati for New York City, Foster became one of America's best known song writers. A bronze statue of Foster still looks down on the Ohio from the Cincinnati hills.

River transportation was important in the development of Ohio, but it was not a complete transportation system. There were many places to which a pioneer could not travel by that means. The lands along the rivers were the first to be claimed and settled, but there were thousands of acres of rich farmland not along the Ohio rivers and streams.

The first travelers through the wilderness went on foot, following the Indian trails, which were the shortest and easiest routes to follow. The more fortunate travelers owned a horse, which could carry his rider at about 20 miles per hour over a 100-mile journey.

As soon as the pioneers discovered that Ohio had much good land not facing a river, they demanded that roads be built through the forest wilderness. Colonel Ebenezer Zane, who scouted the Ohio country before the American Revolution, knew the land of eastern Ohio. In 1796 the U.S government gave him permission to build a road from Wheeling, now in West Virginia, to a point on the Ohio River at Aberdeen.

The men blazed the trees, or cut notches in them, to show where the new road would go. The underbrush was cleared out and the roadway prepared. At first the pack horses tramped down the dirt, and then came the large Conestoga wagons. This first public road in Ohio was soon widely traveled and served as a mail route. It looked almost like part of a circle, beginning and ending at the Ohio River, after running for 200 miles. To the early settlers it was known as Zane's Trace. For building the road, Zane was given tracts of land, one of which is now the site of Zanesville.

There was still no good roadway leading to the Ohio country. In 1811 the U.S. government began to build the National Road, but since it began at Cumberland, Maryland, it was first called the Cumberland Road. By 1818 the road reached the Ohio River.

On July 4, 1825, a public ceremony at the Belmont Courthouse in St. Clairsville marked the beginning of work on the National Road in Ohio. After following Zane's Trace as far as Zanesville, the road went westward to Columbus and Springfield. By 1840 the National Road had crossed Ohio, being 225 miles long and 66 feet wide. By 1852 it had finally reached Vandalia, Illinois. In later years the same route became Route 40.

As the years went by the roadbed was improved until it was hard surfaced. Stagecoaches and freight wagons crossed it as well as the settlers to the new lands of Ohio and the Northwest. Many roads and trails connected with it. Some of the roads leading to it were very poor. Corduroy roads made of tree trunks placed crossways on the roadbed were built if the land was poorly drained. This made for a very rough ride, and dangerous to horses whose hoofs might get caught between the logs.

Rough Corduroy Road.

As it was expensive to keep the National Road in repair, the state of Ohio set up tollgates along the road. Everyone using the road, with a few exceptions, had to pay a toll, used to improve the roadway. There were toll houses where the toll keepers lived. A pole or pike was across the road, and when the fee was paid the pike was lifted up, so the traveler could go on. Such a road became known as a turnpike. Private companies throughout Ohio built most of the early roads and paid for them, hopefully making a profit for the investors.

There were also county roads, and every citizen over 21 had to work on the roads two days a year or pay someone to work for him.

Probably the best known early traveler of Ohio was Johnny Appleseed. Although his real name was John Chapman, he is remembered by his nickname which he received because of his interest in apples and apple trees. Born in Massachusetts in 1775, he arrived in Ohio around 1800.

He built his first nursery at Pittsburgh, where the little apple trees could be cared for until large enough to set out. As Johnny saw pioneers setting out for the Ohio country, he offered them seedlings. Since there were no fruit trees in the Ohio country, Johnny thought the apple would be the best one to have.

When he saw he could not hand his trees out fast enough at Pittsburgh, he put two canoes together, piled them high with bags of seeds, which he collected from apple presses. Throughout Ohio, he started nurseries filled with apple seedlings.

Johnny Appleseed was an odd looking person as he went from cabin to cabin in the Ohio country. Most of his clothing was old and torn, given to him by settlers in exchange for apple trees. He went barefoot, even when snow was on the ground. He wore a tin pan over his long, black hair, which served both as a hat and a cooking utensil.

Johnny Appleseed never harmed an animal or an Indian, so they learned to love him. They thought he was a special kind of white medicine man. He showed Indians how to use certain herbs of the forest as medicine. He was welcome at every tepee and cabin.

Johnny was interested in more than giving away apple seeds and trees. Under his old shirt, he carried a little library of books. Each book he divided into many parts, and he went from cabin to cabin, giving each family a part of a book. Later he would come back and exchange that part for another part. His library was made up of books of the Bible. Johnny thought God had sent him to Ohio to spread the word of God and to plant apple trees.

After 60 years of wandering through Ohio and the Northwest, Johnny Appleseed returned to Fort Wayne, where he had a little cabin, called home. When he heard that some cattle were breaking down a fence around one of his nurseries, some 20 miles away, he went out in the cold, winter weather to repair it. He became tired and ill, and laid down to rest. Some men found him there, and took him back to his farm at Fort Wayne to rest forever.

On July 4, 1825, the same day that work was begun on the National Road through Ohio, another important event took place

105

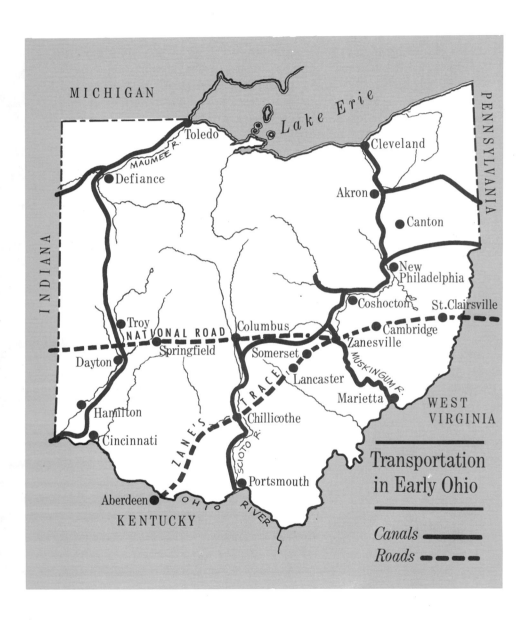

MICHIGAN

Lake Erie

Toledo

Cleveland

MAUMEE R.

Defiance

Akron

Canton

INDIANA

New Philadelphia

Troy

Coshocton

St.Clairsville

NATIONAL ROAD

Columbus

Cambridge

Springfield

Zanesville

Dayton

Somerset

MUSKINGUM R.

Lancaster

Marietta

Hamilton

ZANE'S TRACE

Chillicothe

Cincinnati

SCIOTO R.

WEST VIRGINIA

PENNSYLVANIA

Aberdeen

OHIO RIVER

Portsmouth

KENTUCKY

Transportation in Early Ohio

Canals ▬▬▬▬

Roads ▬ ▬ ▬ ▬

in transportation history in the state. At Licking Summit, outside Newark, Ohio, a group of people gathered. Governor DeWitt Clinton of New York lifted out the first shovelful of dirt from a strip of land that was to become the bed of the Ohio and Erie Canal.

The people of Ohio wanted a system of canals in the state to provide cheap transportation for their surplus agricultural produce. New York state had built a water highway, the Erie Canal, across the state to Lake Erie. Ohio ports on Lake Erie were connected to the Eastern coast and New York City. By building canals to Lake Erie, Ohioans could take advantage of this new route.

The Ohio-Erie Canal was planned to connect the Ohio River and Lake Erie. It would run over 300 miles from Portsmouth on the Ohio through the Cuyahoga Valley to Cleveland.

Canal days began in Ohio in 1825.

To please the people in the western part of Ohio another canal was planned to connect Cincinnati and Dayton, to be extended later to Toledo. This Miami-Erie Canal, as it became when finished, was begun with a similar ceremony with Gov. DeWitt Clinton on July 21, 1825 at Middletown.

Digging the two big canals was no easy task. Forests were cleared to provide the canal bed and a 20-foot strip on either side for the towpaths. Locks and bridges were constructed. The waterway went through various levels meaning the canal boats had to be raised and lowered, through a lock system.

Much of the work was done by farm men and boys. Other workers were the Irish, who left their home land to find new lives and hope in America. The Irish often built shanties along the

107

banks of the canal where they lived as they worked on a section, and when it was completed they would move their shanties on up a few more miles.

Many of the workers became ill with canal chills or canal fever, usually another name for malaria. Others developed pneumonia. Cholera swept the area and many died of this. Accidents took a heavy toll, resulting from powder blasts or even the kick of a stubborn mule. It was estimated that for every six miles of canal built, a man gave his life. The average pay was $10 a month, which included generous allotments of free whiskey.

The canals had a great effect upon the growth of Ohio. Wheat sold for 25¢ a bushel and a barrel of flour brought less than $2. Transported to New York City at a cost of less than $2 a barrel, the flour sold for $8. The canal brought an era of prosperity for Ohio farmers and manufacturers.

Every town on the route of the canals profited from the trade and passenger traffic on it. Some towns developed around the construction sites and the locks which were built required care and maintenance. Akron was one city that developed in this way, and others such as Massillon, Newark, Coshocton, and Chillicothe made rapid strides. Around the locks small factories developed, using the surplus water from the locks, which was enough to turn mill wheels. Another by-product of the canals was the cutting of ice in winter off ponds filled with water from the canal. The ice was stored in great icehouses, and packed in sawdust brought in from lumber mills along the canal. The ice found ready sale in the summer.

The canal furnished employment for many people. Some of the Irish immigrants who helped build it, stayed on to become owners and captains of the canal boats. Young boys found work on the towpaths riding and guiding the horses or mules pulling the canal boats. One of these James Garfield, later became president of the U.S.

In 1842 a young English author, Charles Dickens, arrived in Cincinnati from Pittsburgh. He came down the Ohio River on a steamboat. As he traveled through the United States and Ohio he took notes of the things he saw, and when he returned to England published them in a book called "American Notes." His observations of travel through Ohio are interesting even today.

As he came down the Ohio River, he wrote that every few miles he saw "a log cabin with its little space of cleared land about it." Most of the cabins had a small field of wheat planted around it. The pioneers stopped their work when they saw the steamboat coming down the river.

At Cincinnati, Dickens transferred to a stagecoach which took him through much of Ohio. He complained that the roads were narrow and muddy, and that many of the streams had to be forded. The stagecoach went bumping along and the ride was a hard one. At places corduroy roads were in use. Traveling along the road there were some travelers on horseback, and some in carriages. Big freight wagons, loaded with tons of produce, were on their way to city markets.

Stagecoach travel in early Ohio.

Most of the people who traveled inland away from the canal routes, went by stagecoach. These were operated by companies and run on regular schedules. Most stagecoaches carried 12 passengers, and permitted each to carry about 15 pounds of baggage. The brightly-colored stagecoaches were drawn by four horses, changed about every 16 miles.

The stagecoach drivers stopped at taverns, where passengers obtained food and lodging for the night. Charles Dickens stopped at one called the Golden Lamb, still in operation at Lebanon.

Near Lebanon, he stopped at a Shaker settlement, where he met a group of people with unusual religious beliefs. He described his visit in this way: "We walked into a grim room, where several grim hats were hanging on grim pegs. The time was grimly told by a grim clock."

In describing his trip in the stagecoach from Columbus to Upper Sandusky, Dickens noted: "At one time we were all flying in a heap at the bottom of the coach and at another we were crushing our heads against the roof."

At Tiffin, Dickens found a new way of travel in Ohio. He and his wife boarded the coaches of the Mad River and Lake Erie Railroad to take him to Sandusky, on Lake Erie. There he took a steamboat for Buffalo. The steamer followed the Lake Erie shore. Of one place he wrote: "We lay all Sunday night, at a town, and a beautiful town, too, called Cleveland, on Lake Erie." Here people came on board to greet the popular writer. Dickens then went to Buffalo, and Canada, and returned to his English home.

Even as canals were still being dug, a new kind of transportation was being developed. A steam locomotive was invented which could pull many cars at a speed of 20 miles an hour. Wood was used to heat water, which made steam, causing the big engine to move. While this new form of transportation was not as cheap as the canal, it was faster and more convenient. A locomotive could go anywhere there was a track, and it could go in any kind of weather, and at speeds four and five times faster than a canal boat.

Ohio's first railroad was planned in 1832, but it was not until 1836 that it was completed. It operated only a few miles in Ohio, for its tracks ran from Toledo to Adrian, Michigan. It was called the Lake Erie and Kalamazoo Railroad.

An early train pulls into an Ohio station to take on wood and water.

The first rails were of oak, and its cars were pulled by horses. Soon a thin strap iron covering was put over the oak rails, and in 1837 a steam locomotive was put in operation. It carried the U.S. mails, and had a "Pleasure Car" to carry passengers.

A Charter was granted by the General Assembly of Ohio in 1832 to the Mad River and Lake Erie Railroad, which was to begin at Dayton and end at Sandusky. During this time many other charters were granted, but the proposed railroad lines could not obtain the necessary funds to complete the projects.

By 1838, 16 miles of the Mad River and Lake Erie line were laid south of Sandusky, but it was not completed until 1848. In 1846 this line connected with another one, the Little Miami Railroad. Over 200 miles of track now connected Cincinnati with Sandusky, and the Ohio River was linked to Lake Erie by rail.

Other connecting lines were under construction, so that by 1850 Ohio had 300 miles of railroads, which had grown to 3,000 miles in 1860. In 1851 the Cleveland, Columbus and Cincinnati road became a reality. Ohio's 4,000 miles of railroads in 1873 had grown to 6,000 miles in 1880. Railroad building swept the state like a fever. Every town wanted to be on a railroad, and tied to the life of the nation by this new, rapid means of transportation. A trip which had taken two days by stagecoach between Cleveland and Columbus, now required only five hours by the "Steam Cars" as they were known.

Freight could now be moved ten times faster by rail than by canal. Many shippers found this an important advantage regardless of increased costs. The canals reached their peak in 1851, and by 1857 they reported to the state that they were operating at a loss. By 1860 the railroads were carrying twice as much freight as the canals. Passenger traffic chose the railroads over the four or five-mile per hour canal packet. The railroad also brought about a rapid decline in steamboat traffic.

People liked the cars so well that towns and cities began to adapt them to urban use. First tracks were laid and small cars were pulled on them by horse or mules. These horsecars were found in many places. They gave way to the trolley, which ran on tracks, but which received its power from an electric wire overhead, provid-

111

Horsecars, running on tracks, were the first city transportation systems.

ing mass transportation in urban areas at a low cost, and with power that did not pollute the air, as did the large locomotives. In recent years some areas have considered returning to this form of urban transportation.

As the railroad became the most important means of transportation they began to charge higher rates. The State and federal government then regulated their operation by setting up the Interstate Commerce Commission in 1887.

While still very important to Ohio and the nation in carrying freight, and making industry possible, the railroads carry very few passengers. Automobiles, buses, and airplanes have taken over much of this traffic. Most railroads decided to do away with passenger service as they were losing money on it.

The U.S. government, hoping to improve passenger service and encourage people to use this means of transportation, set up the Intercity Railroad Passenger Service, which has been named Amtrack. It took over rail passenger service in 1971, and since that time has worked to improve rail service to Ohioans.

The nineteenth century introduced great advances in mass transportation, that is ways of travel carrying many people at one time. Yet, as far as the individual and family were concerned, the travel was still on horseback, or by horse and buggy. Most Ohioans welcomed a new means of personal transportation. However, one group of respected, hard-working Ohioans, preferred to keep the horse and carriage, which they use to this very day. The Amish

Modern Amtrak locomotive.

Cab of an Amtrak Turboliner.

people who reside largely in Holmes and its surrounding counties, still ride in a horse-drawn carriage. They still farm using old-fashioned methods, but their crops are among the best in the world. These plain people live by their deep religious beliefs.

As the Twentieth century began, a new means of transportation appeared in Ohio. At first, the vehicle looked like a carriage without a horse, and was called the "horseless carriage." Some Ohio factories which made carriages, fearing the competition of the new automobile, tried to add gasoline engines to the carriages to make them self-propelled. Some bicycle works tried to get into the new industry by making automobiles.

Some of the first automobiles were driven by steam engines, but a light, gasoline engine was invented, which was easier to use on an automobile. Charles Duryea of Massachusetts built one of the first in the U.S. in 1892, but the next year Henry Ford was driving one he built in Detroit.

Ford continued to improve his car, and learned how to build them to travel the rough, country roads and sell at a low price. Other people tried to compete with Ford. No one knows exactly how many different firms have made cars, but in Cleveland over 80 different cars have been produced. Probably the best known was the Winton.

To show how fast his cars could travel, Henry Ford hired a young driver from Toledo, Barney Oldfield. He had to race against Alexander Winton, another Ohioan, whose car was favored to win. When the race was finished, Barney Oldfield in the Ford 999 had won.

While Ohio did not become a leader in the automobile industry, it did become a major supplier of automobile parts and supplies. Its steel went into automobile bodies, and its rubber industry prospered from the demand for tires. A young chemist found a way to use low-grade rubber to make tires, which everyone could afford.

In 1871 the rubber industry began at Akron, and it grew slowly at first. With the increased demand for tires due to the mass production of automobiles, it became the rubber capital of the U.S.

An Ohio farm boy, born near New Londonville, Charles F. Kettering made many contributions to the improvement of the automobile.

Horse and carriage of the Amish people.

Early Ford motor cars.

Educational Affairs Dept., Ford Motor Co.

MODEL A
FIRST FORD MOTOR COMPANY CAR
1903

MODEL B TOURING CAR
FIRST FOUR-CYLINDER FORD
1905

MODEL K TOURING CAR
FIRST SIX-CYLINDER CAR
1906

MODEL T TOURING CAR
FIRST FORD MODEL T
1909

As automobiles became more and more common, one great problem remained.

A new ignition system was needed, for at that time a person could not step on a starter or turn an ignition key to start a car. The car had to be cranked, which was hard to do. Many people did not drive for that reason. Those who cranked cars often ended up with a broken wrist or arm. Kettering decided to invent a self-starter.

Within two years "Boss Ket" as his men called him, had made a self-starter. The first starter was used on the 1912 Cadillac, and within two years most cars had them.

Kettering started a company called the Dayton Engineering Laboratories Company, shortened to Delco.

His invention brought him to the attention of General Motors Corporation and he was asked to head their research department. As automobile engines improved, a better grade of gasoline was needed. He found it in what he called Ethyl. He found better paints for cars. In all he made over 100 inventions.

Kettering was interested in research all of his life. When a new city was founded where Kettering had lived and worked, it was named in his honor— Kettering, Ohio.

Orville and Wilbur Wright operated a bicycle shop in Dayton, but the young brothers were interested in building a machine that would make a new way of transportation possible. They believed that a flying machine was possible. The only person who had faith in their accomplishing this was their devoted sister, Katherine Wright.

The two young scientists studied everything they could find about flight. From the time their father had brought them home a toy glider, they felt that the glider held the key to manned flight. They studied many gliders, and developed the biplane (two-winged) glider. To study glider flight, the Wright brothers built a wind tunnel, which helped them experiment with different shapes of wings and rudders.

Finally the two brothers built a glider that included all their ideas. They found out that Kitty Hawk, North Carolina, was the best place for their experiments. Their glider flights taught them many things, but they soon came to the conclusion that if a glider were to be useful, it would have to have an engine on it.

In 1902 they began work on an airplane with a four-cylinder, 12-horsepower, gasoline motor. It was larger than the one used on automobiles at that time.

In the fall of 1903 the Wright Brothers returned to Kitty Hawk. On December 17, they took their plane up. Only five people came to see see the Wright Brothers experiment. Wilbur climbed into the plane. The engine started, and two men pushed the plane. Slowly it gained height, and the wheels were high off the ground. A plane weighing 1000 pounds was flying. Orville started his stopwatch as the plane left the ground, and stopped it as the plane landed. The flight had lasted 59 seconds, and the plane had flown a distance of 852 feet, reaching a speed of 30 miles per hour.

It took many years for the Wright Brothers and their airplane to be recognized as a revolution in transportation. At first it gained national attention through its use by daredevil fliers. They gave exhibitions, showing how high, far, or fast an airplane could fly. The government made early experiments to see if it had any military value, and used planes for carrying air mail.

An Ohio boy from Columbus, Edward V. Rickenbacker, demonstrated its use in World War I. Rickenbacker's first interest had been in racing automobiles, and at 19, defeated another famous Ohio racer, Barney Oldfield in an important event.

During World War I Rickenbacker became a pilot in the Air Service and his daring career ended with his becoming the Ace of Aces of the war, and all the honors that went with it. During World War II he was involved in another heroic air story.

An Ohio pilot, Jerrie F. Mock of Columbus gained fame as the first woman to fly solo around the world in a single-engine plane.

Ohio today is carrying on the tradition of the Wright Brothers. Wright-Patterson Air Base is one of the nation's most important Air Force installations. The Air Force Museum is located near Dayton. Ohio ranks third in the number of registered aircraft and fifth in the number of certified pilots. The state has almost 500 airports.

Ohio's record as the Birthplace of Aviation, perhaps led to the developing of a special interest in space on the part of her citizens.

Wright brothers invention changed transportation.

Ohioans played an important part in the conquest of space, and one of her sons was the first to step on the moon.

Born in Cambridge in 1921, John Glenn spent his boyhood in New Concord. One of his hobbies was building model planes. In high school he was interested in sports and music, as well as a girl, Anna Castor, who became his wife. At Muskingum College, Glenn took part in the Navy flying program, but he later transferred to the Marines.

During World War II and the Korean War, Glenn flew over 120 combat missions. After the war, he became a test pilot, and was the first man to fly faster than the speed of sound.

Due to his training and experience, Colonel John Glenn was chosen as an astronaut. He was given the assignment to man the Atlas-Mercury space vehicle, known as Friendship 7.

On February 20, 1962, he began his orbital flight, which took him three times around the earth, at a speed of 17,000 miles per hour.

July 20, 1969, marked the date that Neil Armstrong became the first man in world history to set foot on the moon.

Born at Wapakoneta in 1930, he graduated from the high school there and enrolled at Purdue University, where he studied aeronautical engineering. He joined the United States Air Force and as a fighter pilot flew 78 combat missions over Korea.

After the war, Armstrong became a member of the National Aeronautical Space Administration, NASA, acting as test pilot for the experimental X-15 plane, which reached speeds up to 4,000 miles per hour.

He was accepted in the astronaut program, and piloted Gemini 8 when it first docked in space. Due to his skill in flying and his calmness in face of danger, he was selected to be Commander of Apollo 11, with the mission to land on the moon.

The command module, which carried the three men on the historic space adventure, was named the Columbia. The lunar landing module was named in honor of the U.S.'s national emblem, the Eagle. As the world listened they heard Armstrong announce, "The Eagle has landed." Then the television camera showed him step upon the moon's barren surface.

119

While not as exciting as space exploration, the improvement of the St. Lawrence-Great Lakes waterway and the Ohio River have been major engineering projects of recent years.

In 1954 the St. Lawrence Seaway act passed Congress. By construction of the St. Lawrence Seaway, Lake Erie port cities would become world ports. The United States and Canada worked together to build this great seaway, which cost about one billion dollars. Giant earth-moving machines lifted and moved about 200 million tons of rock and dirt. Great dams were built, towns moved, highways and railroads rerouted.

When opened to ships in 1959, the St. Lawrence Seaway became the longest inland waterway in the world, over 2300 miles long. Since it has been so successful, plans are always underway for its improvement.

Today such lake ports as Cleveland, Ashtabula, Conneaut, Lorain, Sandusky, and Toledo are ocean ports. Ohio products or needed raw materials pass through these ports. Ships from all parts of the world can be seen at Lake Erie ports.

The Ohio River, the first highway into the state, has not lost its importance in the state's transportation system. At first it appeared that the railroads would do away with the need for river traffic, but more and more coal was mined along the river. The cheapest way to transport the coal is by river barge. By 1890 over 10,000,000 tons of coal were shipped on barges.

To make it possible for the Ohio River to carry traffic at all seasons, a system of new dams was needed. Steamboats and freight barges were dependent upon the water flow in the river, usually highest during the spring when snow melted, and in the autumn when rains fell. In 1885 the Davis Island Dam was built with the help of the U.S. government. This helped, but more dams were needed.

During World War I, the U.S. decided that more than railroads were needed in the Ohio River Valley. By putting a string of barges behind one towboat, freight could be carried at a much lower price than by rail. One towboat could pull as much weight as twelve locomotives.

To improve the Ohio River for navigation, a series of 46 dams was planned. This project was completed in 1929. With the use of the new diesel towboats more and more barges go up and down the river.

Another project was planned to build 19 high-lift dams. It was begun in 1961, and recently completed. The new Ohio Waterway was a billion dollar project.

Ohio's system of highway transportation began with the building of the National Road. Now in miles of surface highways, Ohio, ranks fifth in the U.S. Ohio is still the Gateway State. Americans use Ohio highways to travel from East to the West.

A new interstate highway system began in Ohio with the Ohio turnpike, opened in 1955. It crossed northern Ohio spanning 241 miles from the Pennsylvania to the Indiana border. Ohio has been an important state in the Interstate Highway System. I-71, I-75 and I-77 carry traffic north and south, while I-70, I-80 and I-90 are major east-west arteries. Circle freeways such as 270, 271, 275 and 475 carry traffic around large cities.

Ohio's location at the nation's crossroads keeps the state in an important position in rail traffic. Amtrak passenger lines cross the state, and much freight moves along the rails. Ohio has more railroad track for its size than any state in the U.S. Despite recent consolidations of rail lines, Ohio has almost 8,000 miles of track. All sections of the state are served by the railroads.

A study of the Ohio Transportation Map published by the Ohio Department of Transportation will provide a good review of the state's major transportation facilities. In addition to showing the detailed road and highway system of the state, it shows where the airports are located, the Amtrak routes, and deep sea and interstate ports.

The map legends contain symbols which are important to every traveler. Through a color key the various types of highways are shown, indicating their condition and size. A mileage chart gives distance between various points in Ohio.

Interstate Highways are shown in green with the number interposed. These carry the greatest amount of traffic, including the Ohio turnpike. With your finger trace these major routes through the state.

Since the nation is turning to the metric system, the new map shows how to convert miles to kilometers, and carries a scale.

121

The Delta Queen, now joined by new Mississippi Queen.

Every future driver in Ohio will need to understand how to read a road map and how to use it. It is a driver's best tool.

Finding the closest route between two places becomes more important as motorists conserve gasoline and oil. Using the mileage chart is a fast way to do this.

No state has a better or more modern transportation system than Ohio. It is a system built to serve Ohio in the future, and to serve its young people, who will live in that future.

Sometimes in Ohio with its long history, the past and the present meet. This is true of the steamboat. Remembering the steamboat days, Ohioans did not want to lose that touch of the past. The Delta Queen, which had been built in 1926, and first saw service on the Sacramento River in California, was brought to Cincinnati. It operated out of Cincinnati, providing cruises down the Ohio and Mississippi Rivers for those who wished to relive a part of the nation's past. For many years before her death, Captain Mary Greene made the Delta Queen her home, and the Greene Lines continue to operate the "Queens."

On May 11, 1976, a new steamboat, the "Mississippi Queen" made its maiden voyage from the home port of Cincinnati. It was the first steampowered sternwheeler built in over 30 years in the U.S. The new "Queen" is 384 feet long or 100 feet longer than the Delta Queen. It is the largest and safest steamboat ever built, being of all steel construction. Its 214 guest cabins take Americans on a voyage into the past.

Communication

The early settlers of Ohio were cut off from the outside world. They lived a lonely and isolated life, looking forward to a traveler or a peddler who might bring some news of other people.

Some of the news they heard from the travelers was probably just gossip, while some of it was reliable, but it was always interesting. Important notices, such as an approaching marriage, were often posted on a tree or a wall of a building. Some early towns had a big blackboard placed at the intersection of the two busiest streets where notices and news items could be written or posted.

If a person wanted to learn what someone else thought, a book would provide a means of communication between one mind and another. The pioneer did not have many books to read, but each one was treasured and read over and over. Books were exchanged among neighbors before libraries were organized. Pamphlets and almanacs were widely used as sources of current information.

Letters from one person to another were, and still are a means of personal communication. In the early days of Ohio, letters kept families in touch with each other. Letters were sent through the mail, carried by horseback in saddlebags, and then by stagecoaches. Post offices opened as soon as possible. At one time all the mail for the Northwest Territory came to Cincinnati, and people traveled by horseback for miles to get a letter.

Ohio's first mail went by saddlebag.

The people who settled in Ohio were used to newspapers, for they began almost as soon as the nation. The first newspaper published at Cincinnati in 1793, was called the "Centinel of the North-Western Territory." William Maxwell was the publisher. The Centinel was sold, and moved to Chillicothe in 1800, where it was published as "Freeman's Journal" before consolidating with the "Scioto Gazette." The Gazette is still published each day in Chillicothe. When the "Centinel" left, Cincinnati started another newspaper.

The early Ohio newspaper were small in size, the same as a sheet of school writing paper, 8½ by 11 inches. Paper was hard to obtain and editors sometimes had to wait for a supply to arrive before printing the paper. The early papers were not printed well because paper, ink, and printing presses were small and hand operated. They appeared once a week. The editor wrote most of the news himself, and printed all the new laws and letters from subscribers. For the national and world news, the editor subscribed to eastern newspapers and copied the news from them. This meant the news was often late and old.

Since the subscription rates were so low, the newspaper owner had to depend upon advertisment to pay most of the cost of printing. Patent medicine filled much of the advertising space.

Today there are almost 100 daily newspapers in Ohio, 20 with Sunday editions. Most Ohioans receive a newspaper. There are many weekly newspapers published in smaller communities. Some weekly newspapers depend upon advertising to pay their cost and the papers are given away.

Editors used to take very strong positions on political questions. A newspaper was often the voice of a political party. Fist fights between editors with opposing views were not unusual. Sometimes many people did not agree with the editor, and a mob would attack the building where the paper was published. At times presses were broken, or the building set on fire. This happened in a few places in Ohio over the question of slavery.

In 1837 Samuel F. B. Morse sent the first message over a wire. His new invention, called the telegraph, brought about a communications revolution. Newspapers could receive news of the outside world in a matter of minutes. The first telegraph wire was stretched between Washington, D.C. and Baltimore, Maryland.

During the 1840s telegraph wires were strung across Ohio, until every community had contact with other Ohio communities and the eastern seaboard. Many people learned the Morse Code, a system of dots and dashes, which spelled out letters. It is still in use. By translating these into words, instant communication became possible. Finally a cable was laid on the floor of the Atlantic Ocean, making possible telegraph connections with Europe.

Telegraph service was desired by every important newspaper. Now everyone in the U.S. could know what was happening a short time after the event. Through the sending of telegrams business men could communicate with each other in much less time than by letter. Any person could send a telegram by going to the nearest telegraph station. Here a telegrapher would translate his message and send it clicking on its way. Messages were delivered by bicycle riders.

When special news came over the telegraph wire, the newspaper stopped the presses, and on the front page printed the story. Then news boys would grab up the papers and take them out, yelling "Extra, Extra, Read All About It." In the early days, Ohioans called the telegraph the "Lightning wire."

Since it was possible to send dots and dashes over a wire, inventors began to ask why the voice could not be sent the same way. Elisha Gray, born at Barnsville in 1835, began to work on this idea as a professor at Oberlin College.

Just two hours after Alexander Graham Bell applied for his patent on a telephone on Feb. 14, 1876, Elisha Gray filed his application covering the same invention. After a long battle in the courts, Gray lost his claim, but began his own company, known today as Western Electric, to manufacture equipment and make improvements on both the telegraph and telephone.

Gray continued his work, and he did get credit for inventing the telautograph. This machine enabled a person to write something by hand at one place, and at the same time automatic pens made a copy of what was written somewhere else.

In 1878 the telephone arrived in Ohio. The first switchboard was set up in Cincinnati, with lines running out the windows of the building to connect with various places of business which first saw the benefits of a phone. It wasn't long until people wanted phones in their homes. Soon telephone wire stretched across Ohio.

Now almost 7,000,000 telephones are in use in the Buckeye state. The largest number belong to the Ohio Bell Telephone Company, whose cables are linked to those of the American Telephone and Telegraph Company. However, in many smaller communities and in the rural areas, Ohio telephone service is often provided by independent telephone companies, of which there are over 50 in Ohio.

Born in Milan, in 1847, Thomas Edison became Ohio's greatest inventor, as well as the greatest inventor in history. He is credited with over 1,000 patents, the most important being the invention of the incandescent electric light, but he also made several contributions in the field of communication.

From the time he was seven years old, Edison was interested in science. He set up his first laboratory in the basement of his home. One day when he was fifteen, he was out walking and noticed a small boy crawling along a railroad track. Tom saw a train coming and rushed over and pulled the boy out of its way. As a reward for saving the boy's life, his father, who happened to be the telegraph operator at the station, asked Edison what he would like as a reward. Edison's request was an unusual one. He asked the telegrapher to teach him how to operate the instrument.

Tom learned fast and soon was a telegraph operator himself. He became interested in how it worked. One of his first inventions was the telegraph repeater, which slowed down the speed, so that it could be more accurately copied down. Later he invented the automatic and multiplex telegraph. His first big invention was the improvement of the stock ticker, used to print stock prices. For this he was given a check for $40,000 with which he equipped his first laboratory.

The telephone soon came to Edison's attention. The first telephone used the same piece for one to talk into, and then holding it to the ear, listen to the reply. Today the transmitter is at one end and the receiver at the other. Since the first phones sent out a weak sound, Edison invented a carbon transmitter to make the voice come through loud and clear.

In the early years when using a phone a person would answer

Telephone and Radio revolutionized communication.

An early day telephone.

with a long question, such as "Can you talk now?" As Edison was working on improving the telephone, he did not have time to waste words, so one day he simply answered, "Hello." That was the first "Hello," and it has been used ever since.

Working with both the telegraph and telephone, Edison studied sound waves, and how they operate. It occurred to him that he could make what he called a "talking machine." He wrapped some tin foil around a cylinder, then cranked the cylinder by hand. He used a pin to make impressions on the tin foil. With the little cylinder revolving Edison spoke into a horn, reciting, "Mary had a little lamb." Then he replaced the pin with a needle, and the machine actually repeated the verse— it talked. Today Edison's machine is called a phonograph, but most people call it a record player.

The phonograph meant a voice or music could be recorded and replayed time and time again, even when the person was no longer living. It was a great advance in communication. An artist can make a record and you can listen to it in private.

Edison noted that roll film had been developed for use in a camera. Using the new film, Edison believed it could be used in a motion picture camera. He made such a camera called the kinetograph, and a projector, the kinetoscope. From this developed the modern motion pictures, another means of communication. Edison also developed the first microphone for making records, which became useful in radio broadcasting.

Edison also made the first mimeograph,which being a simple reproduction process, made possible a cheap printing process for small organizations, schools, and other groups. It improved communications within groups, for many depend on mimeograph letters and bulletins. Edison is credited with recording some scientific ideas in his notebooks, which led to the development of the transistor, an important element in modern communication devices.

Radio and Television

The next great advancement in communication came with the transmission through the air of the human voice. With a proper receiver, called a radio, every family could bring the outside world into their home just by the turning of a dial, or in the early days, the turning of several dials.

With the beginning of the twentieth century, scientists began to experiment with voice broadcasting, but regular broadcasting did not begin until 1920 when KDKA of Pittsburgh broadcast the election returns announcing that Warren G. Harding of Ohio was the new president of the U.S. Not many Ohioans received the station for the few sets in use were homemade, powered by batteries. There were no speakers, the listeners wore earphones, and if two listened each shared an earphone.

WHK of Cleveland, still broadcasting, is credited with being the first licensed station on the air in Ohio. This was very early in 1922, and in March, 1922, WLW of Cincinnati was given government permission to use the air waves. Powell Crosley, who founded WLW which at first operated out of his home, went into the business of manufacturing radios. His first one, the Harko, was built for the Christmas trade of 1921, and would receive KDKA. It was a simple crystal set, but sold faster than Crosley could make them. Soon many inventive Ohioans were building their own crystal sets.

An early day radio.

The year 1922 was the year when radio became an important part of America's communication system. In January of that year only 28 stations were on the air, but by December of 1922, over 570 stations were listed. Radio became a national pastime, and people stayed up to all hours to test how far they could reach with their radio sets. The program wasn't important, but the location of the station was the main interest. In 1923 WLW had a contest to see how far its signal reached, and listeners from 42 states answered.

This changed, and programming became the main interest. News soon became an interest of listeners. By the mid-twenties, networks were organized and programs broadcast nationally. By 1927, WLW began to originate network programs. In 1928 WLW raised its power to 50,000 watts, building a new transmitter at Mason. On May 2, 1934, President Franklin D. Roosevelt pushed a gold key, and WLW's new 500,000 transmitter went on the air. WLW became known as the nation's station and was the most powerful ever to broadcast in the U.S. It was later reduced to 50,000 watts.

WLW also became known as the "cradle of stars" and many famous radio personalities began their careers at the station.

In 1946 Crosley's TV station, W8XCT began to broadcast experimental programs. In 1948 it became WLWT and the first TV station to sign a contract with NBC-TV as an affiliate. Since no network or cable existed, WLWT had to televise kinescopes. In 1949 WLW-C in Columbus and WLW-D, Dayton, were put on the air.

The antennas of more than 300 radio and TV stations now puncture the skyline of Ohio. Every community has its own AM or FM voice, and is within viewing distance of a TV station.

Where TV is more difficult to receive there are Cable TV companies, which make possible a clear, strong picture. Cable TV also has many other possibilities. It represents the latest development in communication.

CHAPTER V

Education and Culture

When Samuel Lewis became Ohio's first State Superintendent of Schools, he was unhappy at what he found. In the year 1837, Ohio had very few free schools. Most of them were run on a subscription basis, which meant teachers were paid by parents for their work and for school supplies. If parents could not afford to pay tuition, the children had to stay home.

When Congress passed the Ordinance of 1787, it made provisions for a system of free schools. The Ordinance provided: "Religion, morality and knowledge being necessary to good government and the happiness of mankind, schools and the means of education shall forever be encouraged."

The government surveyed the land, dividing it into one mile square sections. It took 36 sections to make up a township.

Township and Section plot.

6	5	4	3	2	1
7	8	9	10	11	12
18	17	16	15	14	13
19	20	21	22	23	24
30	29	28	27	26	25
31	32	33	34	35	36

Section

Township

Section 16 of each township was set aside for the support of public schools. The school lands were sold, and the money invested. This money was appropriated for the schools. Although over 700,000 acres of land were set aside for school support, the income was never enough to support a school system.

The early subscription schools provided education in Ohio for a quarter of a century. The schooling usually lasted 12 weeks, called a term. If the money gave out before the term ended, the teacher left.

Most of the early teachers in Ohio never attended college. In fact, some of them had only completed the eighth grade. Anyone could be a teacher, and most were men, who taught in the winter and worked as farmers in the summer, on their own farms or hiring out to others. Some of these teachers knew little about children or education. They were often cruel to the children. Children were punished for doing many things which were not bad. They were often beaten and mistreated. Corporal punishment was common.

The teacher was expected to teach every day. There were no vacations, except perhaps, Christmas day. To get a day off, the children would plan a lock-out once a term. They would lock the teacher out of the school or refuse to let him in. The teacher had to promise a treat and a day off after a lock-out. A lock-out would usually occur near the end of the term.

The children studied the basic subjects, often called the 3 Rs: "reading,'riting, and 'rithmetic." Spelling was studied as a game, and developed into a contest between schools. Spelling matches were held in the classroom, and spelling bees became popular as one school challenged the best spellers of another school. People came for miles around to a spelling bee, and the winners were awarded prizes. Sometimes the same idea was used with arithmetic. These were called "ciphering" matches. If a teacher had a good voice, to earn extra money, he would conduct a singing school one evening a week.

School supplies were limited. Unruled paper, called foolscap, was used sparingly. Each pupil had a ruler, which some friendly carpenter had made for him. Using a bar-lead pencil, the pupil

133

A typical one-room Ohio school.

Consolidated schools. Pupils transported by bus.

had to rule his own paper. A goose quill made a good pen, and sand was used to blot the ink. The teacher mixed the ink from ink powder, and poured it into the pupil's ink bottle.

Each student made a copybook, of foolscap, cut into one size and stitched together, with a brown-paper cover. Arithmetic was usually done on the pupil's slate with a slate pencil. Good spellers used a dictionary as their textbook.

The schools did not have different grades, they were ungraded. All came to the one-room school, some six years old and some eighteen. Brothers and sisters were in the same room. A teacher had many classes each day. When it came one group's turn to be with the teacher, that group came forward to what was called the recitation bench. Most of the day they worked on written assignments. The older students often helped the younger ones.

The school rooms were not very comfortable, for in pioneer times the benches were made of logs, split in half. The pupils had no desks as today. They kept their books beside them on the bench. The boys often lined their pants with buckskin to protect them against the splinters, and the schoolmaster's hickory stick.

Ohio State Superintendent of Schools, Samuel Lewis tried to get the people interested in education. The General Assembly passed laws in 1821 and 1825 setting up school districts with provision for electing school officers to run the schools.

The people of Ohio preferred to make out with what they had, rather than tax themselves to educate all children. Some Ohioans said that children should stay at home and help with the work. Others thought it was the responsibility of parents to pay for the education of their own children. People without children saw no reason for them to pay for education of other people's children.

By 1838 only Cincinnati had public schools. The people of the Queen City were interested in education, building a schoolhouse in 1790. However, the first schoolhouse in Ohio was built by the Moravian missionaries. Bathsheba Rouse became the first woman schoolteacher in Ohio when she set up a school in a log cabin in Belpre.

While the schools for the children of early Ohio were much like those of the other states, Ohio made a special contribution to education. Cincinnati was an important book publishing center. Here millions of school textbooks were printed, with the most important ones being written by Ohio authors.

William Holmes McGuffey, a professor at Miami University at Oxford, wrote a graded series of readers, known as McGuffey Readers. These were the most widely used readers in the nineteenth century.

Born of pioneer parents, McGuffey struggled for an education. Being poor, he had to work his way through college. He became a professor at Miami University when he was a young man, and soon his students recognized him as an excellent teacher. He made his classes so interesting that very few pupils failed.

One day a Cincinnati publisher asked McGuffey to write a set of readers. At that time only one book was used in the schools of Ohio. It was called Webster's Blue Back Speller, a text for both spelling and reading.

Since McGuffey had often taught younger children in the village of Oxford, he knew that new books were needed. He wanted to write a set of books that would do more than serve as readers. He wished to write stories that would teach boys and girls how to do the right things, or as he said, books that taught morals.

In his work room, McGuffey had an odd desk, which can still be seen at the McGuffey Museum at Miami University. It had eight sides, with a drawer in each side, and it turned. As McGuffey gathered his stories for his readers, he would put each one in a drawer, according to its difficulty. Each drawer held the stories for one book, and there was to be a book for each level. From this came the idea of putting children in grades, according to the book they were reading.

Once published the books became very popular, as McGuffey kept revising them. They were read by most of the boys and girls in the west, and ranked next to the Bible and dictionary in sales.

William McGuffey wasn't the only Ohioan to write school textbooks. A teacher from Cincinnati, Joseph Ray, wrote arithmetic books. Platt Spencer became famous for his beautiful handwriting. He made a handwriting book, and school children all over the nation copied from it, trying to learn to write like him.

McGuffey taught in one of Ohio's first colleges. Miami University was chartered in 1809, and a few years later classes were held in its first building for high school students. It wasn't until 1824 that university classes were taught. Ohio University, the oldest college west of the Allegheny Mountains, was founded in 1804, but graduated its first college class in 1815.

The first building erected to provide higher learning was the Muskingum Academy founded in 1797, which later became Marietta College.

Many church groups set up colleges in Ohio where their young people could obtain training for the ministry or for various other professions. Kenyon College, founded in 1824, ranks as the state's third oldest, with Western Reserve at Cleveland founded only two years later. Denison at Granville, and Xavier at Cincinnati opened their doors in 1831.

Oberlin, since 1833, has been recognized not only for its fine educational program, but by being the first in Ohio to welcome Black students and women to study on its campus. Otterbein, founded in 1847, was coeducational.

Edwin C. Berry, a noted sociologist, and Carl Thomas Rowan, journalist and later Ambassador to Finland, represent the achievement of two of Oberlin's early Black graduates.

Among the first colleges for Negroes in the United States was Wilberforce, built in 1856. With church support, it was named for William Wilberforce, who worked in Great Britain to end the slave trade. The college, now interracial, is still a leader in Ohio education.

America's most important educator, Horace Mann, came to Ohio in 1853 as president of Antioch College at Yellow Springs. Here he spent the last six years of his life building a new kind of college program. He made the study of teaching or education a part of the regular college curriculum. His school was open to both women and Black students.

The state's largest university, Ohio State University, developed out of the Ohio Agricultural and Mechanical College, opened in 1873. Its College of Medicine dates back to 1833, then a separate institution. In 1878 the official name became Ohio State

University and the state of Ohio began to provide financial support.

Ohio cities began to open colleges for their residents. The University of Cincinnati is the oldest one in the U.S., but Akron and Toledo later opened similar institutions.

Ohio is a leader in higher education, ranking seventh in the U.S. in the number of universities. It has many which were supported by religious groups, and twelve supported entirely by state funds, while another group is given state assistance. There are also many Junior Colleges, or Community Colleges, which provide two-years of training. A student can then enter a four-year institution, or in many fields graduate with training in one of many specific technical careers.

Ohio is proud of the fact that about every young person in the state lives within 25 miles of an institution for learning beyond high school. Nearly any profession or trade can be pursued in these schools.

Since few books were brought to the Ohio country, they were one of the things missed most by the pioneer. During the long winter evenings, there was little else to do for recreation. The pioneers had no extra cash, but decided by pooling their resources, they could set up libraries. Then all could borrow and read books. As early as 1796 the village of Belpre started a library.

The people of Ohio's largest town at that time, Cincinnati, were able to put together $340 to start a subscription library in 1802, and Dayton opened one in 1805. Everyone who subscribed, or contributed money, could borrow any of the books. Marietta also started a subscription library.

In 1803, the year Ohio became a state, the citizens of Ames township in Athens County held a meeting to discuss building roads. Before the meeting was over, they talked over other problems, one of which was the lack of a library. They didn't have the money to buy books, but one person suggested a new idea. Since the woods were full of raccoons, foxes and skunks, there were animals to be trapped. Their furs could be taken to market and sold, and the money earned, used to buy books.

After the furs were collected, one of the pioneers took them to Boston. There he was given $37.50 for them. Dr. Manasseh

Cutler helped select 51 books to be brought back to Ohio. Since the library fund was raised in such an unusual way, the library was known as the Coon-Skin Library. After that dues were paid in coonskins, so more books could be purchased.

Governor Thomas Worthington was very careful in spending state funds, and in 1817 announced that he had saved enough money to start a state library. This state library which began with some 500 books has grown today to almost 1,000,000 books. Through inter-library loan these books are available to Ohio citizens through their various public libraries.

Every Ohioan is only a few miles from a library. In the state the libraries operate under various plans. There are also school libraries to serve all of Ohio's students. For people who live in very small villages or in the rural districts, Bookmobile service is provided.

Libraries not only help Ohioans get an education, but it makes it possible for them to continue to read and learn all of their lives. In addition to the public and school libraries, there are over 100 special libraries, providing books and other resources on any subject.

A very valuable library collection for people interested in Ohio culture is the Ohioana Library, founded by Martha Kinney Cooper, the wife of an Ohio Governor. She started this collection in 1929, which included works of Ohio authors and composers. Each year awards are made to encourage Ohio writers, and an attractive yearbook is published on some Ohio topic.

A large collection of books, magazines, newspapers, and original documents are found in the library at the Ohio Historical Center. It has over 80,000 volumes.

The Ohio Historical Society began as a private organization in 1885 to preserve the history and archeology of the state. In 1891 it became a state organization with some state support. Ohioans can become members of the society, and those who do receive certain privileges, and a newsletter and magazine.

The Ohio Historical Center at Columbus is near the site of the Ohio State Fair, an annual event which draws large crowds. The Fair is a tribute to Ohio agriculture and plans events of special interest to farmers and to rural boys and girls. Exhibits interest both rural and city dwellers.

Counties, towns and cities also have historical museums which preserve the past of a local area.

Ohio has several notable art museums, housing collections worth millions of dollars. One of the most beautiful is the Cleveland Museum of Art, whose collection shows many cultures and periods in world history. It maintains a large research library. Cleveland also has the Cleveland Institute of Art.

At Cincinnati there are two art centers, the Cincinnati Art Museum and the Taft Museum. Columbus has a Gallery of Fine Arts and the Bryson Art Gallery. The Toledo Museum of Art has a special collection of glass, for which the city is noted. Dayton, Akron, and Canton are among the many cities in Ohio which boast of art museums and centers.

Even before Ohio became a state, an artist, George Beck, who was a scout with General Anthony Wayne, began to paint the Ohio landscape. He was followed by Thomas Cole, who began his career as a traveling portrait painter. Since the photography had not been developed, many pioneers paid to have their portraits painted. Cole later continued his education in painting and created beautiful landscapes. John Neagle made portrait painting popular in Cincinnati, and is still remembered by his painting of "Pat Lyon" and the "Blacksmith.".

By the middle of the nineteenth century Cincinnati was the leading art center of the West and was the home of several noted artists. Frank Duveneck, born in Covington and educated in Europe, returned to Cincinnati as dean of the Art Academy, and consultant for the Art Museum. He attracted many artists to the Queen City to study under him, including Herbert W. Fall, a native Ohioan, who provided some of the illustration for this book.

John Twachtman, born in the Queen City, in 1835, studied under Duveneck. While in Europe, he became interested in the French impressionist technique, and brought this idea back to Cincinnati. He used it in his realistic landscapes, especially those of winter.

Cincinnatian, Robert Henri, after studying abroad, returned to the U.S. to introduce realism into art. He painted America as it was and did not cover up anything unpleasant. He inspired George Bellows to use his own American style. Since Bellows had been an athlete at Ohio State University, he was interested in sports. Some of his best pictures portray prize fights and athletic events.

Elizabeth Nourse, born in Mt. Healthy, a Cincinnati suburb, was that city's first woman artist. She studied at the Cincinnati Art Academy and in Paris. In 1891 she presented an art exhibition which brought national attention. Her work is now exhibited both in the U.S. and in France.

In more recent years, Frank N. Wilcox became the leader of a group of artists in the Cleveland area who specialized in water colors. His books "Ohio Canals" and "Ohio Indian Trails" contain hundreds of historical sketches. William Sommer and Henry Keller were also part of this Cleveland group.

A native of Ashtabula, Charles E. Burchfield painted rural scenes with stark reality, and in later years turned to wildlife and forest trees. John A. Ruthven, a Cincinnati artist, is now prominent in this field.

Historical events caught the eyes of some Ohio artists. William H. Powell painted the huge canvas of Oliver Hazard Perry's victory on Lake Erie during the War of 1812. Charles T. Webber painted the "Underground Railroad" showing Cincinnati's participation. The "Signing of the Treaty of Greenville" is the work of Howard Chandler Christy, a Morgan County artist. Henry Farney who did his best work at his home in Cincinnati left a treasure of art work portraying Indian life. Robert Duncanson, a noted Black painter, did a canvas of the Little Miami River.

The most notable historic painting and the one most often reproduced in the U.S. came from the brush of an Ohio artist, Archibald M. Willard. He was born in Wellington. His painting is "The Spirit of 1776."

More and more sculpture is being seen around Ohio. The most famous piece is on the grounds of the Capitol at Columbus entitled, "My Jewels Monument" a tribute to Ohio heroes by Levi T. Schofield.

Among early sculptors was Hiram Powers who began his study in Cincinnati. His statue of the Greek slave is considered one of the best produced in the U.S. He also made many statues of noted American statesmen. John Q. Ward's the "Indian Hunter" in Central Park, New York City, is one of his many pieces.

Edmonia Lewis, born in Ohio in 1845, was the state's first important Negro artist, and the first Black sculptor to gain national fame. She obtained an education at Oberlin College, where she was active in the Abolitionist movement. Here she met William Lloyd Garrison, prominent in the movement, who noted her gift as a sculptor and introduced her to one of his friends in Boston, also a sculptor.

Her first famous bust was of John Brown, a bitter anti-slavery man, who was hanged. The one of Col. Robert Shaw, of the first Negro Civil War Regiment, was considered an outstanding work. A statue entitled, "Forever Free" expressed the feelings of Black man gaining his freedom. She made other busts including those of Lincoln and Longfellow.

William Farrow, born in Dayton in 1885, was an artist of importance in Ohio.

Music

On the frontier, music served as an important part of recreation. People had to make their own entertainment. The fiddler (violinist today) was one of the most important individuals in the community, for he furnished the music for the dances. Schoolmasters went from one town to the other organizing singing schools. One of these masters, also a teacher, was Benjamin Hanby, who first introduced his popular "Up on the Housetop" at a singing school in New Paris.

In early Ohio, Cincinnati played a major part in the development of music education by introducing it into the schools in 1845. Since so many German immigrants settled in the Queen City, this led to a great appreciation of music, for Germany was a musical nation. They loved orchestras, bands, choirs and concerts. In the early 1870s Cincinnati began the famous May Festivals, to which choral groups from all over southwestern Ohio came. Out of the great interest in this event in 1895, developed the Cincinnati Symphony Orchestras. In 1920 Summer Opera began at Cincinnati at the Zoological Garden, but is now on the stage of the remodeled Music Hall. Each spring the Metropolitan Opera Company of New York visits Cleveland.

Today's Cleveland's Philharmonic Orchestra traces its beginning to 1918 when conductor Nikolai Sokoloff led its first performance. In 1968 it opened a new home, the Blossom Music Center, where summer concerts are enjoyed. Other cities such as Toledo, Columbus, Dayton and Youngstown boast of a civic symphony as do many smaller communities.

The first Ohio colleges to become nationally known were the Oberlin Conservatory of Music and the Cincinnati Conservatory of Music, founded by Clara Baur. Both were opened in 1867.

The list of composers from Ohio is a long one. Oley Speaks born at Canal Winchester, wrote many beautiful songs of semi-classical nature. Homer Rodeheaver wrote religious songs, while Daniel Emmett composed folk songs, such as "Dixie." Tell Taylor of Findlay is remembered for "Down by the Old Mill Stream."

Authors

Ohio's authors have gained national attention. The McGuffey Readers were a literary treasure house. Uncle Tom's Cabin, by Harriet Beecher Stowe was the best seller of the last century. Zane Grey, born and raised at Zanesville, wrote a popular series about the old West. He also wrote the story of his ancestor, the heroine of Fort Henry, in the book, "Betty Zane."

The earliest Ohio writers were concerned with recording history. Caleb Atwater of Circleville wrote the first "History of Ohio." Daniel Drake, a physician, wrote not only on medical topics, but about his city, Cincinnati. Timothy Flint's, "Recollections of the Last Ten Years" (1826) describes frontier Ohio. Henry Howe traveled throughout the state of Ohio to interview and record the reminiscences of its early settlers. In 1846 he compiled his famous "Historical Collections," which were revised in 1889, making them the most complete historical record of the state.

Among modern writers of Ohio's history are Harlan Hatcher and Walter Havighurst. Conrad Richter and Allan W. Eckert have brought back life on the frontier in their novels. Dick Perry's books on Ohio have a humorous touch and a wide appeal.

Edward Judson, who edited a magazine in Cincinnati, wrote tales of the West under the by-line of Ned Buntline. One of the stories he preserved was that of the riverman, Mike Fink. One of the first writers of the historical novel in Ohio was Mary H. Catherwood. Charles W. Chestnutt of Cleveland was a well-known Negro novelist.

Writing both history and novels, as well as serving as a critic, William Dean Howells was one of America's leading literary men at the beginning of the century.

In the field of the short story, Sherwood Anderson, O. Henry, and Ambrose Bierce have become well known. Anderson's "Winesburg, Ohio" is still studied as a classic. James Thurber was a popular humorist. Louis Bromfield, born in Mansfield, produced over 30 books in his lifetime, one of them winning the Pulitzer prize. Some of his books are based on life in Ohio. He loved rural life, and lived on a working farm near Lucas, Ohio, which he called Malabar Farm.

Dorothy C. Fisher and Fannie Hurst were popular novelists, and millions of Americans enjoyed their books. Ben Ames Williams published over 500 short stories and novels, some of which were about Ohio.

While poetry is no longer as popular as it once was, Ohio was the home of many poets. Two sisters, Alice and Phoebe Cary of Hamilton County won national attention. Their home, Clovernook, today serves the blind and is open to the public. Other poets include Edith Thomas, Hart Crane, and Ridgely Torrence.

One of Ohio's most important poets was Paul Laurence Dunbar, born in Dayton in 1872. His parents had been given their freedom during the Civil War. Dunbar showed his talent early in life, beginning to read at the age of four, and write short verses at six.

When Paul was 12 years old, his father, Joshua Dunbar, died, leaving his mother to support the family.

After he graduated from high school, Dunbar went to work as an elevator operator, to help support his mother. During his spare time waiting for passengers, he began to write short verses.

When a group of writers planned to meet in Dayton, one of Paul's former teachers, asked him to write the welcoming verse. The writers were pleased with the poetry written by the young Black man.

Dunbar soon had enough poems for a book, which he published as "Oak and Ivy Poems." Many people read and enjoyed the poems. Soon he was receiving invitations to read his poems before groups of people.

When he published his next book, an Ohio critic, William Dean Howells read it. He told the nation about it, and encouraged Paul Laurence Dunbar in his literary work. He soon was famous, and was asked to go to England to read his poetry. When he returned to the U.S. there was a surprise awaiting him. He was made a member of the staff of the Library of Congress.

Before he died in 1906, in his short life, Dunbar had written 18 volumes of poetry, some fiction and many uncollected poems and articles. No one ever recorded Negro dialect in verse as well as he. His home at Dayton is now a state museum, and one of his verses is on a plaque at the Dayton Public Library.

Another Black poet, Langston Hughes, began his writing career as a student at Central High School, Cleveland, starting as a poet, but becoming a master of many forms of writing.

Performing Arts

The theatre brought entertainment to early Ohioans, just as it does today. The first stage play in Ohio was presented at Cincinnati in a shed at Fort Washington in 1801. It was musical comedy titled, "The Poor Soldier," a popular play of its day. By 1830 both Cincinnati and Columbus had two theatres. Soon stages were being built in large halls in various buildings, so that traveling players could put on a performance. The play most widely presented during the last century was "Uncle Tom's Cabin," a dramatization of the book.

With the coming of the steamboat on the Ohio River, the Showboat made its appearance. Seating from 200 to 1,000 these boats presented plays, vaudeville acts and minstrel shows.

Daniel D. Emmett of Mt. Vernon is credited with originating the minstrel show, composing many of the musical numbers used in the productions. John Robinson developed the circus as it appears today under the Big Top. He sold out to Ringling Brothers.

The theatre grew in popularity near the end of the last century. Opera Houses were erected throughout the state. Famous names in the theatre appeared on Ohio stages. Magic shows were also popular, with Howard Thurston, of Columbus, reaching the top of his profession.

Born in a log cabin near Greenville, Phoebe Mozee, as Annie Oakley became one of the nation's top entertainers as well as the world's most famous markswoman.

When her father died, Annie took down his old gun from over the fireplace. The ten-year old girl loaded the gun, and went into the woods. In a short time she returned with a rabbit which provided meat for supper. Soon Annie was shooting other game such as quail and pheasant.

When she shot quail, a small bird, she learned to shoot it through the head, so that the best meat of the bird was saved, and those eating the quail did not bite into shot. Annie learned that she could sell her quail to hotels in Greenville, Dayton and Cincinnati, shipping them by stagecoach.

One day in 1874, Frank Butler, champion sharpshooter, arrived in Cincinnati. The manager of the Gibson Hotel, who bought quail shot by A. Oakley, did not know she was a girl, and sent for the person betting he could outshoot Butler. Although surprised when the expert shot turned out to be Annie, the match took place. Everyone was in for another surprise, for Annie won. She became Frank Butler's shooting partner, and eventually his wife.

The two joined the popular Buffalo Bill Cody's Wild West Show, and toured the nation. An Indian who was with the show gave Annie her nickname, "Little Sure Shot." The show also toured the major European cities. When she retired from show business, Annie returned to Greenville.

Her glamorous life became the basis of one of the most loved musicals, "Annie Get Your Gun." The music from the show is on records, and may still be enjoyed. Mementoes of her life are on display at a Greenville Museum.

Elsie Janis, described by one writer as that "lanky, lovely lady from Columbus," was another noted Ohio entertainer. Although a great success in shows in New York and London, she gave this up to spend her time entertaining the American soldiers overseas during World War I. She was the first woman revue artist that the army permitted at advanced bases, close to the front.

After the war, she returned to the stage in several productions, which she wrote and produced. Later she wrote other plays and books, and appeared in films.

One of America's favorite quartettes for many years has been the Mills Brothers, who started singing in their father's barbershop in Piqua. Their father, before becoming a barber, had been a concert singer, and trained his boys to sing in harmony.

The Mills Brothers made their first professional appearance at Mays Opera House in their hometown. One day an orchestra leader arrived in Piqua, and hearing about the boys went to the shop for a haircut. He liked their singing, and asked them to appear on a Cincinnati radio station. They became so popular that they were invited to New York.

The Mills Brothers was the first Negro act to be hired to do a sponsored network radio program. Using a guitar for accompaniment the group can imitate many instruments with their trained voices. The quartette has made albums since 1931. The Mills Brothers have toured the world, appearing in many places including the famous Trivoli Gardens in Denmark.

Joe E. Brown, the comic with the big mouth, was born in Holgate, starting his career with the circus as an acrobat. He became a famous comedian, appearing in many motion pictures. During World War II, he traveled over 150,000 miles to entertain the troops.

147

Just as Joe made people laugh, Ted Lewis from Circleville, made them dream as they listened to his band and his popular songs.

Bob Hope, who grew up in Cleveland, has provided entertainment for Americans for many years. His movies, the famous "Road" series and television programs made him one the of best known entertainers in the U.S. For many years he visited American troops presenting shows.

Harry Warner, a bicycle repairman in Youngstown, bought a print of "The Great Train Robbery"— America's first motion picture with a real story line— in 1903. He took this film on a tour of Ohio, showing the film anywhere he could find an audience, who would pay 5¢. From this beginning came Warner Brothers Pictures.

It was an Ohioan, Clark Gable, born at Cadiz, who played the lead in "Gone With the Wind," still playing, making it America's leading box-office attraction. Tyrone Power, a Cincinnati native, starred in 26 movies. Doris Day, another Cincinnatian, is a popular vocalist as well as a film, and television star.

The Gish sisters, Dorothy born in Dayton, and Lillian in Springfield, were early motion pictures stars. The daredevil automobile racer, Barney Oldfield, also played in the movies.

One of America's favorite cowboys on the screen and television, Roy Rogers, came from Hamilton County. Son of a farmer, Roy raised pigs, did farm chores, and was a member of the 4-H Club.

The theatre is still very important to Ohioans as part of their cultural heritage. When the shows from New York stopped touring the Ohio theatres, people began to organize their own theatre groups to give live stage presentation. There are over 50 theatre organizations in the state. These groups give young people an opportunity to appear on the stage, and at the same time provide entertainment for those who come to see the productions.

Some of these theater groups are made up of professional performers, such as those of the Cleveland Playhouse, while others use all amateurs. Children's Theater groups throughout the state stage good plays for young people. In addition, the universities have theater groups and present many interesting programs.

Ohio is a land of culture. To bring all these activities to the attention of the people of the state and to encourage them to take part in the activities is the purpose of the Ohio Arts Council.

The General Assembly of the State of Ohio created the Council in 1965 as a state agency. The Ohio Arts Council keeps a record of all the state's cultural resources. It also encourages the development of new cultural programs in Ohio.

CHAPTER VI

Work and Careers in Ohio

When pioneers arrived in Ohio, they found a dark, forested country.

At the most, 15,000 Indians once hunted the wild game from which they obtained their food. Today almost 11,000,000 Ohioans live in the state, and most of the forests are gone. Less than 15 percent of the land is covered with trees.

Building a great state has been the accomplishment of Ohio's hardworking people, beginning with those who lived on the frontier. It was not easy—work built Ohio. Through work a great nation grew out of a wilderness. Work never ends—there is still much to be done. Work not only helps a state, but it also helps a person.

Everyone helps Ohio by doing some kind of work. This is the way a person makes a living. Through work, an individual earns money, which is a medium of exchange. With this money a person buys the things needed to provide food, clothing, and shelter.

While soil is the most important natural resource of Ohio, the state has a great variety of other resources. Minerals, rocks, clay, sand and gravel have been a foundation for many Ohio industries. As the years have passed they have become even more important. People, through work, convert Ohio's resources into products which are sold all over the U.S. and the world.

Through education young people are trained to become producing members of Ohio's economic system. At first, students learn the basic fundamentals of communication, reading, writing and mathematics used in all jobs. Then they need to learn how to do specific kinds of work. This may be done in professional or technical training programs. The wise young person studies to find out where he will be needed in Ohio's future, and then plans a

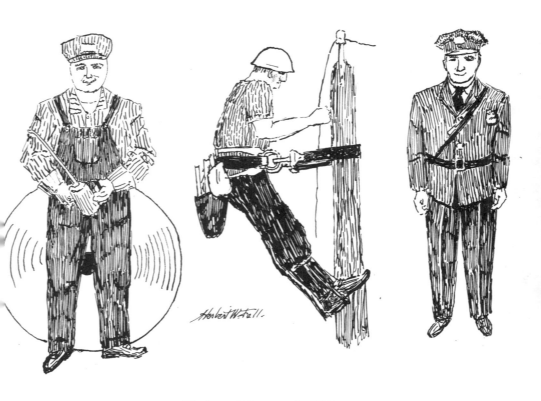

Work and Careers in Ohio.

career in the field that has the most interest. There are hundreds of careers from which to choose.

Agriculture

When Ohio was first settled, about everyone made a living from farming, or agriculture. The soils of Ohio are varied. Some result from the weathering of rocks, and others were transported here by glaciers which covered parts of the state.

The first settlers came to Ohio to make a better living for themselves and their families. The soil of New England was rocky and produced a poor yield. In the South many small farmers were not able to compete against the big plantations and slave labor, and the land wore out from growing cotton. Land in the East sold for $25 to $50 an acre, while Ohio land was $2 an acre.

The Ohio farmer of the last century worked long and hard. Here he is bringing in the hay.

It wasn't long until the people of the East found out about the rich Ohio soil. So many farmers in the East left that some areas were almost deserted. Businessmen, and owners of small industries did not like to see so many people leaving. Thousands of immigrants were soon in Ohio, planning a new life.

When farmers arrived in the Ohio country, they brought with them the same farming methods they had used in the East. People from New England often settled in northeastern Ohio. They brought their sheep and cattle, raised hay and began dairying. The farmers from Pennsylvania found Ohio much like the western part of their state. From foreign lands came the Swiss and Finns who preferred northeastern Ohio, the French liked Gallia County, and the Welsh, the Miami Valley.

Since early farming was done without modern machinery, the farms usually did not exceed 160 acres, and many were smaller than that. Horses and oxen furnished the only power outside that of the work of the farmer and his family. To do the heavy jobs, the farmers often traded labor. One family would help another, and then the favor would be returned.

Butchering is a good example. This was heavy hard work, and usually two or more families would work together, making the work go faster. Handling the animals required the strength of more than one man. Animals had to be killed and bled, then strung up. They had to be scalded, and the hair scraped from the skin.

Butchering day on the farm.

The carcass was cut up. Some of the meat was ground for sausage, with each family having its own favorite way of seasoning. Hams and shoulders were cured in the smokehouse, where they were salted, then smoked over a slow fire. The meat was preserved in this manner, for there was no refrigeration as there is today.

Meat that could not so easily be cured, was divided up with the families, who helped with the butchering.

Before Ohio's transportation system was developed, the farmer found it difficult to sell the surplus. He wanted to do this for there were things which the family needed. Money was also required to pay for the land, and to pay the taxes.

The first major crop of the Ohio farmer was corn. Corn could be planted among the tree stumps, which were often left to rot out. Seed corn brought from the East did not grow as well in Ohio, with its shorter growing season. It did not fill out well before frost. The Indians used flint corn, but the farmers did not like it because of its small yield per acre. Farmers began to experiment. It was found that by crossing flint corn with that from the East, a new variety resulted. The pioneers soon had a better corn than the Indians or the Eastern farmers.

Corn among tree stumps.

154

Ever since that time, farmers have desired better and better corn crops. New varieties are still being developed. Now hybrid corns are grown all over Ohio, and farmers can pick from a large variety. The harvesting of corn used to be a long, difficult job, but now it is done easily and rapidly with a mechanical corn picker.

In pioneer days, corn was difficult to get to market. Farmers raised it and fed it to pigs and hogs, or to cattle. The livestock was often driven on foot to markets by young men. The hogs ate the nuts out of the forests as they walked to market. When the roads and canal were completed, the hogs were butchered and the meat packed in salt or brine in big barrels, and shipped to market. Hams were smoked and cured. Beef was also sent to market.

Much corn was used in making whiskey, consumed in the towns or shipped to market.

Farm boys earned spending money by trapping wild animals for their skins, or by killing unwanted animals for a bounty. A bounty was a money prize for killing such dangerous animals as wolves and panthers. Girls searched out wild herbs and roots which sold well. They also helped their mother make cheese or butter which sold for cash at the grocery stores in the villages.

Wheat was a cash crop. It was sold in town, where millers ground the wheat into flour for the local market, and shipped the surplus to distant cities. Ohio produced a soft winter wheat, particularly desired in making bread and pastry. In early days every town had its bakeries, but most farm women baked their own bread.

Ohio farmers not only produced a better corn, but they also improved their livestock. In 1833 the Scioto Valley farmers began raising improved Shorthorn cattle, while Butler and Warren County farmers, better swine. The Poland-China hog, highly prized in its day, was shipped all over the West. Today a monument to this breed of hog can be seen at Blue Ball. Ohio with hay and grain, and good grazing land, became a leading livestock producer.

By 1850 Ohio ranked first in the U.S. in agriculture. It stood first in the production of corn and wool, and in raising sheep and

155

horses. It was second in wheat production and the raising of cattle.

Today Ohio ranks fifth as an agricultural state, so farming is still important. Almost 20 percent of Ohio's income is from agriculture and its related activities. Agriculture has now become what is referred to as agribusiness. This includes the businesses and industries based on agriculture. Farmers produce a crop, but it must be hauled to market by trucks or railroads. Grain can be fed to livestock or shipped and processed. Corn becomes cornmeal, but also hundreds of products are now made from corn. Wheat becomes cereals and flour, which in turn is baked into bread. Meat, from animals fattened in Ohio, must be processed and delivered to the store where the consumer purchases it.

Hybrid corn in Ohio.

It is estimated that over 750,000 workers in Ohio help in agribusiness. It takes training and skill to be a farmer today. Many farmers graduate from the Agricultural College at Ohio State, one of the best in the nation. Scientists work to improve agriculture, such as at the Ohio Research and Development Center at Wooster.

Agriculture keeps changing like everything else. Since 1945 the number of farms in Ohio has declined by one-half, but at the same time the size of the average farm has doubled. With modern machinery one person can do much more work than in the pioneer days. As long as people eat, farmers will be needed.

Mechanical corn picker enables Ohio farmer to grow and harvest more corn.

This photo shows contour stripcropping.

The major agricultural activity in Ohio is the growing of crops. Corn is still the most important crop to Ohio farmers. Soybeans are becoming more important, being in demand on world markets. The soybean is an old crop, which was raised in China 5,000 years ago. The first soybeans came to the U.S. around 1800 from China, but little was done with them. Much later it was discovered that soybeans could be used for automobile parts, such as door handles, steering wheels and radio cases.

People already discovered that soybeans were a good substitute for such foods as meat, cereals, cheese, milk, salad oil and other protein foods. At first it was used in the making of pet foods and cattle feed, but today it has found its way into the American diet. Each year the demand grows for soybeans in the U.S. and around the world, and Ohio farmers plant more and more of them.

While wheat does not make up over ten percent of Ohio's farm income in any county, wheat makes a good crop in rotation with corn and soybeans, and modern farmers rotate crops to improve the soil. Not only is crop rotation part of farming, but contour stripcropping is also practiced in rolling areas, so that the soil does not wash away. Farmers realize that soil is Ohio's most important natural resource.

Oats is a grain fed to animals in Ohio, and is a leading crop in several counties. A small amount of rye and barley is grown in Ohio. Popcorn, so popular with young people, is an important crop in Ohio. Potatoes provide a good cash crop for farmers, and they find many uses as a favorite food of Ohioans, such as potato chips and French fries. Sugar beets are also on the list of Ohio crops.

While concentrated in a few Ohio counties — Brown, Adams, Gallia and Lawrence — tobacco is a good money crop. Ohio is also a producer of fruit, with apples being the main crop. However, grapes for wine were most important in Ohio's past, and are again becoming an important crop. Some peaches and cherries are produced.

Commercial vegetable production is an important source of income. Many of these vegetable crops are produced in areas

158

around the major urban areas, with one-half the sales in ten counties with large cities. The vegetables are grown on what are called truck farms, being trucked into town, or sold at a roadside stand. Some of the vegetables such as cabbage for kraut, tomatoes, and cucumbers for pickles are canned in Ohio and shipped to other states.

Since many people enjoy fresh vegetables the year around, Ohio is one of the leading states in the production of greenhouse vegetables. Greenhouse farming has been important in Ohio since early days. Flowers are also grown in the greenhouses, both cut flowers and plants. Thousands of people work in greenhouses and nurseries, a demanding job requiring great technical skill.

The care and feeding of livestock is a major agricultural activity. Cattle and calf sales bring in almost as much money as that of growing of corn and soybeans. Livestock is found in greatest numbers in southeastern Ohio, but western Ohio also raises cattle. Hogs are important in livestock farming, with southwestern Ohio the leading producer. Poultry and egg production, along with turkeys, provide cash income.

Dairying is a major activity in Ohio.

Ohio farms use modern machinery.

Dairying is an agricultural activity throughout Ohio, with about one-fifth of the farmers engaged in it. Large dairy farms are found around all the cities to provide milk and milk products for the city dwellers. Milk and ice cream are popular and healthful foods. Ohio's climate produces grass for grazing and good hay crops. Rolling lands and gentle hills make pasture lands ideal for cattle.

Forest Resources

Geography, which gave Ohio a good climate, rich soil, and level to rolling lands, make it an agricultural state. Geography was good to Ohio in other ways.

At first the pioneers wanted to destroy the trees which covered most of their farmland. Often they did not try to clear the hilly areas of the farm, but left them with the trees. Most of the trees were hardwoods, excellent for making furniture or framing of houses. Trees also provided firewood to keep the fireplaces going before the days of central heating and coal.

Wood was also burned in the boilers that kept the early Ohio locomotives running.

Farmers close to cities found a demand for firewood, and chopped, and took it to the city to sell. Every community had a sawmill, and with the building came a demand for lumber.

After all the years Ohio has been a state, lumber and wood products are still produced by some workers. Land which can not be used for farming is being reforested.

Mineral Resources

Under the good earth of Ohio, lie minerals of vast importance to the state's economy. These make up what is known as extractive industries, or mining industries. The most valuable of these underground resources is the solid black mineral substance called coal. Thirty-two Ohio counties have coal reserves, but Belmont, Harrison and Jefferson counties are the most important producers. One third of all mineral production in Ohio is coal.

Coal has been of great use in building the industry of the state. It is a major source of energy and power, and unlike petroleum and gas, there are vast reserves in Ohio. Just how great the reserves is not really known, but at the present rate scientists report that Ohio has enough coal to last at least 400 years.

Coal was first used in Ohio to supply heat for the home. Then it was used in small industries such as the blacksmith shops and foundries. Coal fires were also used to evaporate brine, to make it into salt. As early as 1835 coal mined in Ohio was shipped down the river to New Orleans for use in the sugar refineries. As wood to make charcoal gave out, it was replaced by coal in Ohio's early blast furnaces.

With the energy crisis in the U.S. today, coal is even more important. Coal can be used as a substitute for petroleum in generating electricity. In fact, Ohio, fortunately kept most of its coal generating plants rather than converting to oil.

Ohio's coal is easy to mine. Most of it can be obtained through strip mining. While this is a problem in destroying land, good practices can reclaim the land. Coal can also be converted into artificial gas, which will be needed as natural gas reserves are depleted.

In early days a man could dig the coal out of the ground, put it in a wheelbarrow and sell it to steamboats coming down the

161

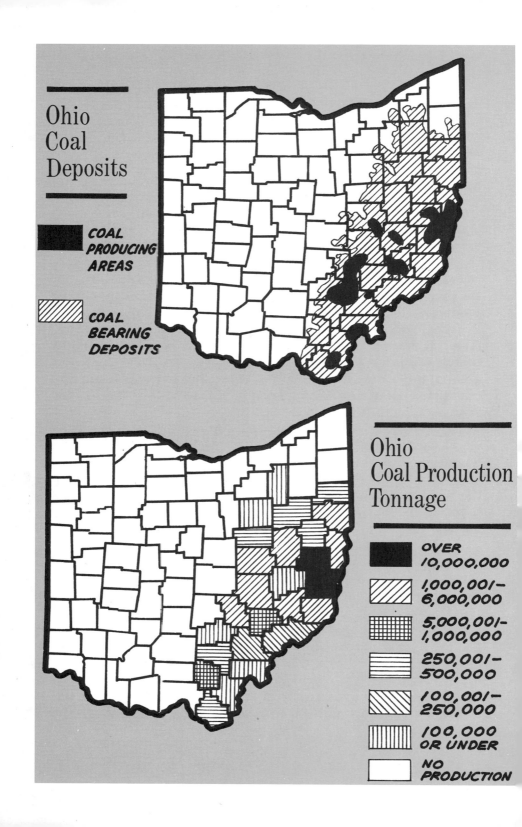

Ohio
Coal
Deposits

COAL
PRODUCING
AREAS

COAL
BEARING
DEPOSITS

Ohio
Coal Production
Tonnage

OVER
10,000,000

1,000,001–
6,000,000

5,000,001–
1,000,000

250,001–
500,000

100,001–
250,000

100,000
OR UNDER

NO
PRODUCTION

river. Jake Heatherington was such a coal dealer, but when he got tired of the wheelbarrow, he bought a mule named Jack to pull a cart. Business grew and finally Jake became wealthy. He remembered his faithful mule, Jack, who helped build his coal business. Jake and the mule retired to live in the oddest house ever built in Bellaire. It was built so that Jack could live in it with his master. People of Ohio called it the "House that Jack Built."

Railroads move out most of Ohio's coal, but trucks are becoming more important. The most unusual way of moving coal is the pipeline built to carry coal in powdered form from Cadiz to Cleveland.

Coal is not only used to produce energy, but also in the manufacture of chemicals. Coal also plays a part in the manufacture of plastic, nylon, drugs, fertilizers, and even perfume.

The same year, 1859, that oil was discovered in Pennsylvania, the search was underway in Ohio. It was found that Lima was built over an oil field. Oil was discovered in Ohio as early as 1814, when two men drilling for salt brine in Noble County ran into oil. To them it was just in their way.

In 1880 many oil fields were in production in Ohio, and by 1890 over 15,000,000 barrels of oil a year were being pumped from under Ohio. With Ohio an oil producer, the refining industry began in the state and today one of the largest refineries in the nation is at Toledo.

In 1836, a driller searching for water near Findlay, ran into gas. It wasn't until the 1880s that Findlay realized how important natural gas could be. It was of use as a fuel, and for lighting. Gas was also discovered at Toledo. Since a steady hot, and cheap fuel was needed for the making of glass, Ohio had the basis of another industry.

Although Ohio must depend upon other sources for oil and gas, it is still a producing state. Drilling continues, for more oil and gas may be found in deeper wells.

Before the pioneers came to Ohio, the Indians had developed the salt industry. They took the water from saline springs, and evaporated it, getting salt crystals. The refining of table salt as well as providing salt for livestock is an Ohio industry. Rock salt

This "grasshopper-like" pump pulls oil from the depths of Ohio's rich earth.

lies under about one-fourth of the state, with most of the production now in underground mines in Cuyahoga and Lake Counties.

Important for flavoring foods, salt had many other uses, especially in the chemical industry. Scientists have found almost 15,000 uses for this basic mineral, which along with limestone, is the basis for the state's chemical industry.

Limestone is a rock of great economic importance, for it has many uses. Limestone is used in the blast furnaces in the steel-making process. It is used in the cement industry, as well as in the manufacturing of glass and paper. The construction industry uses limestone.

Ohio has been a producer of limestone for a long time, and located near Barberton is the deepest limestone quarry in the world. Only Illinois supplies the nation with more limestone. Ohio's reserves of this rock are almost unlimited.

The largest sandstone quarry in the U.S. is at South Amherst. Most of the sandstone used in building comes from Ohio quarries, for Ohio's sandstone is of high quality. Sandstone also has many industrial uses.

Shale ranks third in importance of rocks underlying Ohio. It is used in the manufacturing of clay and cement products.

Since early days clay has been a major resource of Ohio. Pioneers found large deposits of clay in many areas, and around these developed the brick-making industry. These bricks were used to build the towns and cities of Ohio, and while not the same high quality of bricks as manufactured today, they withstood many years of service. The most important industry based on Ohio's almost unlimited clay deposits is that of pottery, tile, and pipe manufacturing.

While sand and gravel seem to be common materials to an Ohioan, they are important raw materials. Gravel paved the early mud roads of the state, making transportation easier. Gravel and sand are still the major construction materials of highways, bridges, and dams, and are used in all types of modern buildings.

Growth of Industry

During the nineteenth century, Ohio grew from an agricultural state into an industrial state. Villages and towns grew up on crossroads, starting with a general store, a tavern or stagecoach stop, a blacksmith shop, and other businesses to meet the needs of the farmers.

Towns that were near a stream, river, or canal soon utilized the power from running water to turn a waterwheel. Waterwheels were Ohio's first source of energy. A typical Ohio town would have some business man who would develop a small industrial center. This would consist of a group of mills along the millrace, which brought water to run the waterwheels.

The most important early mill was the gristmill. By changing the millstone, a grist mill could grind wheat in flour, or corn into cornmeal. This was a convenience to every farm family, for it saved the work of grinding grain in a hand mill. Sometimes these mills were erected on a stream, such as the Bambo Harris gristmill in Hamilton County built in 1800. Harris was a skilled Black mechanic and operated one of the first mills in the state.

In a small village, the gristmill might be the only one, but in a larger place there would be a sawmill and a woolen mill. The

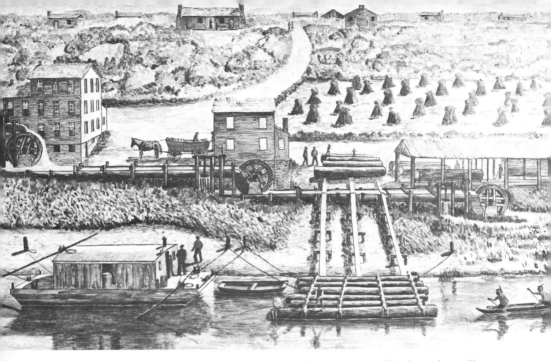

Beginning of industry in an Ohio town. The woolen mill, the grist mill, and the sawmill fed by the same race.

Bambo Harris Grist Mill in 1800.

Meat packing was Ohio's first big industry. Cincinnati was called "Porkopolis."

gristmill helped prepare grain for food. The woolen mill processed wool sheared off the farmer's sheep for making cloth, while the sawmill cut logs into lumber for homes and barns.

Springfield is an example of how a small pioneer settlement grew into an industrial city. In 1799 the first log cabin was built at the site, and before long there were eight cabins. In 1803 the town was platted, named Springfield after a large spring nearby. Simon Kenton built a gristmill and a sawmill. Then Cooper Ludlow built a tannery, which processed hides of cattle into leather. Local shoemakers made the leather into shoes. In 1809 a powder mill was built, suppling farmers in Ohio with an explosive to blow out the stumps from the fields that were cleared. Springfield also had a cotton and woolen mill.

In 1838 the National Road had reached Springfield, which was then at the end of the road. Springfield was in the center of a great farming region, so it developed an industry to supply the needs of the farmers in Ohio. In 1838 James Leffel produced sickles, axes, and knives in his machine shop. He also invented a double turbine waterwheel, and since water was then the main energy source at that time, the wheel sold throughout the West.

Obed Hussey of Hamilton County invented a reaper to cut the wheat of Ohio, and a manufacturing plant to produce the reaper was built in Urbana. Then William Whitely invented a combined reaper and mower with a self rake, which he called the Champion. A factory was built at Springfield to make the new reaper. In one year the Champion Machine Company built 160,000 reapers and Springfield was known as the Champion City. Later Champion became part of the International Harvester Company of Chicago.

As farmers began to use machinery on farms, it replaced the need for much of the farm labor. Hired hands were the first without work, then even the farmers' sons no longer were needed. They went to the city to find work. Ohio changed from a rural state to an urban state, and manufacturing became the way that most Ohioans made a living.

Although Ohio began with manufacturing farm machinery, the state developed into a major supplier of all kinds of machinery. Today more Ohio industrial workers are employed in firms making machinery and electrical equipment than in any other kind of manufacturing.

Machinery and electrical equipment require large amounts of iron and steel. Ohio began early in the iron industry. The state had some deposits of iron ore. Trees were cut to provide a source of charcoal, which was used to smelt the iron ore. As early as 1797, John Young, who had settled in the Mahoning Valley, platted a town, which he named Youngstown. He used the iron ore he discovered nearby to feed a small furnace. Out of this small beginning grew the iron and steel industry of the Mahoning Valley.

In 1825 John Means began to develop the iron industry in the Hanging Rock area, for the hills contain iron ore, with limestone deposits near, as well as clay for making bricks to line the furnaces. As charcoal ran out, he turned to the coal of the region. Starting with a furnace called the Union, it wasn't long until many furnaces were in operation. By 1850, 22 blast furnaces could be found in the Hanging Rock area.

168

Ironmaster James Campbell found a way to make better pig iron at Hanging Rock, but the demand was so great for his product that he needed to increase production. He organized the Ohio Iron and Coal Company, bought 400 acres of land about three miles from his old furnace, and platted a new town. At this new site, Ironton, Campbell built new furnaces, one of which, the Etna, was at the time, the largest blast furnace in the world. With the coming of railroads, more iron was needed. The Hecla Furnace turned out iron for locomotive wheels. It also produced iron and steel to make cannon and guns for the Civil War.

The iron industry shifted from northern to southeastern Ohio due to the rich iron ore found in the Hanging Rock area. Just as the best ore was being used up, a great iron ore field was discovered in Minnesota. This ore could be shipped to northern Ohio by way of the Great Lakes. With great amounts of fuel needed, charcoal gave way to coal, which was also available in northern Ohio.

Cleveland, still a small city of 45,000 in 1860, was a lake port and on the main rail lines across the country. It was a good site for the steel industry. Steel mills were built, along with steel fabricating plants, and Cleveland became and remains a leading steel producer.

Today Youngstown, the site of the first charcoal furnace in Ohio, and Warren, in the Mahoning Valley, are steel towns, as are Canton, and Steubenville in northeastern Ohio. Outside of that section of the state, there is another steel center in southwestern Ohio at Middletown and Hamilton.

It was a Middletown inventor, John B. Tytus, who invented a new way to make steel. After years of study, and with an investment of $10,000,000 by Armco Steel Corporation, Tytus set up a continuous wide strip mill which turned out better steel at a lower cost. It speeded up the manufacture of steel so that it would have a wider use in the economy. It has been called one of the ten greatest inventions of modern times.

Another Ohio inventor, Charles M. Hall, became interested in the wonder metal aluminum when a boy in high school. It was a lightweight metal, and strong, but unlike steel would not rust.

The age of steel and welding in Ohio industry.

Aluminum was too expensive for general use.

Hall entered Oberlin College, and using the laboratory there, worked on the problem of how to make cheaper aluminum. Finally in his own workshed workshop, he found how to use electricity to produce a cheaper product. Aluminum is a major U.S. industry, and some is used in the Ohio fabrication industry. A wide variety of metal products are manufactured in the state, including metal cans, tinware, tools, cutlery, and general hardware.

The inventions of Thomas A. Edison, already noted, and Charles Brush helped to develop the manufacturing of electrical equipment in the state. Both of their inventions led to generating plants and the production of other electrical supplies.

After graduating from college, Brush set up a laboratory at Cleveland. He wanted to put electrical energy to work for man. He built a dynamo that produced a current which would light several lamps. Some of these lamps produced as much as 4,000 candlepower and would light up the night. Seeing the value of light to make city streets safer, for gaslights were weak and produced long shadows, Brush set up the first electric street lighting system in the state at Cleveland. On an April night in 1879 Brush's invention brightened the streets around Monumental Park. Soon other cities bought the Brush system putting lights atop tall towers. Gaslight was on the way out.

Brush also discovered that streetcars would run by the same electrical power. Soon he had an electric streetcar in operation on a Cleveland street, and this replaced the horsecar. The traction or trolley car, as the people called it, would furnish a new means of transportation in cities and between cities. Later Brush's electric company became part of the General Electric Company, which has several important manufacturing plants in Ohio.

A janitor at Canton, who couldn't stand dust, decided he would find a better way of sweeping rugs. Murray Spangler went to work to improve the sweeper by putting an electric fan on the brush of the sweeper, which collected the dirt but also caused more dust. He then put a bag on the sweeper. In 1908 he obtained a patent on his new electric suction sweeper.

He met Henry W. Hoover, a Canton businessman, who was running a factory that produced harness and saddles. Thinking that the sweeper might have a better future than his business with the growing acceptance of the automobile, he went into partnership with Spangler. It wasn't long until the new sweeper caught on, and Canton had a new industry.

Ohio is a major producer of glass products. While the first glass factory was started at Cincinnati in 1814, and another at Moscow in 1815, it was the discovery of natural gas that made Ohio a leader in this line of products. Both Findlay and Fostoria saw the value of natural gas for glass production, becoming the site of many glass works.

When Edward D. Libbey, who owned a glass company in Massachusetts, heard of the discovery of natural gas around Toledo, he decided to move to that city. He built his new plant among the corn shocks at the end of a gas line. The Libby Glass Company turned out the first tableware at the new plant in 1888.

One day Michael J. Owens, a glassblower from Pittsburgh, arrived in Toledo and asked Libbey for a job. He saw the need to speed up production as the demand for glass kept growing. After making several minor inventions to that end, in 1903 Owens built a bottle-making machine. The company became Libby-Owens.

Captain John Ford, a riverboat man, turned to glassmaking and discovered a method of making the stronger plate glass. With a son he started the Pittsburgh Plate Glass Company, sold it, and built a factory in Wood County. This later was merged with the Toledo works, and became Libbey-Owens-Ford, one of three major glass producing companies today. Toledo is known as the "Glass Capital of the World."

Closely related to glass making is the pottery industry. Centering on East Liverpool in eastern Ohio is the area in which pottery is manufactured. Much of the best pottery clay in the world is found here.

East Liverpool began with one kiln in 1841. James Bennett, a young pottery maker from England, stepped off a steamboat at the small village, and went out for a short walk. He saw clay on the hillside, and as a potter, he recognized it as the best. He started his own plant and then went out and sold his pottery. Soon the whole area became a pottery center, with kilns at such towns as Roseville, Crooksville, Zanesville, and Scio.

During the great Depression of the early 1930s the pottery industry suffered greatly. People were not buying the product. Lew Reese, who had worked at the potter's wheel, thought that there should be a way to make pottery by machine, and thus lower the cost of pottery and tableware to the consumer.

He found a pottery at Scio which was closed. He bought the plant and installed the new machinery which he designed and built. It would make cheap white chinaware ten times faster than the old method. Soon he was getting orders from all over the U.S. for his chinaware.

Lew Reese was very fair to the people who worked for him at the pottery, and they worked to help him make a good product.

Under our economic system in the U.S. we call the boss and his helpers, management. The people who work in the industry are called labor. Management and labor want the same thing, for the company must succeed or there will be no jobs for anyone. Most of the money made goes to pay the workers and to buy the raw materials needed to manufacture the product.

Some of the money goes to pay the men who run the business of the industry. To stay in business, it is necessary to keep buying new machinery and improving the plant itself. After all bills are paid the money that is left is called profit and it is divided among the stockholders. These are the people who used their savings to buy stock, which provided money to start the plant and to make major changes and additions to it. Unless a profit is made people will not buy stock or will sell what they have.

The story of John D. Rockefeller, who built one of Ohio's biggest companies, illustrates how the American economic system works. John D. Rockefeller was born a poor boy, the son of a peddler. As a young boy, his parents moved to Cleveland, and Rockefeller graduated from Central High School.

Rockefeller's first job was as a bookkeeper at $20 per month. Each pay day he saved a little from his pay, for he wanted to go into business for himself. He saved the money so that he could build up capital, which is money used to start a business. A man who uses the money he saved in this manner is called a capitalist, so Rockefeller was a capitalist. All Americans who own stocks or their own business are capitalists. Without capitalists our country would not have its great industries, which all started small. Industries and business create jobs and thus make it possible for young people to plan careers, and obtain a job when they leave school.

With $1000 that Rockefeller saved, and another $1000 that he borrowed, he had enough capital to go into business for himself. The business succeeded. If it had not, the money would have been lost. This is known as taking a risk, and every person who starts a new enterprise takes a risk. A business must make money, or it will go broke or bankrupt, and close its doors. If this happens the people who invested in it, lose their money, and workers lose their jobs.

When Rockefeller heard about the discovery of oil, he decided to sell his business, and go into a new one, the petroleum industry. Oil could be used in many ways. It would replace whale oil which was burned in lamps, and lubricate the new machinery being invented.

In 1862 a small refinery was started in Cleveland, and within five years Rockefeller's refinery was the biggest in the city. By 1870 Cleveland was an oil town, where one-third of the nation's petroleum was refined. Coal oil or kerosene was used in lighting homes.

Rockefeller saw that there were too many small refineries in Cleveland, and he began to buy them and consolidate them into one big company. He called his company the Standard Oil Company of Ohio, which carries the nickname, Sohio. When he formed his new company he started with a capital of $1,000,000, and it was the largest oil company in the world. Later on it was divided into several companies.

The oil industry grew and so did the steel industry of Cleveland. From 1850 to 1880 Cleveland's population increased ten times, but it still wasn't as large as Cincinnati. By 1900 the Census figures showed that Cleveland had outgrown Cincinnati and had become the largest city in Ohio, which it has remained.

Even before Ohio became a state, a small printing industry had begun. As more newspapers were started, there was a demand for paper. This created a need for a paper industry in Ohio, for it was too difficult and expensive to bring all the paper from the East.

In 1806 three businessmen from Pennsylvania organized the Ohio Paper Mills and built a mill at what is now East Liverpool. When they began operation, there were perhaps a dozen printing presses in the state, so one mill could not meet the demand.

Christian Waldsmith set up a paper mill on the Little Miami River in the Miami Valley and began to make paper in 1811. The paper industry grew in the Miami Valley and it remains a major industry in the Hamilton-Middletown area as well as in other southwestern Ohio cities.

Daniel E. Mead became an important figure in the paper

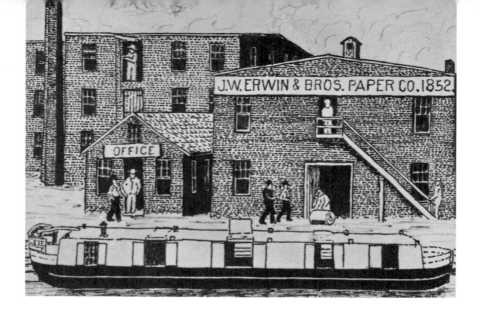

industry. The Mead Paper Company began in Dayton, and then purchased the paper mills at Chillicothe. Today there are over 300 paper plants in Ohio. Ohio ranks third in paper production in the U.S.

Another industry had its beginning in Dayton. John Patterson built the National Cash Register plant there. It became the largest employer in Dayton, but due to advances in computer technology new plants to meet the demands of changes in production were built elsewhere.

Ohio's industry has changed through the years, for industry exists only to meet the demands of the consumer. As these demands change, industry must change with them, or go out of business.

Ohio cities have also changed down through the years. At present many large Ohio cities are not growing, but actually losing population as people move to suburbs. For example, Cleveland lost over 100,000 people in ten years, but cities near it, such as Euclid, Lakewood, Parma, and Loraine have made gains in population.

Columbus, the state's capital, replaced Cincinnati as the second largest city in the state in the Census of 1970. However, Cincinnati is only a core city, serving the needs, and often supplying jobs, for people in northern Kentucky as well as many suburban communities to its north. Cincinnati is noted for its large soap manufacturing industry, Proctor and Gamble, dating back to canal days. It is also a major producer of transportation equipment, and serves as a food processing center. The paper and printing industry is also of importance, as is the production of chemicals.

Columbus's industry is very well diversified, but it is noted for transportation equipment and instrument plants.

Toledo, ranking fourth among Ohio's cities, is of growing importance as a lake port on the St. Lawrence Seaway route. Glass and petroleum refining are still major industries. In Akron, fifth in population, the production of rubber products still employ almost half its workers, but fabricated metal products are also important.

Cleveland and Toledo, World Ports

Between Cincinnati and Dayton is almost one continuous metropolitan area with different manufacturing plants. Kettering and Moraine, just south of Dayton, have grown rapidly. Dayton has a diversified economy, which includes the areas of paper and printing, rubber and plastics, machinery, electrical equipment and appliances.

Youngstown continues to be important in steel production along with Canton and Steubenville.

Today Ohio ranks third in the nation according to value added through manufacturing. One out of every three of its workers is employed in some manufacturing activity. Almost half the income of the workers of the state comes from manufacturing.

The young person looking for a career in Ohio has many choices. Many will want to enter some form of manufacturing, for making a product used by other people is a good way to spend one's time. Making products interests many young Ohioans. This takes intelligence and skill. More people in Ohio earn a living in manufacturing than in any other career.

Taking a natural resource, or several natural resources, and making them into a primary product, such as steel, paper, soap, or glass, requires the labor of many skilled people. Ohio has over 450 industrial laboratories in the state, which require scientific minds to keep them in operation. Research is part of every important industry.

Transportation and the maintenance of utilities such as gas and electric, telephones and water services make up another important group of jobs.

The construction industry employs skilled men and women in many activities. Bringing products to the consumer is the activity of the wholesale and retail trade group of jobs. Finance, insurance and real estate provide other careers of a specialized nature.

Ranking second in Ohio employment opportunities, is a fast growing group of careers, known as service occupations. Nurses, teachers, doctors, lawyers, firemen, policemen all provide a service for their fellowmen. In the future it is expected that more careers will open up in this area of work.

There are many job families. Study the one which interests you the most. Find out how a person prepares for a special field of work.

It is never too early to begin to think about the future. Your future can be an interesting career in the Ohio of tomorrow.

177

CHAPTER VII

Government: State and Local

Early Government

When people live together in groups they form a society. Any society must have rules and regulations which its members must respect and follow. If they do not, the society disintegrates. These rules and regulations when agreed upon by the members of the society become its laws. In some early societies these were unwritten, but today laws are written down and printed, filling many volumes of books.

The laws by which a society lives and means of enforcement of these laws is known as government. The government is the power or authority that is created to carry out or enforce the laws. Without this authority, called government, some people would ignore and refuse to obey the laws. This would lead to a land without laws, or anarchy. Only the very strong would be safe, and even they would have to live in fear.

The study of government and how it operates is called political science. Men and women who study the law and use it to settle disputes and maintain a peaceful society are called lawyers. People who are elected to run or administer the government are called politicians.

When the Europeans came into the Ohio country, they found evidence of a government. It was not the same kind of government that the explorers and pioneers had known. The pioneer and Indians did not understand each others' government. This often led to misunderstanding.

One of the major differences in their government was the idea of private property. The American colonists under their governments had the right to own private or individual property. The Indians thought all land belonged to all the people. They did not even understand that land could be owned by one person or tribe and sold. When a treaty was made, with a payment made for the land, the Indians did not understand that they were to leave that land forever. Since Ohio was the hunting grounds or preserve of many tribes, no one tribe had real control over a particular part.

For very important matters, such as going to war, the Indians of Ohio were divided into two Confederacies. The Algonquin Confederacy was made up of three tribes: Miami, Delaware and Shawnee. The Iroquois Confederacy was composed of four tribes: Erie, Wyandot, Ottowa, and Seneca, or Mingo.

The Confederacy was a very loose governmental organization. When a very important problem faced its people, a big tribal council would be held, and a decision would be made.

A Tribal Government

The smallest, or basic unit, of each tribe's government was the family. The family is the basic unit of Ohio's government. A family is a group of related people living together and sharing the same dwelling, where each care for the other.

It would not be safe for one family to live alone in the Ohio forests, so the Indians lived in clans. These clans were each made up of several families, who were usually related to each other. When members of the clan were ready to marry, they chose their husbands or brides from other clans.

Each clan used the name of an animal or a thing which meant something special to it. This was their name or sign which they called a totem. Little Turtle, the great Miami chief, was a member of the turtle clan. Within one tribe would be several clan names. Among the most popular totems were turtle, deer, bear, hawk, eagle, elk, beaver and wolf.

An hereditary chief, meaning the title was passed from father to son, headed some clans. In other clans, the chief was elected. In the more democratic clans, both men and women voted for members of the Council and the Chief.

When a special problem came up, a Grand Council was held. Each clan sent its Chief to the Tribal Council, which was the government for that group of clans. The Council made the decisions as to tribal policy. The leader of the tribe was elected by

179

the chiefs of the clan, and was called the Sachem.

Some of the problems faced by the Council were settlement of disputes among the members of the clans or with other tribes. They also handled such things as murder or theft. They made the decision as when to go to war, or when to make peace.

As the Tribal Council debated, there would often be many visitors attending the meeting. The important leaders, the chiefs and medicine men, stayed at the ceremonial lodge, but the visitors had to camp out. Such meetings were usually held in the summer.

Sometimes delegates would come from other tribes or other confederacies. If the Americans wished to discuss a problem with the Indians, they would attend the council meeting, and speak to the Indians through an interpretor.

Although not written down, the decisions made at the council meetings were accepted by the Indians as law.

A New Government

Just as soon as the American Revolution ended, and a peace treaty was signed between the new United States and England, many Americans wanted to settle the western lands. In 1784 Thomas Jefferson proposed to Congress that the territory northwest of the Ohio, or the Northwest Territory, be divided into several states. These were to be admitted to the Union after reaching a certain population. They were then to enjoy the same rights as the original states.

Congress continued to work on a plan of government for the new territory, and finally in 1787 the Northwest Ordinance was adopted.

The Ordinance of 1787 was really a plan of government or a Constitution for the new territory. It was a plan made by Congress, which provided for the creation of new states.

At first the Northwest Territory was to be under a temporary government, whose officers were appointed by Congress. They were a Governor, a secretary, and three judges. The laws for the new territory were taken from those of the original states and approved by Congress. This would be the first step.

When a section of the territory reached a population of 5,000 free male inhabitants over 21 years of age, the men were given the right to elect the lower house of a representative assembly. Congress chose the upper house. The Territorial Governor had the power to veto any law passed by the assembly. When the population of any section obtained a population of 60,000 adult males, the people were to draw up a Constitution and apply for statehood.

The Northwest Ordinance also contained sections promising the settlers of the new territory their rights. They were to enjoy freedom under the law, and have the legal rights enjoyed by all Americans. They were promised freedom of worship. Slavery was not permitted in the territory. The Ordinance promised that "the utmost good faith shall always be observed towards the Indians."

The most unusual article contained this statement: "Religion, morality, and knowledge, being necessary to good government and the happiness of mankind, schools and the means of education shall forever be encouraged." From this promise grew the free, public school system, a new idea in history.

Only four months after the first settlers arrived at Marietta, Governor Arthur St. Clair, with his official appointment from Congress, spoke before the people of that small community, July 9, 1788. The Territorial capital was at Chillicothe, and Ohio's first stage of development under the Ordinance of 1787 began. Serving under Governor St. Clair was his secretary, Winthrop Sargent, and three judges.

The first task of Governor St. Clair was to make a list of good laws for the territory and to set up a system of law courts. Knowing that every society must have rules, the people of the Ohio Land Company had made a list of regulations to govern themselves before the Governor came. This was called the Marietta Code, and it was nailed on a big tree where everyone could read it.

Governor St. Clair studied the laws of Pennsylvania and Massachusetts, and picked out the best laws from their codes. Some time, in 1795, all the laws in use in the new Territory were set up in type by Ohio's first printer, William Maxwell at

Cincinnati. They made up the first book printed in the West, and were called Maxwell's Code.

Governor St. Clair also set up counties, and picked out a town for the county seat, where the county government was to be located. St. Clair also appointed the judges and sheriffs for the new counties. The people soon felt that Governor St. Clair had all the power, so they were dissatisfied. Many had fought in the American Revolution for their rights. Ohioans couldn't wait until they became a state.

The Governor was in no hurry to give up his power, but he saw the people were angry. He agreed that a census would be taken and the census showed that Ohio had 5,000 voters. In December 1798 the first election was held in which 22 men were chosen for the Territorial House of Representatives. The Assembly met and passed several new laws, but the people were still not satisfied.

In May, 1800 the U.S. Congress approved the division of land of the Northwest Territory that was to be Ohio. When the second Territorial Assembly met in 1801 it accepted petitions for statehood. On April 30, 1802, President Thomas Jefferson signed the Enabling Act for Ohio to become a state.

Before Ohio was admitted as a state, it had to submit a Constitution to Congress. A Constitutional Convention was called for Nov. 1, 1802. At the Capitol building at Chillicothe, 35 men met to write this important document. Lawyers, merchants, farmers, and people representing other occupations, came from all over Ohio. They voted 34 to 1 for Statehood. After a month of hard work, their new Constitution was ready.

It began: "We the people of the eastern division of the territory of the U.S. northwest of the river Ohio...." It contained eight articles, or main parts. The two longest articles outlined the legislative powers of the General Assembly, and the rights of the people. Under this Constitution, the Governor had very little power, for the people were disgusted with the power exercised by Governor St. Clair. The Constitution provided that slavery be forbidden. It set up the steps by which the people could amend the Constitution.

Three important ideas of government were contained in Ohio's first Constitution, and these are still important today in a democracy. The people are the reason for government, and all power comes from them. In Europe at that time much of the power came from the ruler, or King. Americans did not like this idea. They felt that everyone should be governed by his own consent.

Another idea was that a government is only possible if good laws are made, and then if everyone obeys the laws. Every person has rights under the law, and the courts see that each is treated equally and fairly.

To prevent the government from becoming too powerful, the powers of the three branches—the Legislative, the Executive and the Judicial—should be separated. Each should balance the other. To do this the Constitution set up one branch to make the laws. This was called the General Assembly. The second branch was to carry out or enforce the laws that were made. This was the Office of the Governor and his aides. The third branch applied the laws and made judgments about the laws through a system of Courts.

The new Ohio Constitution was much like the U.S. Constitution. While the U.S. Constitution listed the powers of the federal government, the Ohio Constitution did not do this. The state's powers were known from the Constitutions of the other states of the union. An amendment to the U.S. Constitution also defined these as follows: "The powers not delegated to the United States by the Constitution, nor prohibited by it to the States, are reserved to the States respectively or to the people."

The United States Constitution is the law of the land, and no state can make a law that conflicts with it. Each Constitution covers a different part of government, and its special functions. The U.S. Constitution clearly defines the function and power of the Federal government, while the Ohio Constitution outlines the function and power assumed by the state.

The Constitution of 1802 was presented to the U. S. Congress and approved by them on Feb. 19, 1803. An election was held for the General Assembly. On March 3, 1803, Ohio became the nation's 17th state.

Edward Tiffin was elected Governor. He was born in England and at the age of 11 came to Virginia with his parents. In 1798 he emigrated to Chillicothe. Tiffin married Mary Worthington, sister of Thomas Worthington who also emigrated to Ohio at the same time, and was to become the sixth governor of Ohio. Tiffin served two terms as Governor then went on to serve the national government. Tiffin, Ohio, is named in his honor.

With statehood, Ohioans began to think of a capital city, and a Capitol building for the state. Governor Arthur St. Clair set up his government at Marietta in 1788, and in 1790 moved the capital to Cincinnati, nearer the center of the large territory he governed.

When Congress divided the Northwest Territory, Chillicothe was selected as the capital of the eastern part. In 1800 a square, two-story Capitol building was erected, which although used as a state Capitol for only a few years, served other functions until it was demolished in 1852.

In 1808 the state legislature undertook the study of the best location for a capital. From 1809 to 1812 the Ohio government was at Zanesville, and a statehouse was erected there. Then in 1812 the state government was moved back to Chillicothe.

Realizing that northern Ohio would develop and desiring a location that would put the state government in the center of the state, the legislature decided to find a new location for its work. The site chosen was along the high east bank of the Scioto River, opposite a small village called Franklinton, laid out in 1797.

The new town was called Columbus, in honor of the Italian admiral who discovered the new world. The first Capitol building, of stone and brick, had two large chambers for the House of Representatives and the Senate to meet, several committee rooms, and a gallery. It contained several offices for state officials, and even room for a state library.

The General Assembly held its first session in the new Capitol in 1816. Ohio's population grew so rapidly, that the Capitol building was soon too small. In 1838 the legislature named a committee to plan a new one. A contest was announced and prizes offered to the architects who submitted the three best plans. Over 50 plans were submitted. Henry Walter of Cincinnati won first prize, but parts of the other two plans, which the legislators liked, were incorporated into the final drawings. The committee decided on a Greek Revival stone building with Doric columns. The large blocks of limestone used to build the Capitol were taken from a quarry on the west bank of the river.

While it was planned to complete the Capitol in six years at a cost of $400,000, it actually took 22 years and cost over three times that much. It is such a good building and so well planned that it has been noted as one of the outstanding types of its kind of architecture in the U.S. Many famous people have walked across the floor of its beautiful Rotunda. Lincoln spoke here on two occasions, and his body lay in state in the Rotunda after his death.

In the center of the Rotunda dome is the Great Seal of Ohio. Stairways lead up to the House of Representatives at one end, and to the Senate at the other end. In these chambers of the General Assembly, the laws of Ohio are made.

The most important monument on the Statehouse grounds is that of "Cornelia and her Jewels" at the northwest corner. The woman Cornelia represents the state of Ohio, and around her are seven sons, Ohioans who served our nation during the Civil War. They were Generals Grant, Sherman, Sheridan, Garfield and Hayes, three of whom became president, and two men, Stanton and Chase who served in Lincoln's cabinet. The story of Cornelia can be found in Roman history.

When the Statehouse became too small, the legislature had a Supreme Court Annex added. It is to the east and is connected to the Capitol building by a walkway. Since that time other office buildings have been built near the Statehouse to provide office space for Ohio's expanding state government.

New Constitution

Just as Ohio's government outgrew its building space, it also had to change its Constitution. The first Constitution had given

■ Distribution of Constitutional Power

STATES MAY

Control elections, local governments, public health, safety and morals, within their boundaries (includes such things as marriage, divorce, education and general voting qualifications).

STATES MAY NOT

Interfere with functions of the federal government, such as making war, writing treaties with foreign countries, maintaining armies or navies, printing their own money.

FEDERAL GOVERMENT MAY

Regulate commerce over state lines and with foreign nations. Ratify treaties and carry on foreign relations. Maintain postal systems, grant copyrights, coin money, declare war, and raise, support and make rules for the regulation of an army and navy.

FEDERAL GOV'T MAY NOT

Favor one state at expense of another. Grant titles of nobility, or restrict an individual from knowing the statement of charges against him or prevent him from the right of a speedy trial, except in cases of rebellion or invasion.

BOTH MAY

Levy taxes.
Build roads.
Borrow money.
Spend money for the general welfare.

BOTH MAY NOT

Deprive persons of life or property without due process of law, or pass laws incriminating persons for acts that were not illegal when committed.

too little power to the Governor, he could not act for the good of the people. The Judicial system was too weak to do a good job. There were not enough courts, and the court system worked too slowly. The powers of government were not really balanced, for the General Assembly had most of the power. It could borrow all the money it wished, and the state was in debt.

Ohioans decided they needed a new Constitution. Delegates were elected and the Convention met in Columbus in 1850. After the delegates completed their work, the people of Ohio voted to adopt the new constitution, which went into effect Sept. 1, 1851.

This Constitution is still in effect today. The historic document begins with this Preamble: "We, the people of the State of Ohio, grateful to Almighty God for our freedom, to secure its blessings and promote our common welfare, do establish this Constitution." This is followed by Article 1, the Bill of Rights.

The Bill of Rights begins: "All men are, by nature, free and independent, and have certain inalienable rights, among which are those of enjoying and defending life and liberty, acquiring, possessing, and protecting property, and seeking and obtaining happiness and safety."

The second section states that political power is vested in the people in these words: "Government is instituted for their equal protection and benefit, and they have the right to alter, reform, or abolish the same, whenever they may deem it necessary. . . ."

The articles in the Bill of Rights guarantee to every Ohioan the right to assemble in a peaceable manner; the right to bear arms for their defense; trial by jury; freedom from slavery and involuntary servitude; freedom of religion; freedom of speech, and the right to own property. Other articles promise a citizen his rights in the courts.

General Assembly

The Ohio Constitution sets up the framework of its government. The General Assembly is given the legislative power, and is to consider and make laws for the good of its citizens. It is made up of two houses: the Senate with 33 members, and the House of Representatives with 99 members.

Anyone 18 years of age or older may vote for members of the General Assembly after meeting the rules in his community for becoming a voter. This may require registration. Senators are elected for four years, and House members for two years. Their terms begin the January following their election.

Sessions of the General Assembly usually run six months or more. The Governor may call the General Assembly into special session to act on a particular item of business whenever he thinks it is necessary.

At the beginning of each session, the General Assembly elects its officers and sets up its committee assignments. Much of the work is done in committees, and every member serves on several committees. The House of Representatives elects a Speaker, or presiding officer. The Lieutenant Governor is the presiding officer of the Senate.

Students who visit the Statehouse, as the Capitol is called, enjoy visiting the chambers where the General Assembly meet. One of the things they like best is the chair in which the Speaker of the House sits. It is hand-carved, with a carving of the Great Seal of Ohio at the top of the mahogany chair, first used in 1857. Seven Ohio Presidents of the U.S. — Ulysses S. Grant, Rutherford B. Hayes, James A. Garfield, Benjamin Harrison, William McKinley, William H. Taft, and Warren G. Harding — have sat in the chair. The other Ohio president, William H. Harrison, died before the new Statehouse was built. When Lincoln addressed the General Assembly he, too, had the honor of sitting in the chair.

So that all Ohioans are equally represented, re-apportionment is made after the federal Census is taken every ten years. That means that the boundaries of a district which a member of the General Assembly represents changes every ten years.

Besides making the laws, the General Assembly also levies taxes and decides how the money will be spent. This is called making appropriations. The state is expected to raise enough money by taxes to pay its bills. It is very limited in the amount of money it may borrow. All appropriation bills must start in the House of Representatives, but other bills may begin in either house. Each bill must be approved by both houses before it becomes a law.

By following a bill through the General Assembly, an Ohio citizen can understand how carefully each new law is considered. A typical bill is introduced by a member of the House of Representatives, but before he does, he must have the Clerk assign a number to it. The bill may be referred to by its number and title at the first reading, and if three-fourths of the members agree, the whole bill need not be read.

The bill then goes to the Reference Committee, which examines it to see if any others like it are being studied. If not, the bill is ordered printed. It is ready for its second reading.

After that it goes to one of the Standing Committees, depending on the subject of the bill. The proper committee arranges a public hearing of the bill. This way anyone or any business affected by the bill can appear before the committee and give their arguments for or against it. After the hearing the committee may approve the bill or reject it. If they do this, it is called pigeonholing. Only a majority vote of the House can get the bill back for reconsideration.

Our bill was approved, and sent to the Rules Committee, which puts it on the schedule of the House for a third reading, for under the Ohio Constitution each bill must be read and studied three times in both houses before it becomes a law. Making a law is very important, and must be carefully done.

The bill is read for the third time before the House, and voted upon. Since our bill received a majority vote in its favor, it is sent to the Senate for action.

Just about the same steps are repeated in the Senate. Fortunately for our bill, the Senate, too, voted favorably for its passage. It was signed by the Lieutenant Governor for the Senate and the Speaker for the House.

If a bill does not pass the Senate, it may go to a Conference Committee of the House and Senate, and be changed to make its passage possible. A compromise may be worked out.

Our bill passed without any problems and went directly to the Governor. The Governor, upon receiving the bill has three choices: he may sign the bill and it becomes law; he may not sign it, and within ten days it becomes law; he may veto it. If he vetoes a bill, it takes a vote of three-fifths of the members of each branch of the General Assembly to pass the bill, or override his veto. The Governor signed our bill.

Executive Department

Article III of the Ohio Constitution reads: "The executive department shall consist of a governor, lieutenant governor, secretary of state, auditor of state, treasurer of state and an attorney general, who shall be elected on the first Tuesday after the first Monday in November by the electors of the state, and at the places of voting for members of the General Assembly."

It is the duty of the Governor to carry out the laws of the state and to see that the provisions of the Ohio Constitution are followed. He is the chief executive of the state. While the Governor may not make a law, he may make recommendations for laws to the General Assembly. It was also noted that the Governor may veto a law, a power given him by an amendment to the Ohio Constitution in 1903. In 1912 another amendment gave the Governor the power of vetoing an item of an appropriations bill. This is called the item veto.

The Governor submits a budget to the General Assembly every two years; it is called the biennial budget. He reports to the legislature on the general conditions of the state.

Since Ohio has a large population, the Governor needs help in carrying out his executive duties. These people serve in the Governor's Cabinet. Each of the appointees oversees a department of state government. The Finance Department has control of state spending as authorized in the budget. A Director of Commerce supervises banking. The State Fire Marshal sets state fire safety standards. Some 20 departments are represented in the Governor's cabinet.

In addition to the Cabinet, the elected state executives assist the Governor. The Lieutenant Governor, presiding officer of the Senate, keeps himself informed about state government and is always ready to take over the affairs of state in case the governor is no longer able to do so, because of death, disability, impeachment or resignation.

The Secretary of State is the chief election officer of the state and prepares the rules and regulations regarding elections. He maintains a current list of all elected officials, and issues the certificate of election. It is his duty to keep all the records of the state.

The Treasurer handles state money, but the Auditor keeps an exact record of every financial transaction. His department also audits the books of all Ohio governmental divisions, including those of school boards. The Auditor must issue a warrant for all money withdrawn from the state treasury. The records of the Treasurer and Auditor must always be in balance.

The Attorney General is really the state's lawyer, and any official agency may request his legal advice. In case the state is named in a court action, he represents it.

While the Governor is commander-in-chief of the military forces of the state, he delegates this to his Adjutant General. This is a man with military experience. The National Guard is an old organization, which began as the state militia. The militia was organized in 1788 at Marietta to protect settlers against the Indians. In the spring of 1812, it was ordered to Detroit to protect the fort against the English. Since that time, it has taken a part in every war fought by the nation.

In both World Wars, the soldiers of the 37th Buckeye Division gained recognition for their bravery. One of them, an Army Sergeant, so distinguished himself that he inspired the World War II song, "The Ballad of Rodger Young." He is buried at Green Springs.

Today the guard is organized into two groups: The Ohio Army National Guard, and the Air National Guard.

Judicial System

Article IV of the Ohio Constitution provides: "The judicial power of the state is vested in a supreme court, court of appeals, court of common pleas, and such other courts inferior to the supreme court as may from time to time be established by law."

Although decisions of the state courts may be appealed to the federal courts and the Supreme Court of the U.S., most legal problems are settled in the state court system.

The Chief Justice and six associate justices elected by the voters, make up Ohio's Supreme Court. Justices are elected for a six-year term. Most of the work of the Supreme Court is to review and make a final decision on cases appealed to it from the Court of Appeals.

The state is divided into appellate districts, each of which has a court of appeals, consisting of three judges. The judges are elected. It studies the cases appealed to it, and it may make the decision that the lower court was correct in its ruling, or it may reverse that decision. The Court of Appeals hears cases referred to it from the Court of Common Pleas.

The Court of Common Pleas is the one that most citizens will know most about. There is one in every county. This court has original jurisdiction over cases involving both civil and criminal action. Civil cases refer to disputes between people that may involve money or property that need to be settled. These result in a settlement rather than in imprisonment or punishment.

Criminal cases involve the disregard of a law, and may result in a prison sentence. Robbery and murder are two examples. A Grand Jury meets and makes a decision over whether a crime has been committed. If so, the Prosecuting Attorney presents a case against the person involved. The Court listens to the case.

The Common Pleas Court considers all serious criminal cases. Minor offenses may be decided in inferior courts. It may be used to appeal civil cases or other cases decided in an inferior court.

The Probate Court was set up under the Constitution of 1851 as an independent Court, but in 1968 an amendment made it a Division of Common Pleas Court. The main work of the Probate Court is to take care of a person's business after death. It settles the estate, and sees that the money or property of the deceased person is distributed according to law. Many people have wills which tell the court how the estate is to be settled.

The Probate Court also issues marriage licenses, oversees the adoption of children, and considers problems of people no longer able to handle their own business.

Juvenile Court may be a part of this Court if no separate Juvenile Court has been established. This would depend upon the size of the community, as it would in the case of a Court of Domestic Relations.

A County Court system was established by the 102nd General Assembly which replaced the Justice of Peace court. This court has jurisdiction outside that of the Municipal Court. Its judges are elected by the people to a four-year term. The number of judges elected depends upon the population of the county.

The Municipal Courts are very important in Ohio for so many people live in urban areas. The court hears civil cases, and those involving minor criminal action. Municipal judges must have been engaged in a law practice before election by the people under the court's jurisdiction. The number of judges elected is based upon the people served by the court. For most Ohioans, the Municipal Court is the one with which they would have contact, and which would settle most of their legal problems.

County Government

The Ordinance of 1787 permitted the Governor to establish counties and appoint officers to run them. Ohio was divided into counties before it became a state, but these were a few large counties, which have since been subdivided. The General Assembly was given the power over determining county boundaries after Ohio was admitted to the Union.

The county has always been an important part of state government. It is organized as the basic unit of government, which receives all its powers from the state. Under the Ohio Constitution the General Assembly can only pass laws which treat all counties the same. The powers and duties of county officers are set up under the laws of Ohio.

There are 88 counties in Ohio, each of which has its own officials and government. Each has a county seat, the town or city where there is located the courthouse and offices of the county officials.

193

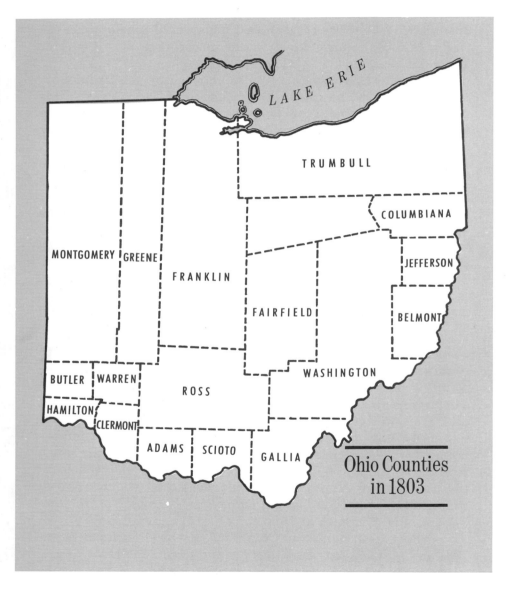

LAKE ERIE

TRUMBULL

COLUMBIANA

MONTGOMERY GREENE

FRANKLIN

JEFFERSON

FAIRFIELD

BELMONT

BUTLER WARREN

WASHINGTON

ROSS

HAMILTON

CLERMONT

ADAMS SCIOTO

GALLIA

Ohio Counties
in 1803

Each county has the same officials. The Board of County Commissioners is made up of three people, elected at-large by the voters of the county. They are elected for a four-year term, which begins the first Monday in January after their election. The terms are set up so that not more than two are elected at one time. The commissioners serve as the executive of the county.

The power of the County Commissioners is clearly outlined in the state Constitution. Their main work is to administer the law in their area. Their salaries are based upon the population of the county.

County officials chosen by the voters in addition to the three Commissioners are those of Probate Judge, Prosecuting Attorney, Clerk of Courts, Sheriff, Coroner, Engineer, Auditor, Treasurer, and Recorder. The work of the Probate Judge and Prosecuting Attorney has been discussed. The Clerk of Court keeps records of the Common Pleas Court and the Court of Appeals. The Clerk also records all licenses, certificates of title to motor vehicles, and files the Coroner's reports.

The Coroner, a licensed physician, keeps a record of all deaths in the county. In case of a death resulting from violence the Coroner may examine the body and give his opinion as to the cause, which could lead to court action.

The sheriff's duties include preserving the peace, enforcing the laws, and taking care of legal papers of the courts. He is in charge of the Courthouse, and the county jail.

The auditor oversees the finances of the county, but he does not have custody of the money. The County Treasurer keeps the public funds, and collects and pays the county bills and obligations. He receives the money from taxpayers. The auditor and treasurer work closely together. Payments made from the treasury must be on a warrant from the auditor. The two provide a check on each other.

The County Engineer must hold an engineer and surveyor's license. He is in charge of making plans and specifications for public roads, bridges, and other public improvements.

The County Recorder is in charge of county legal papers.

All legal documents that are to be recorded under law are in his charge. This includes mortgages, plats, leases, and many other documents. These must also be indexed by this office.

Ohio Counties

Townships

Townships, a small part of a county, are a local unit of government in Ohio and sixteen other states. The township began as a geographic unit under the Ordinance of 1785, land ordinance. It provided that surveyors "proceed to divide the said territory into townships of six miles square. . . ." Then these plats were subdivided into lots one mile square of 640 acres, which was called a section. A typical farm in Ohio was a quarter section.

Governor St. Clair thought that these townships made a good unit for civil government. He appointed township clerks, constables to preserve the peace, and people to care for the poor. When Ohio became a state, the General Assembly set up the township as the local unit of government.

Before modern means of communication and transportation, the early settlers could not travel far. Most of their business was cared for in the township. The township took over the building and maintenance of country roads, with the county and state planning and maintaining the major roadways. The township also set up parks, maintained the cemetery, and took care of other needs of its citizens. Zoning of township land, and providing fire protection have become important duties of township officials.

As the people of Ohio left the country and moved into the cities, it appeared that the township would lose its importance. As the years passed, Ohioans began to leave the large urban centers and move back to the country to build homes and commute to work. The townships around the cities grew in population and their services had to be expanded. The township remains an important unit of government, although some have disappeared due to annexation of land into cities and villages. There remain over 1300 townships in Ohio.

Township voters elect officers on Election Day in November. Terms are set up so there will always be an experienced member. The term of office is for four years. Three people are elected to make up a board to oversee township affairs. It is the duty of the Trustees to compile an annual budget for the township covering the operating costs of their programs.

The township clerk serves as the secretary to the Board of Trustees, as well as keeping an account of all financial transactions.

The Constable does the same work as a police officer in a city or a sheriff in the county. The Constable arrests those who violate the law, and serves papers as ordered by the courts.

Municipal Government

The Ohio Constitution in Article 18 on Municipal Corporations makes this classification: "Municipal corporations are hereby classified into cities and villages. All such corporations having a population of 5,000 or over shall be cities; all others shall be villages. . . ."

Municipalities are given the powers under the Constitution of "local self-government and to adopt and enforce within their limits such local police, sanitary and other similar regulations, as are not in conflict with general laws."

The population of Ohio has grown until today there are over 1,000 cities and villages in the state. These are called municipal corporations. Although people often refer to towns, they are not recognized by the Constitution. As generally used the word, town, means an urban community ranking in population between a village and city. However, under the Constitution when a village reaches a population of 5,000, it automatically becomes a city.

When this figure of 5,000 has been reached, the Secretary of State issues a statement or proclamation, which is sent to the municipality. The Mayor presents it to the Council, and it becomes a part of the record of the municipality. The village then makes the legal changes necessary to become a city.

Village Government

Many villages began where two important highways crossed. Others began around some industrial development. Someone would build a mill, and the workers would build homes around it. At first these villages were in the township, but as they grew the people living in them felt they wanted more services than the township provided. They wanted to run their own affairs.

The Ohio law provides that thirty voters may sign a petition, which is presented to the township trustees. The petition must describe the land included in the proposed village, and a map. After the trustees approve the petition, an election is held. If the voters are in favor of the new village, within six months an election is held and village officials are elected. They are elected at-large for a term of four years, but the terms of council members are staggered.

The Village Council, which is the legislative group of the municipality, may make any laws that do not violate those of the state of Ohio. The laws made by a municipality are called ordinances. Each ordinance must be read three times before it goes into effect.

The chief executive officer of a village is the Mayor. It is his duty to enforce the laws of the village and the state and to oversee the work of the departments of village government. These may include a fire and police department, as well as a street department and others as needed. Each village has a clerk and treasurer. The clerk keeps a record of council meetings, and the treasurer receives and pays out money.

The village may set up boards or committees to provide for a water supply, a sewer system, and a waste collection program. The needs of the village government depends upon its population. The larger it becomes, the more people are needed to help operate the government. When it reaches a population of 5,000, it becomes a city.

City Government

Under Ohio law there are three kinds of city government permitted. They are the Mayor-Council plan; the City Manager plan; and the Commission plan. The last plan is seldom used, so the first two plans will be studied.

In 1912 a home rule amendment was accepted by Ohio voters. It provided that "any municipality may frame and adopt or amend a charter for its government. . . ." This has led to differences among cities as to the exact way they operate their municipal government.

Most Ohio cities use the Mayor-Council plan, with some variations. Under this plan the people elect a Mayor, and Council members. The number of council members may vary from as few as five to over 30. Their pay is usually small and also varies as to the city and the amount of time they may be needed. A city council must meet once a month or may meet much more often.

The Council is the legislative body of the city, which studies and passes ordinances to meet the needs of its people. The City Council has great power within the boundaries of the municipality. The budget of a city may be very large and complicated.

Typical city building during the last half of the nineteenth century. 200

The Council must approve the budget, and levy taxes to pay for its operation. The Council under law is permitted to hire a city solicitor, who advises it on legal questions. He must be a qualified lawyer.

The Council may appoint committees of citizens to consider problems facing the city, and to make recommendations to the Council. Many important citizens work on these committees as a public service.

The election of council members varies from city to city. Some elect a councilman to represent a specific ward, or section of the city. Others elect the councilmen from the city at-large, which means they are voted on by all the citizens and are to represent every ward. Other cities use systems of proportional representation, which is a more complicated voting system.

Under the Mayor-Council plan, the Mayor is the most important person in the city government. He is the chief executive of the city, and appoints supervisors to help him in the day-to-day administration of the city government. With the approval of council he appoints the heads of various city departments. His most important duty is to see that the ordinances passed by the Council are carried out. The powers given the mayor vary from city to city. In some municipalities the mayor has great authority, in others, his power is limited.

The City Manager plan is the newest plan in municipal government. Under this plan there may be a mayor, who performs ceremonial functions, but he is not the actual executive.

The person who administrates, or runs the city government, is the city manager. The city manager is chosen by the council. He has been trained in the university to be a city administrator. A council usually asks for applications from trained people who wish to be city manager. The council interviews and then picks the person they think will do the best job. The city manager is not elected by the people. He is usually not a resident of the city, but moves into the city when he becomes manager. Under this form of government, the most important decision made by the council is the selection of the manager.

The council is still responsible for passing ordinances and

making plans for the improvement of the city. When the council is not satisfied with the city manager, they may fire him, or ask him to leave. It is the council that the people hold responsible for how the city is run.

The story of Dayton serves as a review of municipal government and how it changes through the years. Dayton was the first large city in the U.S., as well as Ohio, to adopt the city manager form of government. Before Ohio was a state, Dayton was a village. When Montgomery County was created, Dayton was made the county seat. In 1805 Dayton was incorporated as a town. In 1840 Dayton had over 6,000 people and the Ohio legislature made it a city.

Dayton had the Mayor-Council plan. There were twelve councilmen, two from each ward. Dayton kept growing, and some local citizens believed there should be a better way to run a municipality. John H. Patterson, a leading businessman of the city, suggested that the government should be run like a business. The people of Dayton asked him to serve as chairman of a committee to see how this could be done. His committee studied the plans of other cities in the U.S.

This committee suggested that a commission of five members be elected by the whole city to represent the people. The commission would choose a city manager. In 1913 Dayton voters approved this new plan, or charter, of government. Since that time many Ohio cities have decided to use the City Manager plan.

Your Government and You

Your local government works for you, no matter where you live in Ohio. All units of government face the same basic problems.

Every community must provide for the safety of its citizens. At first there were few people needed to protect people against criminals who would rob or injure them. As more people moved into cities, police forces were organized. During the 1880's Cincinnati and Toledo began to set high standards for their departments.

As more people crowded into communities, fire became a real

202

danger. Large wooden buildings with no fire escapes resulted in many deaths. The early fire departments were volunteer departments, and it took too much time to reach a fire. Since there were no fire alarms or telephones, it was difficult to notify the firemen. Cincinnati led in organizing a modern fire department, and by 1875 employed regular firemen to man its equipment. Although all larger cities have paid fire departments, volunteer fire departments protect most communities.

Fighting fires took water under pressure. The need for a community water system to supply fire hydrants was one of the reasons for the setting up of municipal waterworks. Too many wells in a city led to pollution and such diseases as typhoid fever. To provide a safe water supply for homes as well as for firefighting resulted in another municipal service.

Sewers were needed to carry away the street water after heavy rains, as well as to provide a sanitary service to homes. Bathrooms were built in homes making necessary both water and sewers.

As the city grew in size, people could no longer live near the factory or business where they worked. The automobile was not yet in use, so people began to demand that the city provide a means of public transportation. At first tracks were laid and horsecars were used. By the late 1880's the electric trolley was operating in Lima and Mansfield and soon all over the state. The next step was for these to become interurban lines connecting most communities in the state in a transportation network.

Industry reduced the working hours to an eight-hour day and a 40-hour week. People had more time than ever before. They wanted things to do, and places to go. Municipalities developed park systems, and set up recreational programs.

In order that growth of a community might be controlled, the city councils set up planning groups and passed zoning laws. Parts of a city were set aside for industry and business, and other parts were reserved for residential or home use.

Health became a problem with so many people living in the same area. Cities set up health departments, and some, non-profit hospitals to take care of the people who became ill.

Before long municipalities were expected to provide more and more services for its people. This all cost money.

Since your government works for you, you must also work for your government. It costs money to provide all the services which are needed in a community. Some of the services such as for water and sewer are billed to the consumer. Each household must pay for the service based on the usage. The government often charges a fee for use of recreational facilities.

Most of the services provided by your community are paid for by all the people. Every citizen is asked to pay a certain amount of money to the government. This is called a tax. There are different kinds of taxes. All local governments collect a property tax, much of which goes to support schools. Income taxes are also paid to local government units, as well as to the state and federal government. Fees for special services, and licenses to provide certain privileges are also a form of tax.

When each citizen pays his taxes, the money is all put together, so that the government can do the things that are needed. One person alone could not afford to do all these things himself. Each family could not hire a policeman to watch his home or a fireman to put out a fire, or a playground helper to oversee the park, or a private tutor to teach the children. All the families pay a tax, which in turn, pays the community helpers.

Ohio's Problems Today

While each unit of government has its special problems, some problems are state wide. The local government must work with the state government, and many times with the federal government to try to solve the problem. This working together on a project is called cooperation.

While cities face the problem of transportation, so do other governments. This is a problem for the state and nation, for our country is tied together by a transportation network. Highways not only connect all parts of the state, but Ohio highways serve citizens of all other states. Usually a new highway is a cooperative effort of all governmental units.

With so many automobiles and trucks on the roads, air pollution is the result. An automobile in poor repair may travel across several governmental units in one day polluting the air.

The decline of passenger service on railroads has led to discontinuing such service in most parts of Ohio. For many people this means the loss of public transportation. Public bus service is also declining. Older people, and those without automobiles, find transportation difficult for them. Most people travel by air, but it is necessary to get to an airport. Large airports may add to air pollution and noise pollution. Ohio has a department of transportation to work on this problem.

The problem of pollution has been a serious one in Ohio. To improve Ohio's air and water quality, in 1972 the Governor set up a department in his cabinet called the Environmental Protection Agency. This department oversees projects which will result in improving the environment.

Great progress has been made in Ohio. Just a few years ago, industries were pouring all kinds of pollutants into the air. Sewage was being dumped into the rivers. Even the future of Lake Erie was in doubt as pollution spread. The pure, clean water that the pioneers found was not safe to drink, and even the fish were dying.

Ohio became concerned about pollution. All government units worked together. Now the streams and rivers are clearing up, fish are thriving and new recreational areas for people are developing.

What do you think happened to this water area? Who would benefit if it were to be cleaned up?

How do you catch a "Litter Bug?"

Did they have to die?

The problem has not been solved, but science, technology and people are working together in Ohio to improve the environment. What is your community doing?

Housing is another problem. Many people find they do not have the money to afford the kind of home they want and need. Government has made improved housing possible by grants and loans to public housing authorities and private builders. Much work has been done to improve housing conditions in the cities, where slums developed some years ago.

Ohio is trying to improve its small cities, so that they can handle increased population. These cities have industry and jobs for people, and this seems a better plan than starting all new cities. By better distributing the population, Ohio can prevent "people pollution."

What is happening to our air?

Is there such a thing as "people pollution?"

There are always those people who due to misfortune or some physical handicap cannot take care of themselves. Ohio has a department of Public Welfare to help the needy, the blind, the disabled and dependent children.

Since eastern Ohio is a major coal mining region, this creates an environmental problem. Much of Ohio's coal is near the surface and mined through strip mining. Giant machines strip off the earth, and the coal is extracted.

Strip mining can damage the topsoil, and make great scars on the earth. Through laws, and working with the mine operators, Ohio is trying to restore the land mined. Then it is reforested. Forest products are still an important resource of Ohio. In hilly lands, tree farming is a good use of the land.

Problems can be solved by state and local governments working together. One such problem was that of floods in the Miami Valley. In March, 1913, more than 12 inches of rain fell in five days. The rain came down so fast, draining into streams and rivers, that they could not carry the water away fast enough. At Columbus, 4,000 buildings had water in them, but the worst damage was in the Miami Valley, centered around Dayton.

The 1913 flood ravaged cities of Southwestern Ohio and resulted in the Miami Conservancy Act.

After the waters went down, Dayton and the Miami Valley residents came together to make plans to tame the Great Miami River. They called in Arthur E. Morgan, a noted engineer, who suggested a plan, which involved eight cities and 200 square miles of farmland. In order to undertake such a large project, a new Conservancy Law had to be passed by the General Assembly.

The project was so successful that no floods have occurred in the Miami Valley since 1913. In 1934 the Muskingum Conservancy District was organized under the same law.

For workers who become disabled while on a job, protection is given them through Workmen's Compensation, another agency in the Governor's Cabinet. Ohio's Employment Services bureau works to put people in jobs.

Taxation is necessary for any government, but it can also be a problem. Some Ohioans complain that taxes are too high, or that they are not fair to some groups. Since schools rely on property taxes for much of their income, there are often requests to increase the tax. This can only be done by people voting for a tax levy.

The biggest problem facing state and local governments is to get the citizen's participation. A democracy can only work for people, if people are willing to work for it. Citizens are needed to serve on committees and to volunteer for community service.

The one thing that every citizen can do to help the government is to study the problems faced by it. A citizen needs to read about the problem and discuss it with others. Through one of the representatives of government, the citizen can let his opinion be known. This may be done in a personal meeting, or by a letter.

Most important of all is the voting responsibility of each citizen when the age of 18 is reached. Although young people were given the right to vote and participate in the government, many have not exercised that privilege.

Ohio state and local governments also welcome the contributions that minorities can make. One of these groups, the Negro, or Black citizen did not always have that privilege in the State. While slavery was never permitted in Ohio, Black people did not have the right to vote until after the Civil War.

209

Even before a Black man could vote, he might be elected to office. John M. Langston of Chillicothe, was educated at Cincinnati and Oberlin to be a lawyer. He was the first Negro in Ohio to be admitted to the bar. In 1855 he was elected Clerk of Brownhelm Township in Lorain County. Later he was appointed U.S. minister to Haiti.

Edward James Roye, a black Ohioan, born in Newark, and educated at Ohio University and Oberlin, emigrated to Liberia. He entered politics in Liberia, and was elected the fifth president of that nation.

Liberia also obtained the services of another Buckeye, Colonel Charles Young of Xenia, a West Point graduate who served with distinction in the Spanish-American War and World War I. Upon retirement he went to Liberia to organize their army.

The Fifteenth amendment gave the right to vote to Black men in 1870.

George W. Williams became the first member elected to the General Assembly in 1879. He later wrote a book on the history of the Negro in the United States. Dr. Benjamin W. Arnett became a member of the Ohio legislature, elected from Green County in 1886. John P. Green, as a member of the General Assembly, in 1890 introduced a bill that established Labor Day in the state.

Carl Stokes, born in Cleveland in 1929, completed law school and was elected to three terms in the General Assembly. In 1967 he became the first black mayor of Cleveland, Ohio's largest city.

At about the same time, Robert C. Henry was elected Springfield's first Negro mayor, while James T. Henry became the mayor of Xenia. Then Robert M. Duncan was sworn in as a justice of Ohio's Supreme Court. A former municipal court judge in Columbus, he became the first Black member of the state's highest court.

Another group of Americans, in fact half the population, were not permitted to vote under either the U.S. Constitution or the Ohio Constitution. These were the women of America and their fight for the right to vote, is known as the suffrage movment. The first convention held of women wanting basic rights was held in Seneca Falls, New York, in 1848, and the second convention was held in Salem, Ohio in 1850. In 1852 the Ohio Woman's Rights Association was formed at Massillon.

In 1869 the Toledo Woman's Suffrage Association was organized to press for equal rights with men. Rosa L. Segur led this group for many years. Women also showed their interest in other matters. In 1873 a group of Hillsboro church women began the war against liquor, and the next year formed the Women's Christian Temperance Union. Eliza Jane Trimble Thompson, wife of a judge and daughter of a former Ohio governor, was its leader.

Victoria Woodhull, born in Homer, Licking County, decided to run for President of the U.S. in 1872, even though women could not vote. She ran as a candidate for the Equal Rights Party, and received only a few votes, but she did keep before the public the idea of women's rights.

Although gaining the right to vote was to take many years, some progress was made in giving women more rights. In 1887 the Ohio General Assembly passed a law giving women the right to own property. In 1893 a law stated a woman could act as a guardian, and in 1894 the law gave a woman the right to settle a relative's estate upon death. In the same year a law was passed which permitted women to vote in school elections.

This led to the election of Harriet Taylor Upton to the Warren School Board in 1898, and she later became its president. She became one of Ohio's most patient and efficient workers for woman suffrage. She was one of the many women working for an amendment to the Ohio Constitution to secure the right to vote. In 1912 the Woman Suffrage amendment to the Ohio Constitution was among the 8 of the 42 proposed, to be defeated. This did not stop the women.

In 1914 the amendment was again voted upon, and went down to defeat under the pencil of the men voters. At this time some municipal charters gave women the right to vote in local elections, which was at least, a step toward suffrage.

In 1917 the General Assembly of Ohio passed a bill, which was signed by Gov. James M. Cox of Dayton, granting the right

211

of women to vote in presidential and municipal elections. A referendum vote was forced, and the bill was defeated, again by male voters.

In 1919 the Nineteenth Amendment to the U S. Constitution which provided for woman suffrage was ratified by the Ohio General Assembly. In 1920 women had won their long battle for the ballot, and went to the voting booth to elect Warren G. Harding from Marion, Ohio, President. In 1920 Harriet Taylor Upton was elected Chairman of the Ohio Republican Women, the first woman in the U.S. to hold such a high office. She is also remembered as an author.

Edith Campbell, who spent her childhood in Ripley, then moved to Cincinnati, was another woman who worked hard for women's rights. As a member of a Board of Education, she gained the attention of Gov. Cox, who appointed her to a committee with two men to survey the needs of Ohio schools. She also helped in the passage of Ohio's Child Labor Law.

After 1920 women began to run for office themselves. In 1922 six women were elected to the General Assembly. The same year brought another noted woman to national attention. Judge Florence E. Allen of Cleveland was elected to the Ohio Supreme Court, the first woman in the nation to reach such a position. She also became the first woman judge of a U.S. Circuit Court of Appeals.

Now the ballot box offers every citizen, regardless of sex or race, the chance to present his opinion and vote for the person who best represents his ideas. Minorities are learning that each group can make its wishes known in the voting booth.

In Ohio voters have the right to circulate petitions. If the petition is signed by a certain number of voters, the proposal is put on the ballot. This is called the initiative, because any voter may start, or initiate, a law.

Then if the General Assembly passes a law that most people do not want, the people can vote to have it repealed. This action starts with a referendum petition, signed by the required number of voters.

The Constitution of 1851 is still being used in Ohio. In 1873 a revised Constitution was drawn up, but it was rejected by the voters. In 1912 another Constitutional Convention was held. Rather than make a new Constitution, it recommended 41 amendments to the old one. All but 8 were passed by the voters, to update and improve the Constitution. Since that time over 60 new amendments have been made to the Constitution. Every 20 years the voters of Ohio are asked if they wish to hold a Convention to change the Constitution. An amendment can be proposed anytime.

School Districts

Each of Ohio's school districts is independent of other local governmental units. Education is one of the most important functions of government. Since it affects so many young people, it is under the supervision of the State Board of Education.

Article VI of the Ohio Constitution in setting up a public school system states: "Provision shall be made by law for the organization, administration and control of the public school system of the state supported by public funds. . . ."

School districts are governed by the local Board of Education, which is elected by the people of that school district.

The organization is much like the city manager form of municipal government discussed in this chapter. The members of the Board of Education hire a professional educator. The person must have a Superintendent's certificate as issued by the state. It requires the completing of a special course of study and experience in the field of education. The Superintendent of Schools operates or administers the school system under direction of the Board. The Board hires the Superintendent for a specified number of years under a contract. If they are not satisfied with the person's work, they need not renew the contract.

The Superintendent may choose his staff from legally qualified personnel. Principals are appointed by the Superintendent and are responsible to him. The Superintendent also appoints the teachers, who must hold teaching certificates issued by the state.

Since so many people are enrolled in the school system from

kindergarten through the university, education requires more funds than any other government activity.

Every home in Ohio is in some School District. A School District may have the same boundaries of a municipality, or it may not. Some school districts include several local government units. When government units were put together to form a school district, it is called consolidation. This is done so that schools can provide the student with a wider choice of studies.

The Citizen's Role In Government.

CHAPTER VIII

Recreation and Travel

Outdoor Recreation in Ohio

The "Wonderful World of Ohio" is more than a slogan to describe the Buckeye State, for many different kinds of recreation are available. The great variety of vacation lands provide an activity for every season of the year. The many state forests and parks offer campers a place of retreat from the daily routine.

Being located at the nation's crossroads, millions of tourists use Ohio highways traveling from one part of the country to another. Many stop along the way to enjoy some of Ohio's recreational facilities. Tourism is an important part of the state's economy. Since Ohio is the oldest state of the Northwest Territory, it has an interesting historic past, much of which has been preserved in museums, or by restoration.

As special attractions there are almost a hundred fairs sponsored by counties and independent groups. The Ohio State Fair held annually since 1850 at Columbus is one of the nation's largest, and each day it is open, offers some outstanding program. Between March and November over 25 festivals are held in various areas of the state, each with a different theme. Something exciting is always happening in Ohio.

The early pioneers had very little time for recreation, but they made their tasks into games, such as corn huskings and quilting bees. The pioneer hunted the game of the forest, and caught the fish in the streams and rivers. Game provided the pioneer with meat for the table and furs to sell.

As the land was cleared, and farm machinery introduced, people had more leisure time. One of the first activities the men enjoyed was horseracing and shooting matches. They enjoyed participation sports such as swimming and boating, sleigh riding, ice skating, horseshoes and bowling. By the 1890s people were bicycling, playing croquet, and lawn tennis.

Today Ohio has 55 state parks, which cover over 85,000 acres, and these are supplemented by local parks, owned by counties and municipalities, using over 75,000 acres. The state's recreational areas provide a wide variety of activities. Most have hiking trails, and some even have trails for horseback riding.

Some of the parks have beautiful lodges, with indoor and outdoor pools, dining rooms, and conference rooms, as well as private rooms with a view of nature. Campgrounds are available at many of the state parks.

Fishing is the most popular outdoor sport in Ohio, with 500,000 people pursuing it. They catch fish in the waters of 25,000 miles of streams, a hundred lakes, and 30,000 farm ponds. In addition there are the waters of Lake Erie and Sandusky Bay. Over 160 species of fish swim in Ohio waters with the most common being carp, catfish, trout, perch, walleye, bass, pike, and bluegill. In the winter, ice fishing is popular in the northern part of the state.

Ohio's favorite outdoor sport.

Ohio's primitive areas attract wild game birds.

Although many years have passed since pioneer times, Ohio's fields and forests still are the home of the whitetail deer, grouse, partridge, pheasant, waterfowl, rabbit, squirrel, fox and raccoon. Hunters roam over fields and forest in hunting season, with their license proudly displayed. If permission is asked, farmers often permit hunting, for they want the animal population and the food available to wildlife kept in balance. Ohio's Department of Natural Resources has a wildlife section, which studies how many animals can be hunted. It protects all wildlife from extinction.

Some people enjoy just hiking in the woods, and many Ohio parks have hiking trails set up, and by following them a person can enjoy the wonders of nature. The Buckeye Trail Association has laid out a trail almost 500 miles long from Cincinnati on the Ohio River to Headlands Beach State Park near Cleveland.

Backpacking, in which the hiker spends at least one night on the trail, is permitted in some special camping areas. Youth may also stay at a hostel overnight.

For those who prefer cycling, there are bikeways in the state. The Amish Bikeway in Geauga County, starting at Punderson State Park is a very unusual one which would acquaint a person with the Amish country. For the people who play golf, they find

more than 200 courses in Ohio, operated by private clubs, municipalities, counties, and the state.

Canoeing is popular in Ohio, and many canoe liveries are
found, especially around Loudonville in the Mohican River Valley, but over twenty other areas in Ohio offer this sport. Boaters
can choose from over 100,000 acres of navigable water open to
them, as well as Lake Erie. Sailing is preferred by many Ohioans
who enjoy sailing over Ohio lakes. At Cincinnati, houseboats
can be rented for use on the Ohio River. In the winter several
places in Ohio are set aside for ice boating, and winter sailors
glide over the ice at speeds over 70 miles per hour.

Even winter offers something for the outdoor sportsman. In
addition to ice boating and ice fishing, sledding is permitted on
some of the hills in many state parks, with some of them even
being lighted. Tobogganing is a family winter sport, and a few
areas have ice chutes. Snowmobiling is permitted in some Ohio

Around 1900, a favorite sport was swimming in the river.

In which season would these people probably go camping?

Don't let it get away!

parks, if the person has a proper license. With parts of Northern Ohio in the snow belt, skiing is becoming more popular. Nature is aided by the artificial snow-making machines, in providing a season for this sport.

Rock Hounds can find a place to pursue their hobby. Rocks may be hunted with the permission of any private property owner with quarries being a particularly good place to hunt. Rock collecting without a scientific collector's permit, is not permitted in state parks except in these three: Cowan Lake, Stonelick, and Hueston Woods.

Young people who have a special interest in nature's wonders will find many here in Ohio. Cedar Bog, a 200 acre preserve in northwest Ohio between Springfield and Urbana is most unusual. Although the great ice sheet retreated from Ohio 15,000 years ago, an underground stream of icy water continued to flow through the bog, which kept many of the ice age plants alive.

With the growth of interest in caves and caverns, Ohio explorers of the underground may wish to visit such sites as Ohio Caverns, Zane Caverns, Seneca Caverns, and Olentangy Caverns. Seven Caves, Perry's Cave, Crystal Cave, Devil's Den Park Cave, and Old Man's Cave are among the best known. The Blue Hole of Castalia represents an unusual freak of nature.

Several different habitats can be observed in a trip through Davis Natural Preserve near Peebles. Mentor Marsh Preserve and Wahkeena, near Lancaster, are two areas worth study.

Spectator sports are popular in Ohio, many people like to watch rather than to participate. In 1866 a group of men, including the Mayor, joined the Cincinnati Baseball Club. In 1867 when the club adopted a uniform, the people laughed at the short pants, red stockings, and caps. They called the players, the Red Stockings. In 1868 the team won every game, and by 1869 the team became the first all-professional baseball team in the U.S. When the National League was organized, the Cincinnati team became a member of it. At about the same time the Cleveland Indians came into professional baseball and eventually became a member of the American League. Both teams represent Ohio in the nation.

After the Rams left Cleveland, there was a demand for another professional football team. An outstanding Ohio coach, Paul Brown, was hired and organized a new team for the city. On the team were Marion Motley, and All-American Bill Willis, the first two Black players in professional football. The team took its name from its coach, and the Cleveland Browns became one of the nation's best teams. In 1968 Paul Brown organized another Ohio team, the Cincinnati Bengals, and built it into a fine team before his retirement.

At the college level, the Ohio State Buckeyes are nationally known. There are many other good university football teams in Ohio.

Professional basketball has never won the following in Ohio that baseball and football have enjoyed. Professional teams play in Ohio, but most sports fans follow with more interest the college basketball squads, as well as the high school basketball teams. Ice hockey is gaining in popularity in Ohio, which is represented by several fast-moving teams.

Other professional events in auto racing, horse racing, boat racing, and golf, attract thousands of spectators. Ohio's most unusual racing event is the Soap Box Derby at Derby Downs in Akron. Through a series of races in various cities in the U.S. as well as other nations, winners are picked. They all go to Akron for the big races. Boys and girls participate each year for prizes which help them with their education. They build their own motorless cars and learn to race them under rules set up by the Derby officials.

All young people like to visit an amusement park. There are over a dozen in Ohio to enjoy. Among the largest are Cedar Point on Lake Erie at Sandusky, and Kings Island, near Cincinnati. Large zoos are found at Toledo, Cincinnati, Cleveland, Columbus and Canton. Children's zoos and other collections of animals are found throughout Ohio.

Both national and state government are working together to provide recreational areas for Ohioans. In southeastern Ohio, the U.S. government manages Wayne National Forest which contains over 100,000 acres covered with timber, providing a home for wildlife, as well as a recreational area for visitors.

221

Ohio is constantly planning to improve facilities at its twelve state forested areas to offer a wider variety of outdoor recreation, as well as providing wildlife refuges. Some parks offer recreational programs for campers, and environmental education programs to visitors. The program of acquisition and development of recreational facilities continues each year.

Travel in Ohio

Ohio is a land with a long history, and citizens interested in preserving the best of the past. The Ohio Historical Society is an organization working and planning for preserving and restoration of landmarks of importance. The Society has identified over 200 major landmarks. Some tour guides of Ohio contain 400 interesting sites to visit. If local museums and landmarks are considered, there would be well over 500 places of interest to tourists.

Since it would be impossible to include all of these, the ones which are best known will be discussed. There are three National Monuments in Ohio. The Mound City Earthworks near Chillicothe was a burial site of the Hopewell Indians, whose civilization reached its peak in the years 550 B.C. to 500 A.D. At Put-in-Bay on South Bass Island, Lake Erie, is Perry's Victory and International Peace Memorial, a tribute to the hero of the War of 1812. Inscription Rock on Kelley's Island in Lake Erie is carved with the strange picture writing symbols of the Erie Indians. On this island are also Glacial Grooves, cut by a glacier in limestone, 25,000 years ago.

The Ohio Historical Society has divided Ohio into five areas, each of which would provide a tourist with a week-end or a week of exciting places to visit. Each area is only a few hours travel by interstate highways from the home of any Buckeye.

Northwest Ohio

Each section of Ohio contains landmarks which take the tourists from the distant past to the present. In Northwest Ohio the tourist is reminded of the days of Indians and frontiersmen to those of the space age. Near Upper Sandusky is the Indian Mill, a turbine gristmill along the Sandusky River. It was built by the U.S. government for use by the Indians in appreciation of the Wyandots remaining loyal to the Americans during the War of 1812. It is one of America's best museums of milling, with exhibits showing how grain was ground in pioneer days.

The Wyandot Mission, Upper Sandusky, was built in 1824 with U S. government funds. It is a fieldstone church used by the Wyandot Indians, who were converted to the Christian religion through the work of Rev. John Stewart, a Black missionary. He was assisted by another Black Christian, Jonathan Pointer, who served as interpretor.

Hoover's Gristmill, named for its original owner, grandfather of President Herbert Hoover, is located just south of West Milton. Its old waterwheel still turns, and is often photographed. In this and other sections of Ohio are other gristmills such as Bear's Mill, east of Greenville, the Grinnell Mill, Clifton Mill in Greene County, and Wilson's Mill on the Cuyahoga River. In 1840 Ohio had 1800 gristmills.

The old millstream, which furnished the power for these mills, became the subject of a song. Tell Taylor wrote "Down By the Old Millstream," about a mill along the Blanchard River at Findlay. A tourist can still walk across a suspension bridge at the spot.

In Darke County is Fort Jefferson, the site of a frontier fort built by Gen. Arthur St. Clair in 1791 as he advanced northward in the Miami Valley. At a battlefield in Mercer County, he suffered a disastrous defeat by Chief Little Turtle and Chief Blue Jacket. President George Washington then appointed General Anthony Wayne to take command of the campaign against the Indians in Western Ohio. On the same site as the defeat, Gen. Wayne built Fort Recovery. Two blockhouses and a museum are now at this site, as well as a 93-foot monument to honor the soldiers killed in the St. Clair campaign.

Gen. Wayne continued his campaign up western Ohio and at the Battle of Fallen Timbers, on a site between Maumee and Waterville, the Indians met defeat in 1794. A statue stands in tribute to Wayne, and Turkeyfoot Rock marks the place where Chief Turkeyfoot made his last stand.

At Perrysburg, Fort Meigs has been reconstructed. This fort built by Gen. William Henry Harrison, withstood two sieges of the British and Indian attacks. Over ten acres are within the walled fortification of the fort. The palisade walls and seven blockhouses, three of which contain exhibits of the War of 1812, make up the largest reconstruction of a fortification in the U.S. South of Fort Meigs is Fort Amanda, another fort used during the War of 1812.

Both Indian life and canal days are recalled at the Piqua Historical Area. Being the farm home of Col. John Johnston, an Indian trader, the site contains the historic Indian Museum in which is recreated the life and culture of the Ohio Indians. The restored Johnson Homestead is furnished as it was in pioneer days. Since the Miami-Erie Canal flowed by the Johnson farm, a mile of the old canal was restored and filled with water. The canal boat, "General Harrison," now carries tourists up and down its course, pulled by mules on the towpath.

A few miles north of Piqua, in Shelby County, are the stone ruins of a system of six locks which raised or lowered boats on the canal almost 70 feet within a half mile distance. The Miami-Erie and the Wabash-Erie, from Indiana, met at Junction, five miles south of Defiance, and then used the one canal to Toledo. At Defiance the boats used the waters of the Maumee, and then re-entered the canal at Independence Lock, which can be viewed today, along with gates in working order.

The Neil Armstrong Air and Space Museum, honoring the first man to step on the moon, as well as other aviation and space pioneers is near Wapakoneta. Here the tourist can take a trip in the future surrounded by air and space hardware.

The Rutherford B. Hayes Memorial on Hayes Avenue in Fremont is the first presidential museum and library built in the nation. It opened in 1916 at Speigal Grove, the estate of the Ohio president.

The Piatt Castles at West Liberty are open to the public, although still owned by descendants of the original owners. Castle Piatt Mac-a-Cheek built in 1864 of native limestone is modeled after a Norman-French Chateau, while Castle Mac-o-Chee is Flemish. Malabar Farm, on 715 acres near Lucas, was developed by Ohio writer, Louis Bromfield. Farm tours are conducted and Bromfield's home is open. Kingwood Center, in the same area, has beautiful gardens open for the public. Edison's humble birthplace is at Milan.

Northeast Ohio

Religion has played an important part in the life of Ohioans. In Northeast Ohio the traveler can visit historic sites which show that Ohio has always been a land of religious freedom. As early as 1772 Moravian missionaries came into Ohio, and established a Moravian Church and mission school at Schoenbrunn, along the Tuscarawas River. It represented the first settlement in Ohio. Today Schoenbrunn Village at New Philadelphia has been reconstructed with the church, school and log cabins on the original foundations.

Founded in 1817 by another German religious group is Zoar Village. During its history a communal society, in which all shared alike, developed here. It reached its peak in 1850 when 500 people were members. The village still remains, and the Ohio Historical Society has restored seven buildings which are open to tourists. One can see the craftsmen at work, as well as visit the formal gardens.

The Amish represent a religious sect who came to Ohio in the 1820's. They are among Ohio's best farmers and finest craftsmen. Millersburg is their main trading center, and a tourist can drive through Amish country, view the productive farms, well-kept buildings, and see the horse-drawn farm vehicles and buggies.

At Kirkland the first Mormon Temple built in the U.S. is still standing. It appears today much as it did when built by Joseph Smith and his followers in the 1830s. They are known as the Church of Jesus Christ of Latter-Day Saints. At Mount Pleasant, in Jefferson County, is the Historic Friends Meeting House. The Ohio Quakers were leaders in the anti-slavery movement. The restored meeting house is furnished in simple Quaker tradition.

Recalling another religious sect, the Shakers, a museum

225

which features their life style is the Shaker Historical Society Museum at Shaker Heights, near Cleveland. Also at Cleveland is the Temple Museum of Religious Art and Music which tells the story of the Jewish people in the U.S. Another museum dedicated to this purpose is the Hebrew Union College Museum at Cincinnati.

The First Congregational Church at Tallmadge stands as a representative of the Federal style architecture brought to Ohio from New England. Many of Ohio's religious groups are restoring and preserving old places of worship of their congregations and keep them as living memorials with services being held each Sunday.

Fairport Marine Museum is housed in a lighthouse at Fairport Harbor. It was erected in 1825 and rebuilt in 1871 of gray limestone. Its white light could be seen for almost 20 miles out on Lake Erie. Sixty-nine steps in a spiral staircase lead up to the observation platform.

The Pro-Football Hall of Fame at Canton was opened in 1963. Being the birthplace of the National Football League, Canton was chosen for this attraction. Not only does Akron have an Art Institute and Museum of Natural History, but several historic sites. Among them is the John Brown Home Museum. John Brown was an abolitionist who led the fight against slavery. Akron also has the Perkins Stone Mansion and Hywet Hall with its 65 rooms. Nearby is the Railroads of America Museum.

Cleveland has many historic attractions. Its Public Square laid out in 1796 provides a civic center as a place for monuments. It has art museums, a natural science museum, a health museum along with a museum of historical medicine. The Western Reserve Historical Society and Museum has outstanding collections. One of the most unusual museums is the only one outside of Romania, the Romanian Folk Museum at St. Mary's Romanian Orthodox Church.

At Bolivar is Fort Laurens, Ohio's only Revolutionary War fort. Named after Henry Laurens, President of the Continental Congress, it was approved by General George Washington. The outline of the old fort can be traced at the 81 acre park, on which has been built a museum. Ohio's part in the Revolutionary period is told in a multi-media screen production.

The McCook House on the Public Square at Carrollton is the home of the Fighting McCooks, a family which had more men serving in the Civil War than any other in the nation. An exhibit pavilion tells the life of another Ohio war hero, Gen. George A. Custer, at his birthplace, New Rumley.

Between Zanesville and Cambridge is the National Road-Zane Grey Museum. This is a museum devoted to telling the story of transportation in Ohio, as well as that of one of Ohio's best known authors, Zane Grey. The Ohio Pottery Museum in East Liverpool features ceramics.

Central Ohio

Columbus, the capital of the state, has many landmarks of interest. The major attraction is the Ohio Historical Center at Interstate 71 and 17th Avenue, across from the Ohio State Fairgrounds. It is a modern structure with exhibits covering every period of the state's long history, including exhibits on archaeology and natural history. The whole story of Ohio is told from the ice age to the space age.

Adjoining the center is Ohio Village, a re-creation of a typical Ohio community, 1800-1860. The visitor can actually see the costumed craftsmen at work, such as the blacksmith, printer, weaver, and many others. One can eat at the American House Hotel selecting food from an old-fashioned menu, and visit the general store to shop.

A section of old Columbus has been set aside for private restoration, where people still occupy the old brick buildings built by German immigrants. Germans came to Columbus in 1812, and by 1852 made up one-third of the population of Columbus, as well as the state. They built so well that over 100 of their buildings are still standing. Hamilton is developing a similar section. Germans were the largest of the immigrant groups to settle Ohio.

In downtown Columbus is the Statehouse, which every visitor must visit, and not far from it is the Center of Science and Industry of the Franklin County Historical Society. All areas of science are represented in the many displays, with a planetarium being part of the museum. Walking down its Streets of Yester-year brings back Ohio as it used to be.

Orton Museum is on the campus of Ohio State University, devoted to geology, and restorations of prehistoric animals. The Gallery of Fine Arts have a fine collection of the paintings of Ohio artist, George Bellows. The Durell Farm Museum, open by appointment, has a unique collection.

Campbell Mound on McKinley Avenue in the capital repre-sents the Adena Indian culture.

Hanby House at Westerville is furnished in pre-Civil War style, and has many of the family's possessions. Benjamin Hanby was the composer of several songs.

The Ohio Railway Museum at Worthington, contains a fine collection of old electric interurban cars of the street railway period. Its trolleys and locomotives are in working order and vis-itors may climb aboard for a ride on steam and electric operated cars.

Between Newark and Zanesville in Licking County is Flint Ridge. It is believed that for over 10,000 years Mound Builders and Indians came to this site to quarry flint. Today the visitor can follow the trails through the flint pits, which cover over 500 acres. Rising above one of the pits, is Flint Ridge Museum, in which the story and uses of flint is told. Flint, harder than steel, is the official gemstone of Ohio.

The Mound Builders once inhabited central Ohio and their presence is felt at the Mound Builders Earthworks and Octagon Mound at Newark, where the Ohio Indians Art Museum is located.

Southwest Ohio

The culture of the ancient Mound Builders is a feature of Southwest Ohio. The Miamisburg Mound, south of Dayton, is the largest prehistoric mound in Ohio, and one of the highest in the U.S. It rises 65 feet, and its top may be reached by a stair-way. Perhaps the most unusual mound in America is in this area —Serpent Mound in Adams County. No one knows the real meaning of this mound which winds across the land for 1,335 feet. From the observation platform it appears to be a giant snake, probably part of some ancient ceremony that may have taken place 3,000 years ago.

The Hopewell Mound Builders are responsible for an earthworks, Fort Hill, in Highland County. Built on top of a hill, it is thought this was a gathering place of people for some ceremony. Fort Hill covers 1200 acres, with 16 miles of nature trails. Here is a museum devoted to Indian history. Seip Mound near Bainbridge, is a flat-topped mound, probably used for burial by the Hopewell people.

Greatest of all the ancient settlements of the Mound Builders is Fort Ancient, southwest of Lebanon. Over 3 miles of earthen walls enclose three forts. This was the center of Hopewell culture in the U.S. and was also the more recent home of Fort Ancient Indians, from which it received its name. People from all over the world come to visit Fort Ancient and the museum on the site to try to unravel the story of the nation's most ancient people. It was Ohio's first state memorial.

At Lebanon a tourist may eat at Ohio's oldest inn, and stay overnight at the hotel still known as the Golden Lamb which has served as host to ten American Presidents. Less than a block from the historic building is the Warren County Museum, which has a collection of Shaker materials and many 19th century shops built around a village green at Harmon Hall. The Ohio Historical Society maintains Glendower at Lebanon, a Greek Revival mansion, which is furnished with Empire and Victorian items.

The quaint old town of Oxford is the home of Miami University at which William Holmes McGuffey was a professor. Here at the McGuffey House, now a museum, is a collection of the famous readers in a home restored to its appearance in the 1830's. Near Oxford is Hueston Woods State Park in which is the Pioneer Farm Museum where all types of farm machinery and tools of the past century are on display.

The struggle against the Indians of western Ohio is recalled at Fort Hamilton established in 1791 by Gen. Arthur St. Clair, from which the city received its name. At Eaton is Fort St. Clair, built as another link in a chain of forts which extended northward. Its 90 acres were developed as Ohio's first nature preserve.

Cincinnati, known as the Queen City, was the first large city of Ohio and the West, with its history dating back to Fort Washington. The oldest museum of Natural History west of the Allegheny Mountains is located here, but today is one of the most modern with a planetarium and outstanding collections. Its art museum has over 100 galleries. The Taft House Museum, is not only a tribute to a noted Cincinnati family which included a President, but a fine museum of art. Kemper Log House, the oldest home still standing in the Miami Purchase area, is located at the Zoological Gardens.

The Harriet Beecher Stowe House at Cincinnati, is the home of the author who created "Uncle Tom's Cabin." The house is now a museum with relics of the anti-slavery period and Black history.

Not far from Cincinnati, on Liberty Hill at Ripley, is the restored home of Rev. John Rankin, a great leader against slavery. His brick house stood as a haven for those escaping from the South.

At Point Pleasant, in Clermont County, stands the one-room cottage where General Ulysses S. Grant, who later became President, was born. Nearby in Georgetown is the two-room school where Grant obtained his elementary education. It is now a museum. Overlooking the Ohio River at North Bend is a sandstone shaft rising in the air over the resting place of William Henry Harrison and his family. He was the ninth president of the U.S., the first from Ohio.

Near Dayton is the nationally famous Air Force Museum, which is the biggest and most complete military aviation museum in the world. It traces the story of flight from the Wright Brothers to the Space Age. Its gigantic museum is filled with actual aircraft. The Wright brothers, inventors of the airplane, are also honored at Carillon Park, Dayton.

Number 219 North Summit Street, Dayton, was the address of one of Ohio's greatest poets and writers, Paul Laurence Dunbar. The house has been maintained by the Ohio Historical Society, just as it was left by the Dunbars. The Dunbar House is now a National Historic Landmark.

The Madonna of the Trail, a tribute to the brave pioneer women who made the trek west on the National Road, is located at Springfield. The Dental Museum at Bainbridge was the site of the first dental school in the U S., founded by Dr. John Harris in 1825.

Adena, at Chillicothe, was built in 1807 by Thomas Worthington, a Governor of Ohio. The restored stone mansion is on a 300-acre estate. It was here that Ohio's early leaders gathered one evening in 1803 in a large log house, before the stone house was erected, to discuss the new state's problems. After talking all night, the next morning they went out for a walk in the garden. The group, which included Governor Edward Tiffin, watched the sun rise up between the hills of Mt. Logan. Taking this to be a good sign, the men designed the Great Seal of Ohio using this background. This area is now part of the Great Seal Park.

Southeast Ohio

At Marietta the first permanent settlement was made in Ohio, so there are many points of historical interest here. The Campus Martius Museum tells the early history of this city which had its beginnings in 1788. Enclosed in one of the museum's wings is the Rufus Putnam house, furnished with pioneer materials. The Land Office, where Putnam kept a record of the surveys and the purchases of land as Superintendent of the Ohio Land Company, is on the grounds of Campus Martius.

Next to Campus Martius are three exhibit buildings which tell the story of the transportation on the Ohio and inland waterways. The Ohio River Museum presents a multi-media program entitled, "The River" in the museum's theater. From the museum, the tourist can step onto the steamboat, "W. P. Snyder, Jr.," anchored in the Muskingum River. One can inspect from stem to stern the 175 foot long boat, with a paddle wheel over 20 feet in diameter. Other historic sites to visit at Marietta are Putnam's Landing, Mound Cemetery, and various old houses.

On the Muskingum River near Stockport is a site called Big Bottom where the Indians and pioneers fought in 1791.

Farther down the Ohio River is Gallipolis, where 500 French emigrants landed in 1790. Their settlement consisted of 80 log cabins surrounded by stockade fence. In 1825 General Lafayette visited this French settlement in the new world and was entertained at "Our House" then an inn, and now a state memorial. Louis Phillipe, heir to the throne of France also stopped at "Our House." Built in 1819, the federal-style brick inn was restored to its original condition, with its tavern furnished as it was when Henry Cushing opened it.

Prehistoric peoples also roamed this section of Ohio. Tarlton Cross Mound in Fairfield County is the only earthwork in Ohio found in the form of a cross. It is in a 17-acre park. The Leo Petroglyph, in Jackson County, is a great rock with mysterious picture writings. It may have been carved by the Fort Ancient Indians, perhaps over 700 years ago.

The early beginnings of the iron industry are found in Jackson County, and the sites of various furnaces are still marked, such as that of the Jefferson Furnace, the Keystone Furnace and others. The Welsh began development of the industry, bringing with them their skills from Wales. Today the Buckeye Furnace State Memorial in eastern Jackson County contains the original stone stack of a Hanging Rock charcoal furnace used from 1851 to 1894. It is typical of the 46 furnaces that once operated in Ohio. On a 270-acre site, the industrial complex has been rebuilt. It is made up of the charging house, charcoal shed, casting house, blacksmith's shop, company store and the ironmaster's home.

In tribute to another industry of the area is the Ohio Ceramic Center near Crooksville in Perry County. Five buildings make up the center. The potter's wheel is operated by skilled workmen as they turn out ceramics for sale.

Near Pomeroy, Morgan's Raiders who invaded Ohio during the Civil War, were cornered at Buffington Island, where a battle took place. It was the only battle of that war fought on Ohio soil. The McCook monument near Portland is a tribute to the oldest soldier of the Fighting McCook family, Dan McCook. At 137 Main St. in Lancaster stands the restored birthplace of two famous brothers, General William T. Sherman, a Civil War General, and John T. Sherman, a U.S. Senator and statesman.

CHAPTER IX

Who's Who in Ohio History

What Makes a Person Famous?

Have you ever thought why a person is famous in our society? Does the accumulation of money or wealth make a person famous? Is it because a person is a great leader, writer, or artist? Does a person who makes a great contribution to our country become famous?

There are many qualities that tend to make a person famous. Often people are not recognized for their achievements during the time they live, but as the years pass on, they become famous. Their achievements take on added meaning. A new generation looking back through time, can judge the contributions of individuals or groups. They can see how that person's life changed history. For example, the influence of the life of both Abraham Lincoln and Martin Luther King became greater after their assassination.

Famous is a word that must be measured in degrees. Some people are considered famous for one contribution or achievement, while others such as Edison, the inventor, may be famous for many. Some people may be considered famous for an accomplishment of less importance than another. Perhaps the best criteria for judging a person's fame is to ask the question: Did this person do anything that benefited the society to which he be-. longed?

The social group or society considered in this book is that of the people who have lived or now live in Ohio. It is impossible to list all those Ohioans who have made contributions. Anyone who lives a good useful, honest life makes a contribution to Ohio. You will make a contribution as you live the life of a good citizen.

However, some Ohioans have made contributions which benefited many other people, that their names are remembered. Ohio is proud to remember these people. They honor them at the

Ohio Historical Society where there is a special Great Ohioans Hall of Fame exhibit.

One of Ohio's Governors, James A. Rhodes, established at the Capitol at Columbus, a "Teenage Hall of Fame." He asked a group of judges to determine what Ohioans had made an important achievement before reaching the age of 20 years. From a list of 200, they picked 30 for this unusual honor. This proves that a person does not have to be old to become famous. For example, Jesse Owens, the outstanding track athlete of the century, and winner of Olympic medals, began his career while a student at a Cleveland junior high school.

There is not room in the book to even list all the famous people of Ohio. As you have read the story of the Buckeye State, you have seen some of the people who made great contributions to Ohio, and the country. The people chosen for this chapter are those recognized by historians and the people of Ohio as having achieved something of importance. They come from all parts of Ohio as having achieved something of importance. They come from all parts of Ohio and have different ethnic backgrounds.

Some may have come from your community. They would be the most interesting to study. Find out about some local people who made contributions to your community. See how many important people you can add to the list in this section.

The "One-a-Day" Research Plan

Try the "one-a-day" research plan for finding out about the people on the list. Work individually or in a committee to look up information on the people on this list. Take down notes and write them up as your teacher directs.

Representative Ohioans

Since all Ohioans can't be listed, representative citizens were chosen. Read these short sketches and find out why these people were considered famous, before you start on your research.

OHIO PRESIDENTS

Ohio claims the title of "Mother of Presidents" having sent eight of her sons to the highest office in the land.

WILLIAM H. HARRISON, 9th PRESIDENT

"We admit of no government by divine right . . ."

First President to die in office, Harrison served the shortest term — one month. The native Virginian had left medical school in 1791 to become an Indian fighter in the Ohio country. His victory at Tippecanoe and his conduct of the War of 1812 in the Northwest made him a living legend. The famous Log Cabin campaign of 1840 was inspired by the log portion of his North Bend mansion.

ULYSSES S. GRANT, 18th PRESIDENT

"Labor disgraces no man."

The first native Ohioan to become President was born on April 27, 1822, in a cottage in Pt. Pleasant. His boyhood was spent on his father's Georgetown farm. Grant's outstanding role in the Civil War assured his election to two presidential terms. Four days before his death in 1885, he completed his memoirs, written to recoup his lost fortune. The work became a best-seller.

RUTHERFORD B. HAYES, 19th PRESIDENT

"Our government . . . is the government of the free man."

Another Ohio boy destined to become President was born in 1822, in Delaware. He left his thriving Cincinnati law office to serve with gallantry in the Civil War. While Governor, Hayes was elected President in the most disputed election in history. He is buried in his beloved Spiegel Grove estate, site of the first presidential library created by a state for its native son.

JAMES A. GARFIELD, 20th PRESIDENT

"All free governments are party governments."

Canaller, teacher, lawyer, Civil War hero, orator, legislator and President, Garfield was born in Orange in 1831. He had served as chief executive for only four months when, on July 2, 1881, an assassin's bullet cut him down. His Mentor home, Lawnfield, is preserved as a museum and he is buried in an imposing tomb in Cleveland's Lake View Cemetery.

BENJAMIN HARRISON, 23rd PRESIDENT

"Great lives never go out. They go on."

He had been a boy of nine, living in North Bend, when his grandfather was inaugurated Pleasant. As a young man he moved to Indiana and rose from lieutenant to general during the Civil War. Service in the U.S. Senate gave him national prominence. Six states were admitted to the Union during his administration from 1889-1893. He is buried in Indianapolis.

WILLIAM McKINLEY, 25th PRESIDENT

"Duty determines destiny."

The second Ohio-born President to be assassinated, McKinley served as President from 1897 to 1901. He was born in Niles on January 29, 1843, taught school when only sixteen, and rose from private to brevet major in the Civil War. He was the first President to campaign by telephone. The red carnation, his favorite, was made the official State flower in 1904.

**WILLIAM H. TAFT,
27th PRESIDENT**

*"The battlefield . . . .
is yielding to courts . . ."*

Taft was the only President to become U.S. Chief Justice, and the first to be President of 48 States. He was born in Cincinnati in 1857. He held many high governmental and educational posts including that of Secretary of War under Theodore Roosevelt. During his own administration, 1909-1913, the income tax amendment was added to the Constitution. He is buried in Arlington National Cemetery.

**WARREN G. HARDING,
29th PRESIDENT**

"Not revolution but restoration."

Three Ohioans ran against each other for the presidency in 1920. For the first time radio announced the results. Harding, born in a humble Blooming Grove cottage, rode to his inauguration as none of his predecessors had before — in an auto. Death claimed him after 2 years and 151 days in office. His Marion home, from which he conducted the famous "Front Porch" campaign, is preserved as a museum.

**JOSEPH RAY, pioneer
educator (Arithmetic)**
Ohio Historical Society and Ohio Bell

**WILLIAM HOLMES
McGUFFEY, pioneer
educator (Reading)**

**HIRAM REVELS, one
time Ohioan and United
States Senator from
Mississippi**
The Bettmann Archive and Ohio Bell

**PLATT ROGERS
SPENCER, pioneer
educator (Writing)**
Ohio Historical Society and Ohio Bell

**JOHN MERCER
LANGSTON, Abolitionist
and Reconstruction
leader**
The Bettmann Archive and Ohio Bell

**LANGSTON HUGHES,
author and playwright**
Ohio Bell

CARL STOKES, former
mayor of Cleveland, and
one of first black mayors
in United States.

MARTIN LUTHER KING,
Champion of Civil Rights

PAUL LAWRENCE
DUNBAR, famous Dayton
poet

JESSE OWENS, renowned track star

Albert B. Graham

Albert B. Graham, founder of 4-H Clubs.

On January 15, 1902, a special meeting took place in a room of the Courthouse at Springfield. It was called to order by the School superintendent, Albert B. Graham, who smiled as he saw so many of his students in attendance. It was held on Saturday afternoon so that farm boys and girls could attend the meeting while their parents shopped in town.

Graham, an Ohio farm boy himself, had thought of the need for a club program for farm youth. It was agreed at the meeting that a club be formed, with the purpose to study projects leading to improved farming and gardening practices. The club's first project was to test soil for farmers.

When other rural youth heard of this club in Springfield, they wanted to form one for themselves, and the idea spread from county to county. Finally officials of Ohio State University heard of the new agricultural club and asked Graham to come to Ohio State as the first Director of Agricultural Extension in Ohio.

In this job he toured the state, as well as publishing a bulletin. In it he wrote of the agricultural clubs he organized in Ohio. Other states read the bulletin and asked him to speak to groups about the clubs. Finally these clubs were organized into a national organization. In 1930 they became known as the 4-H Clubs. As a member of the U.S. Department of Agriculture, Graham watched his clubs spread across the nation.

4-H Clubs help boys and girls to be better farmers, gardeners and homemakers. Today's members can choose from many projects, and many carry out one, even if they live in town. They have exhibits at county and state fairs. When Dr. Graham died at the age of 91, he had attained fame as founder of the 4-H Clubs of America, a movement which has spread to over 75 nations of the world.

Rabbi Isaac M. Wise

Rabbi Isaac M. Wise, a poor Jewish immigrant, arrived in America with two dollars in his pocket. In central Europe he completed studies to be a Rabbi, but felt America offered him more opportunities.

He first settled in New York City, and then went to Albany. where he was assigned a synagogue. Here he organized a night school to teach other immigrants English. He began to write articles about the Jewish religion, and then a book.

Hearing of the work of Rabbi Wise, the Cincinnati congregation asked him to come to their city in which 4,000 Jewish people had settled. In addition to his work at the synagogue, he edited two Jewish papers and continued to write. He wrote of the need for Jews to become part of American life, and to use the English language even in their worship services.

In Cincinnati the good Rabbi found his life's work, and here he spent almost 50 years. In 1873 delegates from many Jewish congregations met in Cincinnati and agreed to work together, and to establish a place of higher learning for training rabbis. In

1875 Hebrew Union College came into being, with Rabbi Isaac Wise as its president. Starting with fewer than a dozen students, the college grew into a major training center of Jewish rabbis.

At first the college students met in the temple, but the college grew into a beautiful campus of fine buildings. He continued an active life until his death, both at the college and at the Plum Street Temple.

Granville T. Woods

Born in Columbus in 1856, Granville T. Woods, a Black engineer, began his career working in a machine shop, but became interested in railroads. Working as an engineer on the railroads, he saw the need for a communication device to prevent accidents. This led to a telegraphic system which cut down on accidents. In all, Woods patented over fifteen devices to provide for safety of passengers on trains and electric railways.

One of his most important inventions was that of the automatic air brake for locomotives, a patent which he sold to a major manufacturing firm. He also worked on the steam boiler furnace, and invented the chicken incubator.

At his manufacturing plant in Cincinnati, Woods produced telephone, telegraph and electrical equipment.

Garrett A. Morgan

Garrett A. Morgan invented the automatic traffic control light which is seen at every busy traffic intersection. The Black inventor sold this valuable invention to a large company for $40,000.

This was not the first invention of the Cleveland man. Turning to inventing in his spare time he designed a safety belt fastener used on sewing machines. In 1914, at the International Exposition of Sanitation and Safety, Morgan received the Grand Prize for his smoke inhalator, which resulted in the saving of lives of men trapped underground or in tunnels.

His smoke inhalator was developed into a gas mask for World War I soldiers which prevented thousands of deaths. In World War II the masks were carried, but no nation turned to gas warfare.   240

Lucy Webb Hayes

Mrs. Lucy Hayes, wife of Rutherford B. Hayes, the 19th President of the U.S. from Delaware, Ohio, was a fine mother and hostess. She was First Lady of Ohio when her husband served three terms as Governor. She was First Lady of the U.S. when Hayes was president. It was said that no White House hostess since Dolly Madison had shown such charm and friendly manner.

She was born at Chillicothe, later moved to Delaware, where she met her future husband for the first time. Hayes was then a young lawyer. The Webb family moved to Cincinnati in 1848, where Lucy graduated from college.

In 1849 Hayes moved his law practice to Cincinnati, and began his courtship of Lucy Webb, which lasted three years. Their marriage was a most happy one. They reared one daughter and four sons.

After serving as a General in the Civil War, Hayes returned home to Ohio, entered politics and was elected Governor three terms. He went on to win the presidency in 1876.

Lucy Hayes was the first woman with a college education to be First Lady. She began the tradition of the Easter egg rolling on the White House lawn. She would not permit liquor to be served in the White House, and some of the men referred to her as "Lemonade Lucy."

Both she and the president were glad to return to their beautiful home in Spiegel Grove, Fremont, now a state memorial. They lived for many years, happy among their flowers, trees and birds. Both are buried on a grassy knoll in Spiegel Grove.

Frank J. Lausche

Frank J. Lausche set a record for being elected Governor of Ohio. He served five terms, and then went on to become U.S. Senator from the state. Lausche proved that a poor boy whose parents were immigrants from central Europe could be elected to the top office of the state. His success should encourage Ohioans of various ethnic backgrounds.

Lausche was born in the steel-making district of Cleveland in 1895. Frank, one of a family of ten children, was twelve years

241

old when his father died. He sold newspapers, became a lamp-lighter, and helped his mother run a restaurant. He still had a little time left for sports.

After serving in World War I, he returned home and studied to be a lawyer. He next became a municipal judge, and later ran for mayor of Cleveland. In 1944 he was elected to his first term as Governor. As Governor and Senator Frank Lausche made many contributions to Ohio.

Daniel Carter Beard

As a young boy, Daniel Carter Beard enjoyed playing along the Ohio River. The Beard family moved to Cincinnati from Lake County, where Daniel was born. When Beard was a boy during Civil War times, there were forests and caves to explore along the river, and trails to follow through the hills where once the Indians had roamed.

With bow and arrow Beard would hide behind trees and dream of the days when Indian and pioneer followed the same forest paths. Beard's favorite pioneer hero was Daniel Boone, who had crossed the Ohio country many times. He read all he could about the famous explorer.

When he grew up Beard never forgot his happy boyhood days. When he became a writer for magazines, he often wrote about them. He became a popular author and illustrator, writing many stories for youth magazines. In 1882 he published the "American Boy's Handy Book," which introduced boys to crafts, telling them how to do and make things. He received letters from boys wanting to know more about the outdoors, hiking, and exploring trips. He decided to organize a club for them where groups could get together and enjoy outdoor activities. These clubs were called the Sons of Daniel Boone.

They became very popular. In England, Lord Baden-Powell read about the Sons of Daniel Boone. He had been interested in boys' clubs and started one in his country, which he called simply, Boy Scouts. Beard thought that it would be best if the two groups, so much alike, would become one. So America's Sons of Daniel Boone became the Boy Scouts of America.

242

Famous People Associated with Ohio

Abbe, Cleveland
Allen, Florence E.
Anderson, Sherwood
Armstrong, Neil
Arnett, Benjamin
Bailey, Anne
Beard, Daniel C.
Bellows, George W.
Bickerdyke, Mary A.
Blennerhasset, H.
Blue Jacket, Chief
Bouquet, Henry
Bromfield, Louis
Brown, John
Brush, Charles
Cary, Alice—Phoebe
Chapman, John
Chase, Salmon P.
Christy, Howard C.
Clark, George Rogers
Cleaveland, Moses
Clem, Johnnie
Cooper, Martha K.
Cox, James M.
Custer, George A.
De Celeron, De Bienville
Drake, Daniel
Dunbar, Paul L.
Duveneck, Frank
Edison, Thomas A.
Foster, Stephen C.
Gable, Clark

Gamble, James
Garfield, James A.
Garner, Margaret
Gish, Dorothy—Lillian
Gist, Christopher
Glenn, John
Glueck, Nelson
Goodrich, Benjamin
Graham, Albert B.
Grant, Ulysses S.
Green, John P.
Green, William
Grey, Zane
Grimke, Angelina—Sarah
Hanby, Benjamin
Hanna, Marcus A.
Harding, Warren G.
Harris, Mary
Harrison, William H.
Harrison, Benjamin
Hall, Charles M.
Havighurst, Walter
Hayes, Lucy W.
Hayes, Rutherford B.
Hope, Bob
Howe, Henry
Howells, William D.
Hughes, Langston
Hurst, Fannie
Hussey, Obed
Janis, Elsie
Kenton, Simon

Kettering, Charles F.
Langston, John M.
LaSalle, Robert de
Lausche, Frank
Lewis, Edmonia
Little Turtle, Chief
Logan, James Chief
McGuffey, William H.
McKinley, William
Mann, Horace
Morgan, Arthur E.
Morgan, Garrett A.
Nourse, Elizabeth
Oakley, Annie
Owens, Jesse
Patterson, John H.
Perry, Oliver H.
Pontiac, Chief
Price, Leontyne
Putnam, Rufus
Rickenbacker, Eddie
Rockefeller, John D.
Rogers, Roy
Rouse, Bathsheba
Roye, Edward J.
Sabin, Albert B.
St. Clair, Arthur
Sherman, William T.

Smith, Joseph
Spock, Benjamin
Stewart, John
Stokes, Carl
Stowe, Harriet B.
Symmes, John C.
Taft, William H.
Tarhe, Chief
Tecumseh, Chief
Thomas, Lowell
Thurber, James
Tytus, John B.
Verity, George M.
Wald, Lillian D.
Ward, John Q. A.
Wayne, Anthony
Williard, Archibald
Williams, George W.
Wise, Issac M.
Woodhull, Victoria C.
Woods, Granville
Worthington, Thomas
Wright, Katherine
Wright, Orville—Wilbur
Zane, Betty
Zane, Ebenezer
Zeisberger, David

CHAPTER X

Looking Back:
How the Social Scientist
Would Look at Ohio

History is sometimes called the memory of man's experiences. If it is forgotten or goes unnoticed, society may decline or fail. Without history and tradition, a society has no knowledge of what it is or how it came to be. The events of history have caused all the emotions, values, ideals and goals that make life have meaning. These things give people something to live for, struggle for and sometimes die for. Events of history have created countries, governments, religions and social classes that all work together to influence present-day society. Ohioans today should view their state's past in order to understand and appreciate the heritage that has been passed from earlier generations.

To fully understand a group of people (a society), it is important that they be studied through the various branches or disciplines of social science. The areas we will deal with in the following pages are: **history, sociology, cultural anthropology, political science, economics,** and **geography.** Each of these areas of social science calls for special study and attention.

The Historian is mainly concerned with recording what happened, when it happened, where it happened, and what the results were. He is concerned with the following key words: **time, period, happening, cause, result, chronology,** and **change**.

The historian asks these questions:
1. What caused this particular event to take place?
2. Were there people involved who could have changed the final result?
3. Were there new ideas or inventions that caused the change?
4. How did the people feel about the issue or event?
5. Was the physical environment a factor in the issue or event?

The Cultural Anthropologist is concerned with studying a group of people (a society) to discover ways in which people are

245

alike and ways in which they are different. He is interested in the ways in which they are different. He is interested in the ways the group meets its needs, and this he calls their "culture."

He is concerned with the following key words: **mankind, culture, values, beliefs,** and **acculturation** (spread or exchange of culture).

He asks the following questions:
1. What is man?
2. How does man differ from other creatures?
3. What are the major needs of this group?
4. What seems to be their way of life with regard to their values and beliefs?
5. What effect does physical environment have on their developed culture?
6. How does this culture meet the requirements for surviving?

The Political Scientist is interested mainly in political leadership. This involves the people or groups who make and enforce the laws or rules under which the political system operates. He is concerned with these key words: **authority, power, influence, government, decision-making,** and **leadership.**

He asks the following questions:
1. How many are involved in the process of choosing political leaders?
2. What does the society look for in people who are selected to fill leadership roles?
3. Who takes part in making political decisions?
4. How does the society determine how much authority to give its leaders?

The Economist studies how the people in a society make choices and how they distribute resources to obtain needed products and services. He is concerned with these key words: **wants, needs, scarcity, exchange, production, distribution,** and **consumption.**

He asks the following questions:
1. What goods and services are produced?
2. How are goods and services produced?
3. For whom are these goods and services produced?

4. How much or in what quantity are they produced?
5. How fast has the economy grown?
6. What regulations have been developed to control this growth?
7. How does scarcity influence the occupational and technological status of this society?

The Geographer is mainly concerned with the plants, animals and minerals that make up the area to be studied. He wants to find out what happens when certain plants, animals, climate conditions, and people with a particular culture are found in an area. He wants to study the effect of environment on the people and to what extent the people have changed or adapted the environment to meet their goals.

He is concerned with the following key words: **place, location, area, environment, areal association.**

He asks the following questions:
1. How is this place different from other places?
2. How is it similar to other places?
3. Why are conditions the way they are in this place?
4. Did the people make any difference in these conditions?
5. Were natural resources important to this place?
6. How wisely were these resources used?
7. Do the people export raw materials or finished products?
8. What kind of things do they receive from other places?
9. What kinds of activities do people take part in? Has it always been this way? Why?
10. To what extent has the terrain contributed to the overall progress of this place (or kept it from progressing)?

The Sociologist is concerned with how the people behave or act as they live in social groups. He wants to study cooperation and conflict among groups and what role the family, the school, the church, and the government have had in the growth of the society. He is concerned with social change, its cause, and its effect on the society. He also wants to study such things as crime, transportation, communication, and population distribution, as they have developed within the society. He wants to learn how this social group promotes loyalty to its beliefs, and how it

247

has organized to protect itself from outside forces. He is concerned with the following key words: **group, social system, custom, conflict, interaction, role, norm,** and **sanction.**

He asks the following questions:

1. Why is this society organized as it is?
2. What systems have been created by this society?
3. What were the purposes and effects of these systems?
4. How do members of subgroups in this society feel toward each other?
5. Why do they feel this way?
6. What has happened to this society as it has been involved with population increase or decrease, automation and warfare?
7. Have the subgroups of this society all changed at the same rate?
8. How does this society regard its aged population?
9. In what ways does this society show an appreciation of culture and its inheritance?

Your Community

You have read about the various branches of social science and how each might be used in the study of a society. Using the same key words and questions that each social scientist would use, make a study of your own community and attempt to find out more about it by answering as many of the questions as possible. When you follow this plan of studying a community, a state, a nation, or any society, you are learning to look through the eyes of all the social scientists. To study only the historian's point of view, for example, would prevent you from gaining an appreciation of the society as viewed from the total social science perspective. Put on the glasses of the social scientist and see things as a total picture. Your understanding of and appreciation for a social group will be much more meaningful to you as a result.

A SUGGESTED MODEL FOR GATHERING
AND ANALYZING DATA

The People
1. Where did they come from?
2. Why did they come?
3. What culture did they bring with them?
   a. Observances (religious, etc.)
   b. Food
   c. Clothing
   d. Political
   e. Economic
   f. Education

The Environment
4. What adaptations to the new environment had to be made in regard to:
   a. Food?
   b. Clothing?
   c. Shelter?
   d. Political?
   e. Economic processes (supply, demand, trade, scarcity, distribution, manufacture)?
   f. Education?

The Institutions
5. What patterns of change are evident in:
   a. Family?
   b. Government?
   c. Education?
   d. Religion?

Analysis and Generalization
6. In analyzing the data found for questions 1-5, what are some generalizations you might draw with regard to:
   a. Family?
   b. Government?
   c. Education?
   d. Religion?
   e. Shelter?
   f. Economic development?

DATA AND RESOURCE SECTION

PART ONE   OHIO IN OUTLINE

I. **Basic Facts About Ohio**
   A. Ohio from Iroquois word, oheo, meaning "beautiful river."
   B. First State carved out of the Northwest Territory.
   C. Ohio became the 17th state of the Union on Mar. 1, 1803.
   D. State's capital is at Columbus.
   E. Capitol Building or Statehouse completed Nov. 15, 1861.
   F. State Legislature is called General Assembly, and composed of 33 Senators and 99 Representatives.
   G. Population in 1970 was 10,652,017, ranking Ohio 6th in the U.S.
   H. Presidents from Ohio are: William Henry Harrison (1841); Ulysses S. Grant (1869-1877); Rutherford B. Hayes (1877-1881); James A. Garfield (1881); Benjamin Harrison (1889-1893); William McKinley (1897-1901); William H. Taft (1909-1913); Warren G. Harding (1921-1923).

II. **Symbols of Ohio**
   A. State Bird is the Cardinal
   B. State Flower is the Scarlet Carnation.
   C. State Motto: "With God All Things Are Possible."
   D. State Tree is the Buckeye.
   E. State Song is "Beautiful Ohio."
   F. State Seal: Sun rising over hills of Mt. Logan at Chillicothe. 17 Arrows symbolize Ohio's being 17th state admitted to Union. Sheaf of wheat shows importance of agriculture.
   G. State Flag: Pennant shaped, with red and white horizontal stripes. Blue triangle at staff and 17 white stars surrounding red center.
   H. Ohio Nickname is the Buckeye state; people called Buckeyes.
   I. State Insect is the Ladybug.
   J. State's Gem Stone is Ohio Flint.
   K. State Beverage is Tomato Juice.

III. **Ohio's Physical Characteristics**
   A. Area is 41,222 square miles, ranks 35th in area among states.
   B. Boundaries of Ohio are:
      1. North—Lake Erie and Michigan.

250

2. South—Ohio River, West Virginia and Kentucky.
3. East—Ohio River and Pennsylvania.
4. West—Indiana.

C. Greatest Length (North to South) 220 miles.
D. Greatest Width (East to West) 225 miles.
E. Highest Point—1,548 feet above sea level, Campbell Hill,
   Bellefontaine.
F. Lowest Point—428 feet in Southwest Corner of state along
   Ohio.
G. Lake Erie is most important lake with 312 miles of shoreline.
H. Growing season varies from 150 to 180 days.
I. Highest recorded temperature was 113° F. (1926).
J. Lowest recorded temperature was -45° F. (1899).
K. Average Rainfall 38 inches per year.
L. Normal wind direction is from the SW.

IV. **Ohio's Largest Cities with a population of over 100,000—1970
Census:**
A. Cleveland—750,903.
B. Columbus—539,677.
C. Cincinnati—452,524.
D. Toledo—383,818.
E. Akron—275,425.
F. Dayton—243,601.
G. Youngstown—139,788.
H. Canton—110,053.
I. Parma—100,216.

PART TWO

Constitution of the State of OHIO

In February 1850, the Ohio General Assembly sent out a formal call for delegates to a Constitutional Convention. The Convention framed a new Constitution, adopted in 1851, and with the additions of many amendments is still in use today. Complete copies are available at any public or school library.

Below are some of the most important provisions. Deletions are indicated by . . . Important excerpts follow.

The Preamble reads: "We, the people of the State of Ohio, grateful to Almighty God for our freedom, to secure its blessings and promote our common welfare, do establish this Constitution."

Article I. Bill of Rights.

I. Inalienable Rights. All men are, by nature, free and independent, and have certain inalienable rights, among which are those of enjoying and defending life and liberty, acquiring, possessing, and protecting property, and seeking and obtaining happiness and safety.

2. Where Political Power Vested; Special Privileges. All political power is inherent in the people. Government is instituted for their equal protection and benefit, and they have the right to alter, reform or abolish the same, whenever they may deem it necessary; and no special privileges or immunities shall ever be granted, that may not be altered, revoked, or repealed by the General Assembly.

3. Right to Assemble. The people shall have the right to assemble together, in a peaceable manner, to consult for their common good; to instruct their Representatives; and to petition the General Assembly for the redress of grievances.

4. Bearing Arms; Standing Armies; Military Power. The people have the right to bear arms for their defense and security; but standing armies, in time of peace, are dangerous to liberty, and

shall not be kept up; and the military shall be in strict subordination to the civil power.

5. Trial by Jury. The right of trial by jury shall be inviolate, except that, in civil cases, laws may be passed to authorize the rendering of a verdict by the concurrence of not less than three fourths of the jury.

6. Slavery and Involuntary Servitude. There shall be no slavery in this state; nor involuntary servitude, unless for the punishment of crime.

7. Rights of Conscience; the Necessity of Religion and Knowledge. All men have a natural and indefeasible right to worship Almighty God according to the dictates of their own conscience. No person shall be compelled to attend, erect, or support any place of worship, or maintain any form of worship, against his consent; and no preference shall be given, by law, to any religious society; nor shall any interference with the rights of conscience be permitted. No religious test shall be required as a qualification for office. . . Religion, morality, and knowledge, however, being essential to good government, it shall be the duty of the General Assembly to pass suitable laws, to protect every religious denomination in the peaceable enjoyment of its own mode of public worship, and to encourage schools and the means of instruction.

8. Writ of Habeas Corpus. The privilege of the writ of habeas corpus shall not be suspended, unless, in cases of rebellion or invasion, the public safety require it.

9. Bailable Offenses; of Bail, Fine and Punishment. All persons shall be bailable by sufficient sureties, except for capital offenses where the proof is evident, or the presumption great. Excessive bail shall not be required; nor excessive fines imposed, nor cruel and unusual punishments inflicted.

10. Trial for Crimes; Witnesses. Except (in special cases) no person shall be held to answer for a capital, or otherwise infamous crime, unless on presentment or indictment of a grand jury. In any trial, in any court the party accused shall be allowed to appear and defend in person and with counsel; to demand the nature and cause of the accusation against him, and to have a

copy thereof; to meet witnesses face to face, . . . and a speedy public trial by an impartial jury . . .

11. Freedom of Speech and the Press; Libel. Every citizen may freely speak, write, and publish his sentiments on all subjects, being responsible for the abuse of the right; and no law shall be passed to restrain or abridge the liberty of speech, or of the press . . .

(Sections 12 through 20 of the Ohio Constitution are technical and refer to rights not generally exercised by most people, although important to some, and Section 20 ends with the statement that "all powers, not herein delegated, remain with the people.")

ARTICLE II Legislative

1. In Whom Power Vested. The legislative power of the state shall be vested in a General Assembly consisting of a senate and house of representatives but the people reserve to themselves the power to propose to the General Assembly laws and amendments to the constitution and to adopt or reject the same at the polls on a referendum vote as hereinafter provided; and independent of the General Assembly to propose amendments to the constitution and to adopt or reject the same at the polls . . .

1.a. The Initiative and Referendum (This section adopted in 1912 describes in detail how these two processes work.)

(Following this section are many relating to the legislative function, membership in the assembly, powers of each house, and rules and regulations of membership.)

ARTICLE III Executive

1. Executive Department. The executive department shall consist of a governor, lieutenant governor, secretary of state, auditor of state, treasurer of state, and an attorney general, who shall be elected the first Tuesday, after the first Monday in November, by the electors of the state, and at places of voting for members of the general assembly. (This article deals with the term of office, the executive powers of the governor, and the powers and duties of the Lieutenant Governor.)

ARTICLE IV Judicial

1. In Whom Judicial Power Vested. The judicial power of the state is vested in a supreme court, court of appeals, courts of

254

common pleas, courts of probate, and such other courts inferior to courts of appeals as may from time to time be established by law.

(This article defines in detail the composition and duties and jurisdiction of various courts, as well as the terms of office appointments, and election of judges.)

ARTICLE V Elective Franchise

1. Who May Vote. Every citizen of the United States . . . who shall have been a resident of the state one year next preceding the election, and of the county, township, or ward, in which he resides, such time as may be provided by law, shall have the qualifications of an elector, and be entitled to vote at all elections.

2. By Ballot. All elections shall be by ballot. (The remainder of this article concerns types of ballot used in Ohio, privileges of voters, and other details. Section 7 provides that "all nominations for elective state, district, county and municipal offices shall be made at direct primary elections or by petitions as provided by law" with certain exceptions.

ARTICLE VI Education

(This article provides for the establishment of the public school system and the raising of general funds to accomplish this program, as well as a state board of education and superintendent of public instruction to oversee the school system.)

ARTICLE VII Public Institutions. (This section concerns Ohio's public institutions for the insane, deaf, blind and the penitentiary system.)

ARTICLE VIII Public Debt and Public Works. (This is a technical article which would interest only a few people. It contains sections dealing with compensation to Ohio war veterans, the issuing of bonds, and aspects of state finance.)

ARTICLE IX Militia. (This article describes the qualifications of the militia, its officers, and how it may be called to active duty.)

ARTICLE X County and Township Organization.

1. The General Assembly shall provide by general law for the organization and government of counties, and may provide by general law alternative forms of county government. . . .

255

2. Township Officers. The General Assembly shall provide by general law for the election of such township officers as may be necessary. The trustees of townships shall have such powers of local taxation as prescribed by law. No money shall be drawn from any township treasury except by authority of law.

(This article provides for county charters, their provisions, adoptions, and the establishment of a county charter commission.)

ARTICLE XI Apportionment. How representatives shall be apportioned to provide fair representation is the subject of this article.)

ARTICLE XII Finance and Taxation.

ARTICLE XIII Corporations.

ARTICLE XIV Jurisprudence.

ARTICLE XV Miscellaneous.

ARTICLE XVI Amendments.

ARTICLE XVII Elections.

ARTICLE XVIII Municipal Corporations.

1. Classification. Municipal Corporations are hereby classified into cities and villages. All such corporations having a population of five thousand or over shall be cities; all others shall be villages. The method of transition from one class to the other shall be regulated by law.

2. General and Additional Laws. General laws shall be passed to provide for the incorporation and government of cities and villages; and additional laws may also be passed for the government of municipalities adopting the same; but no such additional law shall become operative in any municipality until it shall have been submitted to the electors thereof, and affirmed by a majority of those voting thereon, under regulations established by law.

3. Powers. Municipalities shall have authority to exercise all powers of local self-government and to adopt and enforce within their limits such local police, sanitary and other similar regulations as are not in conflict with general laws.

(The remainder of this article discusses in detail the powers granted municipalities.)

Cottontail Rabbit

Wood Duck

Goldeneye Duck

Ring-Necked Pheasant

White-Tailed Deer

Cardinal

Bob-White Quail

Gray Squirrel

Blue Jay

Duck Hawk

Copperhead Snake

Red Fox

GOVERNORS OF OHIO

Term	Governor	County of Residence
1803-1807 — Edward Tiffin		Ross
1807-1808 — Thomas Kirker		Adams
1808-1810 — Samuel Huntington		Lake
1810-1814 — Return J. Meigs, Jr.		Washington
1814- — Othniel Looker		Hamilton
1814-1818 — Thomas Worthington		Ross
1818-1822 — Ethan Allen Brown		Hamilton
1822 — Allen Trimble		Highland
1822-1826 — Jeremiah Morrow		Warren
1826-1830 — Allen Trimble		Highland
1830-1832 — Duncan McArthur		Ross
1832-1836 — Robert Lucas		Pike
1836-1838 — Joseph Vance		Champaign
1838-1840 — Wilson Shannon		Belmont
1840-1842 — Thomas Corwin		Warren
1842-1844 — Wilson Shannon		Belmont
1844- — Thomas W. Bartley		Richland
1844-1846 — Mordecai Bartley		Richland
1846-1849 — William Bebb		Butler
1849-1850 — Seabury Ford		Geauga
1850-1853 — Reuben Wood		Cuyahoga
1853-1856 — William Medill		Fairfield
1856-1860 — Salmon P. Chase		Hamilton
1860-1862 — William Dennison		Franklin
1862-1864 — David Tod		Mahoning
1864-1865 — John Brough		Cuyahoga
1865-1866 — Charles Anderson		Montgomery
1866-1868 — Jacob B. Cox		Trumbull
1868-1872 — Rutherford B. Hayes		Hamilton
1872-1874 — Edward F. Noyes		Hamilton
1875-1876 — William Allen		Ross
1876-1877 — Rutherford B. Hayes		Sandusky

257

1877-1878—Thomas L. Young	Hamilton
1878-1880—Richard M. Bishop	Hamilton
1880-1884—Charles Foster	Seneca
1884-1886—George Hoadly	Hamilton
1886-1890—Joseph B. Foraker	Hamilton
1890-1892—James E. Campbell	Butler
1892-1896—William McKinley	Stark
1896-1900—Asa S. Buchnell	Clark
1900-1904—George K. Nash	Franklin
1904-1906—Myron T. Herrick	Cuyahoga
1906- —John M Pattison	Clermont
1906-1909—Andrew L. Harris	Preble
1909-1913—Judson Harmon	Hamilton
1913-1915—James M. Cox	Montgomery
1915-1917—Frank B. Willis	Delaware
1917-1921—James M. Cox	Montgomery
1921-1923—Harry L. Davis	Cuyahoga
1923-1929—A. Victor Donahey	Tuscarawas
1929-1931—Myers Y. Cooper	Hamilton
1931-1935—George White	Washington
1935-1939—Martin L. Davey	Portage
1939-1945—John W. Bricker	Franklin
1945-1947—Frank J. Lausche	Cuyahoga
1947-1949—Thomas J. Herbert	Cuyahoga
1949-1957—Frank J. Lausche	Cuyahoga
1957- —John W. Brown	Medina
1957-1959—C. William O'Neill	Washington
1959-1963—Michael V. DiSalle	Lucas
1963-1971—James A. Rhodes	Franklin
1971-1975—John J. Gilligan	Hamilton
1975- —James A. Rhodes	Franklin

PART THREE

Ohio's Counties

After the name of each County is the following information — the county seat — the date the county was established — area in square miles — statement as to origin of the county's name.

ADAMS — West Union — 1797 — 588 sq. mi. — John Adams, American patriot, was the second President of the U.S.

ALLEN — Lima — 1831 — 410 sq. mi. — Ethan Allen, leader of the Green Mountain Boys, was a Revolutionary War hero.

ASHLAND — Ashland — 1846 — 426 sq. mi. — Henry Clay, a popular American statesman, lived at Lexington, Ky. on his Ashland estate.

ASHTABULA — Jefferson — 1811 — 706 sq. mi. — The name of the Ashtabula River is from an Indian word, Fish, plentiful in the early river.

ATHENS — Athens — 1805 — 504 sq. mi. — The Greek city of Athens was noted for being a center of learning, a good name for the seat of learning in the Ohio wilderness — Ohio University.

AUGLAIZE — Wapakoneta — 1848 — 504 sq. mi. — The Auglaize River was given its name by the Indians, at one time being filled with "fallen timbers," the English translation of Auglaize.

BELMONT — St. Clairsville — 1801 — 539 sq. mi. — The English translation of the French word Belmont, is Beautiful Mountain, a county of lovely hills.

BROWN — Georgetown — 1817 — 491 sq. mi. — General Jacob Brown, who fought at Lundy's Lane, was a hero of the War of 1812.

BUTLER — Hamilton — 1803 — 471 sq. mi. — General Richard Butler, an officer of the Revolution, was killed in the Indian Wars in 1791.

CARROLL — Carrollton — 1832 — 396 sq. mi. — Charles Carroll of Carrollton died in 1832, the last survivor of those who signed the Declaration of Independence.

CHAMPAIGN — Urbana — 1805 — 433 sq. mi. — A French word, which translated to English means "a level plain."

CLARK — Springfield — 1817 — 402 sq. mi. — General George Rogers Clark conducted the western campaigns during the American Revolution.

CLERMONT — Batavia — 1800 — 459 sq. mi. — The English translation of the French word is "clear mountain," and refers to hilly terrain.

CLINTON—Wilmington—1810—412 sq. mi.—George Clinton, an uncle of De Witt Clinton, served as Vice President of the U.S. under Madison.

COLUMBIANA—Lisbon—1803—535 sq. mi.—Two names were combined in the one word, honoring two people, Columbus, and Queen Anna.

COSHOCTON—Coshocton—1811—563 sq. mi.—The county name is based on the Indian word, Goschachgunk, which translated means Black Bear town.

CRAWFORD—Bucyrus—1820—404 sq. mi.—Colonel William Crawford, fought in both the Revolution and Indian wars, burned at the stake by the Indians in retaliation of the murder of the Christian Indians.

CUYAHOGA—Cleveland—1807—456 sq. mi.—Being a winding river, the Indians used the word, Cuyahoga, or crooked to describe it.

DARKE—Greenville—1816—605 sq. mi.—General William Darke, after serving in the Revolution, came West to serve under St. Clair.

DEFIANCE—Defiance—1845—412 sq. mi.—Fort Defiance was built by Gen. Anthony Wayne to defy the Indians and the English, as part of his successful campaign in 1794 ending at "Fallen Timbers."

DELAWARE—Delaware—1808—459 sq. mi.—The Delaware Indians had migrated west from the area around the Delaware River.

ERIE—Sandusky—1838—265 sq. mi.—The Erie tribe of Indians lived in the region, and were known as the "Cat" nation.

FAIRFIELD—Lancaster—1800—507 sq. mi.—The early pioneers were attracted by its fair fields, which describes its lands.

FAYETTE— Washington Court House— 1810— 406 sq. mi.— General LaFayette, a French General who helped America during the Revolution, assisting in securing French aid, making victory possible.

FRANKLIN—Columbus—1803—539 sq. mi.—Benjamin Franklin was an American patriot, diplomat, and scientist.

FULTON—Wauseon—1850—407 sq. mi.—Robert Fulton was the much admired inventor of the steamboat, important to early Ohio transportation.

GALLIA—Gallipolis—1803—471 sq. mi.—Originally settled by French emigrants, it is the Latin word for Gaul, the old name for France.

GEAUGA—Chardon—1805—408 sq. mi.—The original name of the Grand River was the Geauga River, named by the Indians, and meaning raccoon.

GREENE—Xenia—1803—416 sq. mi.—Revolutionary War commander, General Nathaniel Greene, was in charge of the southern sector of the war, and one of Washington's best aides.

GUERNSEY—Cambridge—1810—529 sq. mi.—Some of the first settlers of the area came from the English Channel island of Guernsey.

HAMILTON—Cincinnati—1790—415 sq. mi.—Alexander Hamilton was Washington's Secretary of the Treasury when the county was formed.

HANCOCK—Findlay—1820—532 sq. mi.—John Hancock was the first patriot to sign the Declaration of Independence in his bold script.

HARDIN—Kenton—1833—467 sq. mi.—General John Hardin, a hero of the American Revolution, met death at the hands of the Indians while on a peace mission for President Washington.

HARRISON—Cadiz—1814—General William Henry Harrison at the time the county was organized was the hero of the War of 1812; he later became the 9th President of the U.S.

HENRY—Napoleon—1820—420 sq. mi.—Patrick Henry was the Governor of Virginia, and the patriot who stated: "Give me liberty or give me death."

HIGHLAND—Hillsboro—1805—554 sq. mi.—Based upon the geography of the county, which is hilly, the name Highland was appropriate.

HOCKING—Logan—1818—421 sq. mi.—At Rock Mills, the Hocking River flows through a narrow passage or "bottleneck" the Indian word now is used both for the river and the county.

HOLMES—Millersburg—1824—424 sq. mi.—Major Andrew H. Holmes was killed fighting in the ill-fated attack on Mackinac Island in the War of 1812.

HURON— Norwalk— 1809— 497 sq. mi.— French explorers originally called the Wyandot Indian tribe, the Hurons.

JACKSON—Jackson—1816—420 sq. mi.—General Andrew Jackson had just emerged as a great hero of the War of 1812 at the Battle of New Orleans when the county was organized.

JEFFERSON—Steubenville—1797—411 sq. mi.—Thomas Jefferson, then honored as author of the Declaration of Independence and later President.

KNOX—Mount Vernon—1808—532 sq. mi.—Henry Knox served as Chief of Artillery in the American Revolution and the first Secretary of War.

LAKE—Painesville—1840—232 sq. mi.—Ohio's smallest county takes its name from the geographical fact of being on Lake Erie.

LAWRENCE—Ironton—1816—456 sq. mi.—Captain James Lawrence, a hero of the War of 1812, before his death commanded: "Don't Give Up the Ship."

LICKING—Newark—1808—687 sq. mi.—The Licking River which runs through the county, named from nearby salt licks, gave the county its name.

LOGAN—Bellefontaine—1817—469 sq. mi.—General Benjamin Logan, a soldier defeated the Indians in 1786 and wiped out the Mac-O-Chee villages.

LORAIN—Elyria—1822—495 sq. mi.—At the request of an early settler, Heman Ely, from whose name came Elyria, the county given the same name as the French province of Lorraine.

LUCAS—Toledo—1835—351 sq. mi.—Governor Robert Lucas took a decisive role in the "Toledo War" a dispute between Ohio and Michigan over a strip of land on which that city and its port were located. His swift military action kept it as part of Ohio.

MADISON—London—1810—464 sq. mi.—James Madison was the fourth President of the U.S., and president when the county was formed.

MAHONING—Youngstown—1846—424 sq. mi.—Translated from the Indian language, mahoning means "at the licks," implying salt licks.

MARION—Marion—1824—405 sq. mi.—General Francis Marion led the American soldiers during the American Revolution in South Carolina becoming known as the "swamp fox."

MEDINA—Medina—1818—425 sq. mi.—A geographical place name in Saudi Arabia, Medina is the sacred city of Islam to which Mohammed fled.

MEIGS—Pomeroy—1819—436 sq. mi.—Governor Return J. Meigs, also served Ohio as Chief Justice, and Senator, and then became Postmaster General of the U.S., first Ohioan to hold a cabinet post.

MERCER—Celina—1820—471 sq. mi.—General Hugh Mercer was killed at Princeton, in 1777, following action at the Battle of Trenton.

MIAMI—Troy—1807—407 sq. mi.—The Miami Indians lived in this part of Ohio, the word Miami in the Indian language, meant "mother."

MONROE—Woodsfield—1813—456 sq. mi.—Formally organized in 1815, two years after being formed, it was named in honor of James Monroe, who became the fifth president of the U.S.

MONTGOMERY—Dayton—1803—465 sq. mi.—General Richard Montgomery was killed in the attack on Quebec in 1775 at the beginning of the American Revolution.

MORGAN—McConnellville—1818—421 sq. mi.—General Daniel Morgan, an outstanding leader of the American Revolution, was first to use the Kentucky long rifle against the British.

MORROW—Mount Gilead—1848—404 sq. mi.—Governor Jeremiah Morrow after serving as governor served in the U.S. Congress.

MUSKINGUM—Zanesville—1804—670 sq. mi.—In the language of the Delaware Indians, the word meant "a town beside the river."

NOBLE—Caldwell—1851—404 sq. mi.—Warren P. Noble was chairman of a committee in the Ohio legislature on new counties at the time this particular county was being organized.

OTTAWA—Port Clinton—1840—269 sq. mi.—Being famous as traders, the Ottawa tribe derived its name from that trait.

PAULDING—Paulding—1820—417 sq. mi.—John Paulding was one of the soldiers in the American Revolution who captured Major Andre, a British spy.

PERRY—New Lexington—1817—410 sq. mi.—Commodore Oliver Hazard Perry was the hero of the 1813 Battle of Lake Erie at Put-in-Bay.

PICKAWAY—Circleville—1810—507 sq. mi.—This represents the misspelling of the word, Piqua, an Indian word meaning "man risen from the ashes."

PIKE—Waverly—1815—444 sq. mi.—General Zebulon M. Pike, was the noted western explorer who discovered Pike's Peak in Colorado in 1806.

PORTAGE—Ravenna—1807—506 sq. mi.—Canoes were carried between two streams over a footpath or portage, this one being between the Cuyahoga and Tuscarawas Rivers.

PREBLE—Eaton—1808—428 sq. mi.—Commodore Edward Preble led the naval attack against the Tripoli pirates in 1804.

PUTNAM—Ottawa—1820—486 sq. mi.—General Israel Putnam fought at Bunker Hill and through the Revolution; a cousin of Rufus Putnam, who led the first settlement at Marietta.

RICHLAND—Mansfield—1813—499 sq. mi.—A geographic designation referring to the rich, productive and fertile land of that area.

ROSS—Chillicothe—1798—687 sq. mi.—James Ross, a Federalist politician, and friend of Gov. Arthur St. Clair was honored by St. Clair's naming the county for him.

SANDUSKY—Fremont—1820—416 sq. mi.—The Indian word for cold water, was San-Doos-Tee, which became Sandusky.

SCIOTO—Portsmouth—1803—611 sq. mi.—The Wyandot Indian word for "deer" was first applied to the "Sci-on-to" River, then the county.

SENECA—Tiffin—1824—551 sq. mi.—The Seneca Indians originally had a reservation on the land.

SHELBY—Sidney—1819—410 sq. mi.—Isaac Shelby, as a Colonel in the Revolution led the frontiersmen at Kings Mountain in defeating the British forces, and later became Governor of Kentucky.

STARK—Canton—1808—581 sq. mi.—General John Stark's victory at the Battle of Bennington in the Revolution was a turning point in the war.

SUMMIT—Akron—1840—416 sq. mi.—Portage Summit was the highest point on the Ohio-Erie Canal route, a landmark during Canal Days.

TRUMBULL—Warren—1800—632 sq. mi.—Jonathan Trumbull was an early Governor of Connecticut, whose wise advice was sought by Washington, and said to be Brother Jonathan, symbol used by the U.S. before "Uncle Sam."

TUSCARAWAS—New Philadelphia—1808—571 sq. mi.—Taken from the Indian word, meaning "open mouth" the word was probably first used by the Indians to describe the Tuscarawas River.

UNION—Marysville—1820—434 sq. mi.—The name refers to the fact that the county was formed by taking parts of four neighboring counties.

VAN WERT—Van Wert—1820—409 sq. mi.—Isaac Van Wert, a hero of the Revolution, one of three men, who captured Major Andre.

VINTON—McArthur—1850—411 sq. mi.—Samuel F. Vinton, an early Ohio statesman, and a U.S. Congressman.

WARREN—Lebanon—1803—408 sq. mi.—General Joseph Warren was an early leader in the movement for independence and was killed at Bunker Hill.

WASHINGTON—Marietta—1788—641 sq. mi.—When the county was organized, General Washington was head of the Constitutional Convention.

264

WAYNE—Wooster—1812—561 sq. mi.—General Anthony Wayne followed his brilliant military career in the Revolution by planning the campaign which led to the Indian defeat and the Treaty of Greenville.

WILLIAMS—Bryan—1820—421 sq. mi.—David Williams was one of the soldiers who captured Major Andre, British spy in the Revolution.

WOOD—Bowling Green—1820—621 sq. mi.—Capt. Eleazer D. Wood of the Engineering Corp. built Fort Meigs for Gen. Harrison in the War of 1812.

WYANDOT—Upper Sandusky—1845—406 sq. mi.—The Wyandot Indians were the last tribe to leave Ohio in 1843.

PART FOUR

RESOURCE REFERENCES

The references listed below are for the use of students. Material useful to teachers is found in the Guide Book.

Bailey, Bernadine. **Picture Book of Ohio.** Albert Whitman and Co. Chicago, Ill. 1967.

Boesch, Mark. **Beyond the Muskingum.** John C. Winston, Philadelphia. 1953.

Breyfogle, William A. **Wagon Wheels—Story of the National Road.** Aladdin Books, New York, 1956.

Carpenter, Allan. **Ohio. Children's Press, Chicago, 1963.**

Chandler, Edna W. **Little Wolf and Thunder Stick.** Benefic Press, Westchester, Ill. 1956.

Collins, William R. **Ohio: The Buckeye State.** Prentice-Hall Inc. New York, 1963.

Crout, George. **Lincoln's Littlest Soldier.** T. S. Denison & Co., Minneapolis, 1969.

Crout, George. **Lucky Cloverleaf of the 4-H.** T. S. Denison & Co., Minneapolis, 1971.

Crout, George. **Seven Lives of Johnny B. Free.** T. S. Denison & Co., Minneapolis, 1961.

Drury, Maxine. **George and the Long Rifle.** Longsman, Green and Co. New York, 1957.

Epstein, Sam. **All About the Prehistoric Cavemen.** Random House. New York, 1959.

Erwin, Paul. **Round on the Ends: A Story of Ohio.** Creative Writers and Publishers. Cincinnati, Ohio, 1964.

Godfroy, Chief Clarence. **Miami Indian Stories.** Life and Light Press, Winona Lake, Indiana, 1961.

Hatch, Margaret G. **Ohio's Official Symbols.** Ohio Historical Society. Columbus, Ohio, 1968.

Havighurst, Walter. **The Midwest**. Fideler Co., Grand Rapids, Michigan, 1965.

Havighurst, Walter. **River to the West**. G. P. Putnam's Sons, New York, 1970.

Holberg, Ruth L. **Restless Johnny**. Thomas Crowell Co., New York, 1950.

Howell, Charles E. Paul Shaw and Thelma Seehausen. **Land of the Great Lakes**. Harr Wagner Publishing Co., San Francisco, 1958.

Knopf, Richard C. **Indians of the Ohio Country**. Modern Methods. 1959.

Lambe, E. W. and L. W. Shultz. **Indian Lore**. Light and Life Press. Winona Lake, Indiana, 1964.

Lauber, Patricia. **All About the Ice Age**. Random House, New York, 1959.

LeSuer, Meridel. **Little Brother of the Wilderness**. Alfred Knopf, New York, 1964.

Martin, Anamae. **Columbus: The Buckeye Capital**. Charles Merrill Books, Columbus, Ohio, 1962.

McCall, Edith. **Pioneers on Early Waterways**. Childrens Press, Chicago, 1961.

McCall, Edith. **Pioneer Show Folk**. Childrens Press, Chicago, 1961.

May, Julian. **They Lived in the Ice Age**. Holiday House, New York, 1967.

Newman, Shirlee and Diane Sherman. **Canals**. Melmont Publishers, Chicago, 1964.

Nolan, Jeannette C. **The Ohio River**. Coward, McCann, New York, 1973.

Ohio Almanac. 1967 Broadway, Lorain, Ohio.

Ohio Cues. Maumee Valley Historical Society, Wolcott House, 1031 River Road, Maumee, Ohio 43537. Monthly Publication for students of Ohio History.

Ohioana Library Yearbook. Martha Kinney Cooper Ohioana Library Assn. 1105 Ohio Dept. Bldg., Columbus, Ohio. Annual publication on Ohio subjects.

Perry, Dick **Ohio**. Doubleday and Co., Garden City, New York, 1969.

Pfeiffer, John. **The Search for Early Man**. Harper and Row, New York, 1963.

Renick, Marion. **Ohio.** Coward, McCann. New York, 1970.

Richter, Conrad. **The Light in the Forest.** Bantam Books. 414 E. Golf Road, Des Plaines, Ill., 1953.

Richter, Conrad. **A Country of Strangers.** Alfred Knopf, New York, 1966.

Roberts, Carl H. and Paul R. Cummins. **Ohio.** Laidlaw Brothers. River Forest, Ill. 1966.

Robinson, Ruth M. and Mary E. Harris. **The Story of Ohio.** Charles Merrill Books, Columbus, Ohio, 1963.

Roland, Albert. **Great Indian Chiefs.** Crowell-Collier Press, New York, 1966.

Scheele, William. **The Mound Builders.** World Publishing Co., Cleveland, 1960.

Shetrone, H. C. **Primer of Ohio Archaelogy.** Ohio Historical Society, Columbus, Ohio, 1951.

Siedel, Frank. **The Ohio Story.** World Publishing Co., Cleveland, 1950.

Smith, Thomas H. (Ed.) **An Ohio Reader.** William B. Eerdmans Pub. Co., Grand Rapids, Michigan, 49052. 2 vols. 1975. (A Collection of Original documents on Ohio History.)

White, Anne T. **The St. Lawrence Seaway of North America.** Garrard Publishing Co., Champaign, Illinois, 1961.

SERIES OF BOOKS: OHIO AND OHIO BACKGROUNDS

Signature Books, Grossett and Dunlap, New York, Books of particular interest to students studying Ohio in this series are: **Annie Oakley, Buffalo Bill, Dan Beard, Daniel Boone, General Custer, George Washington, John Audubon, Mad Anthony Wayne, Stephen Foster, Thomas A. Edison, Ulysses S. Grant.**

Childhood of Famous Americans, Bobbs-Merrill Company, Indianapolis. The books relating to Ohio are: **Annie Oakley: Little Sure Shot; Anthony Wayne: Daring Boy; Dan Beard: Boy Scout; Daniel Boone: Boy Hunter; George Roger Clark: Boy of the Old Northwest; Harriet Beecher Stowe: Connecticut Girl; Oliver Hazard Perry: Boy of the Sea; Stephen Foster: Boy Minstrel; Tecumseh: Shawnee Boy; Tom Edison: Boy Inventor; U. S. Grant: Young Horseman; Wilbur and Orville Wright: Boys With Wings; William Henry Harrison; Young Tippecanoe; William H. McGuffey: Boy Reading Genius.**

Landmark Books, Random House, New York. The following titles will be of interest: **Prehistoric America; Alexander Hamilton and Aaron Burr; Buffalo Bill's Great Wild West Show; Custer's Last Stand; Daniel Boone; Early Days of Automobiles; Erie Canal; Rogers' Rangers and the French and Indian War; Tippecanoe and Tyler, Too!; Wright Brothers; Americans Into Orbit.**

PART FIVE

OHIO TIME LINE

25,000-15,000 B.C.—Glaciers covered Ohio.

11,000 B.C.—First people may have arrived in Ohio.

9,000-6,000 B.C.—Prehistoric people developed a primitive culture.

6,000-800 B.C.—Archaic civilization grew in the state.

800 B.C.-600 A.D.—Adena Peoples developed their culture.

600 A.D.-1400 A.D.—Hopewell culture dominated region.

1500-1655—Fort Ancient and Erie Indian civilization developed.

1655—Erie, or Cat Nation, defeated and destroyed by Iroquois Confederacy.

1669-1670—La Salle reached Lake Erie and the Ohio River valley.

1748—First Ohio Company of Virginia formed to explore area.

1749—De Celoron Explored and laid claim to the Ohio country for France.

1750—The English send Christopher Gist to claim Ohio.

1756-1763—French and Indian War fought in Old Northwest.

1764—Col. Bouquet demanded that Indians return white captives.

1763-1765—Pontiac's conspiracy spread terror on the frontier.

1772—Moravian missionaries made first settlement in Ohio.

1774—Lord Dunmore's War fought on Ohio soil.

1775—American Revolution began.

1778—Fort Laurens, Ohio's only Revolutionary Fort built.

1778-1779—George Rogers Clark conducted brilliant campaign in Northwest.

1782—Betty Zane's heroic deed saved Fort Henry.

1785—Land Ordinance of 1785 passed, setting up survey of Northwest.

1787—Northwest Ordinance of 1787 passed by Congress.

270

1788—First permanent settlement made in Ohio at Marietta.

1788—Second large settlement made at Cincinnati late in 1788.

1791—Chief Little Turtle defeated Gen. Arthur St. Clair in western Ohio.

1793—First newspaper in Ohio published at Cincinnati.

1794—General Anthony Wayne defeated Indians at Battle of Fallen Timbers.

1795—Treaty of Greenville signed by Indians.

1796—Moses Cleaveland laid out city which still bears his name.

1796—Zane's Trace marked out through Ohio wilderness.

1799—First Territorial Legislature met at Cincinnati.

1800—Ohio made separate territory of Northwest Territory.

1803—Ohio's Constitution is approved.

1803—U.S. Congress admitted Ohio as a state.

1805-1806—Plans of Blennerhassett and Burr thwarted.

1811—Gen. Harrison defeated Indians at Battle of Tippecanoe.

1811—The steamboat, "New Orleans" paddled down the Ohio River.

1812-1814—Ohio played major part in war with British.

1813—Oliver Hazard Perry won the Battle at Put-in-Bay, Lake Erie.

1815—Benjamin Lundy started abolitionist society in Ohio.

1816—Ohio capital moved to Columbus from Chillicothe.

1825—National Road construction was begun in Ohio.

1825—Ohio-Erie and Miami-Erie canal construction began.

1833—Oberlin College opened as Ohio's first coeducational college.

1835—Ohio won a boundary dispute known as the "Toledo War."

1836—First Railroad began operation on a 32-mile track.

1840—William Henry Harrison, an Ohioan, elected 9th President of the U.S.

1846-1848—Ohio men fought in the Mexican War.

1847—Akron Law passed by General Assembly to set up graded school system.

1851—Second Ohio Constitution accepted by voters, still in effect.

1852—Harriet Beecher Stowe published "Uncle Tom's Cabin."

1858—Ohioans freed John Price, a slave, stirring up great controversy.

1859—John Brown of Akron, antislavery leader captured and hung.

1861-1865—Approximately 320,000 Ohio men, black and white fought in the Civil War.

1868—General Ulysses S. Grant elected 18th President.

1870—Negro delegates attend a state convention for the first time.

1870—J. D. Rockefeller organized the Standard Oil Company of Ohio.

1873—Ohio State University was opened at Columbus.

1876—Rutherford B. Hayes elected 19th President.

1879—Thomas A. Edison invented the incandescent light.

1880—James Garfield elected 20th President.

1888—Benjamin Harrison, elected 23rd President of U.S.

1890—John P. Green, Black legislator, introduced bill to establish Labor Day.

1896—William McKinley elected 25th President.

1898—Ohioans volunteered for service in Spanish-American War.

1903—Orville and Wilbur Wright made first successful flight.

1908—William Howard Taft elected President, later became Chief Justice.

1913—Flood swept Southern Ohio, taking 438 lives, costing $300,000,000.

1914—Conservancy Law passed to permit Miami Valley to build dams.

1917-1918—About 250,000 Ohio men served in World War I.

1920—Warren G. Harding elected President.

1921—The Bing Act required school attendance to the age of 18.

1929-1933—Ohio suffered from a great Depression.

1938—Muskingum Watershed completed for flood control.

1941-1945—Ohio sent almost 840,000 men and women to World War II.

1950—Korean War was begun, later Ohio's 37th Division ordered to duty.

1953—Ohio celebrated its Sesquicentennial.

1954—Frank Lausche elected to 5th term as Ohio's Governor.

1955—Ohio Turnpike opened across northern part of state.

1959—St. Lawrence Seaway opened, making Lake Erie cities, world ports.

1962—Col. John Glenn orbited the earth.

1963—Ohio military personnel began service in Viet Nam.

1963—William O. Walker became first Negro cabinet member in Ohio.

1965—Mrs. Jerrie Mock was first woman to fly solo around world.

1966—Springfield first large city to elect Black mayor, Robert E. Henry.

1967—Carl Stokes elected Mayor of Cleveland.

1969—Neil Armstrong became first man to set foot on the moon.

1976—State began official observation of the birthday of Martin Luther King.

1976—Ohio joined nation to commemorate nation's Bicentennial.

The State Song

"Beautiful Ohio" which describes the Ohio River that forms the southern boundary of the state, is the official state song. It was adopted by the General Assembly on Oct. 24, 1969. The music is by Mary Earl and the words by Ballard Macdonald.

Beautiful Ohio

Verse:

Long, long ago
Someone I know
Had a little red canoe
In it room for only two;
Love found its start,
Then in my heart,
And like a flower grew.

Chorus:

Drifting with the current down a moon-lit stream
While above the heavens in their glory gleam
And the stars on high
Twinkle in the sky
Seeming in a paradise of love divine
Dreaming of a pair of eyes that looked in mine,
Beautiful Ohio, in dreams again I see
Visions of what used to be.

Reproduced by special permission of the copyright owners:
Copyright 1918 by Shapiro, Bernstein & Co. Inc.
10 East 53rd St. New York, N.Y. 10022

INDEX

277